Japanese Capitalism and Modernity in a Global Era

Japanese Capitalism and Modernity in a Global Era provides an in-depth examination of one of the most central and defining aspects of capitalist modernity in contemporary Japan – the lifetime employment system.

The book investigates the key themes surrounding the system, including the work attitudes and values of Japanese company employees and whether or not Japan is converging on Western forms of capitalist organization. Peter Matanle presents and analyses original documentary data, drawn from extensive research within four large Japanese corporations, in order to explore these issues from the perspective of both management and employees. The findings are then discussed in terms of the development of Japan's capitalism and modernity.

Contrary to the popular hypothesis that the lifetime employment system and the values of the 'salaryman' are changing in response to both the globalization of market capitalism and the achievement of material affluence, this book argues that, while some change has appeared at the margins of the system and employees' values are gradually becoming more differentiated, there has not yet been a fundamental transformation of the system's foundations. Significantly, the book argues that a subtle change in the way management perceives its relationship with employees may herald a more profound and long-term change in the future organization of the Japanese corporation. It will be of interest to researchers of Japanese studies, Business studies and Sociology.

Peter C. D. Matanle is Lecturer in Japanese Studies at the University of Sheffield and has previously worked at Niigata University in Japan. He is the founder and general editor of the *electronic journal of contemporary japanese studies*.

Sheffield Centre for Japanese Studies / RoutledgeCurzon Series
Series Editor: Glenn D. Hook
Professor of Japanese Studies, University of Sheffield

This series, published by RoutledgeCurzon in association with the Centre for Japanese Studies at the University of Sheffield, both makes available original research on a wide range of subjects dealing with Japan and provides introductory overviews of key topics in Japanese Studies.

The Internationalization of Japan
Edited by Glenn D. Hook and Michael Weiner

Race and Migration in Imperial Japan
Michael Weiner

Japan and the Pacific Free Trade Area
Pekka Korhonen

Greater China and Japan
Prospects for an economic partnership?
Robert Taylor

The Steel Industry in Japan
A comparison with the UK
Hasegawa Harukiyo

Race, Resistance and the Ainu of Japan
Richard Siddle

Japan's Minorities
The illusion of homogeneity
Edited by Michael Weiner

Japanese Business Management
Restructuring for low growth and globalization
Edited by Hasegawa Harukiyo and Glenn D. Hook

Japan and Asia Pacific Integration
Pacific romances 1968–1996
Pekka Korhonen

Japan's Economic Power and Security
Japan and North Korea
Christopher W. Hughes

Japan's Contested Constitution
Documents and analysis
Glenn D. Hook and Gavan McCormack

Japan's International Relations
Politics, economics and security
Glenn D. Hook, Julie Gilson, Christopher Hughes and Hugo Dobson

Japanese Education Reform
Nakasone's legacy
Christopher P. Hood

The Political Economy of Japanese Globalisation
Glenn D. Hook and Hasegawa Harukiyo

Japan and Okinawa
Structure and subjectivity
Edited by Glenn D. Hook and Richard Siddle

Japan and Britain in the Contemporary World
Responses to common issues
Edited by Hugo Dobson and Glenn D. Hook

Japan and United Nations Peacekeeping
New pressures, new responses
Hugo Dobson

Japanese Capitalism and Modernity in a Global Era
Re-fabricating lifetime employment relations
Peter C. D. Matanle

Nikkeiren and Japanese Capitalism
John Crump

Production Networks in Asia and Europe
Skill formation and technology transfer in the automobile industry
Edited by Rogier Busser and Yuri Sadoi

Japanese Capitalism and Modernity in a Global Era

Re-fabricating lifetime employment relations

Peter C. D. Matanle

RoutledgeCurzon
Taylor & Francis Group

LONDON AND NEW YORK

HD
5708.45
.J32
M35
2003

First published 2003
by RoutledgeCurzon
11 New Fetter Lane, London EC4P 4EE

Simultaneously published in the USA and Canada
by RoutledgeCurzon
29 West 35th Street, New York, NY 10001

RoutledgeCurzon is an imprint of the Taylor & Francis Group

© 2003 Peter C. D. Matanle

Typeset in Times Roman by The Running Head Limited, Cambridge
Printed and bound in Great Britain by MPG Books Ltd, Bodmin

All rights reserved. No part of this book may be reprinted or
reproduced or utilised in any form or by an electronic,
mechanical, or other means, now known or hereafter
invented, including photocopying and recording, or in any
information storage or retrieval system, without permission in
writing from the publishers.

British Library Cataloguing in Publication Data
A catalogue record for this book is available from the British Library

Library of Congress Cataloging in Publication Data
Matanle, Peter C. D. Japanese capitalism and modernity in a global
era : re-fabricating lifetime employment relations / Peter C. D. Matanle.
p. cm.
Includes bibliographical references and index.
ISBN 0–415–30574–8 (hc)
1. Job security—Japan. 2. Organizational change—Japan. 3. Industrial
relations—Japan. I. Title.
HD5708.45.J32M35 2003
331'.0952—dc21

ISBN 0–415–30574–8

51631310

For my mother and father

Nothing is more difficult than to know precisely
what we see.

Maurice Merleau-Ponty

Contents

List of illustrations   xiii
Preface   xv
Glossary of terms and abbreviations   xxi

1   Introduction: researching Japanese capitalism and modernity   **1**
Work in capitalist modernity 2
Work values 3
Institutions and organizations of employment 5
*Japan, the lifetime employment system, and the Japanese
    salaryman 7*
Research methodology 9
Research strategy 11

2   Japanese capitalism and modernity in theoretical perspective   **14**
A theory for modernity and the individual 16
Tradition and the self in Japanese modernity 20
Modernization in Europe and Japan 24
The self and modern society in the West and in Japan 27
Contemporary social change, globalization, and convergence 29
Conclusion 36

3   Lifetime employment in post-war Japan   **38**
*The origins and establishment of the Japanese lifetime employment
    system 41*
The lifetime employment system in the 1960s and 1970s 46
The lifetime employment system as a transitional institution 67

4   Re-fabricating lifetime employment relations   **71**
The contemporary structure of lifetime employment 72
Field investigations 86
Re-fabricating the Japanese salaryman 100

5   Working under changing employment relations   **107**
Needs, desires, and values 107
Flow 109
Work values in Japan 112
Field investigations 125
Caught between two modernities 144

**6   Conclusion: Japanese capitalism and modernity in a
global era**   **148**
Review and conclusions 151

Notes   157
Bibliography   165
Index   175

Illustrations

Figures

4.1	Average tenures, ages, and ages of entry by gender in the Japanese automotive and retail sectors	75
4.2	Percentage by age of white-collar male regular employees remaining with their original employer	76
4.3	Employment adjustment of excess middle-aged white-collar workers by large Japanese corporations	78
4.4	Actual implementation of and prospects for new personnel management systems	83
4.5	Number of regular employees, Companies A–D, 1989–2002	89
5.1	Male workers' perceived and desired workplace characteristics	114
5.2	What do you think is the most important reason for people to work?	116
5.3	Until when do you intend to work for this company?	118
5.4	Rate of those wishing to change employer by age group	119
5.5	Number of companies worked at since graduation	120
5.6	Reason for resigning from original employer	121
5.7	Desired career path	123
5.8	Reasons for not wanting to change job	124

Tables

4.1	Overview of companies A–D	87
4.2	Personnel system changes at Company A (1960s–1990s)	102–3
5.1	Principal recruiters of Tokyo University graduates (1997 and 2000)	126

Preface

In attempting to understand and explain the connection between the contemporary work consciousness of the Japanese salaryman and the enormous complexity of modern development I have set myself an ambitious challenge. Nevertheless, if we do not set ourselves difficult tasks and invite the possibility for failure then we reduce the potential for reaping the rewards that come from the pursuit and achievement of our hopes and ambitions. These rewards constitute much more than the sum of personal pleasures that come from satisfying our needs and desires. We value them in and of themselves because they assist us in deriving meaning from our lives and because they come from our natural desire to contribute to enhancing the total quality of the human experience for ourselves as well as for others.

In addition, it is an interesting and, at times, unnerving feeling to be researching something from which it is impossible to separate myself. For I am as much a child of this globalizing capitalist modernity as the subjects that have given so generously of themselves for this research. Although this presents me with an interesting problem, the inability to distance and detach oneself completely from one's research material is not confined to the study of sociology. However, if it is impossible to distance oneself from one's research material then how does one deal with trying to negotiate the dilemma that lies between trying to separate the inseparable and becoming a part of the research process itself? For me, there can be only one answer and that is to make efforts to understand myself as an integral part of the process and to contribute aspects of my experiences, feelings, and opinions to this project.

Some reflections on the researcher as respondent

When I first arrived in Japan in 1987 I was frequently asked by Japanese people why I had decided to come to a country so far and so different from my own. In truth, I felt I had somewhat drifted there. Although ostensibly I had made a considered and active decision to go there, I was reluctant to admit that I felt I had gravitated there without a set of clear reasons for doing so. While I viewed the opportunity to live and work in Japan as an inviting challenge with possible but unspecified long-term benefits, I had also gone there for the reason that I felt I had little more challenging, more interesting, and more profitable to do with myself at the time.

Explaining my motivations, I had devised a fairly convincing story that I was interested in experiencing Japan first-hand because it was the only fully developed non-Western society. At that time there were many Western observers eagerly trying to uncover what they perceived to be the secrets of Japan's almost miraculous post-war economic success and such an answer was plausible enough that conversation often flowed. Although I was indeed interested in how Japan had managed to develop, it was not really why I had originally gone there. Basically, I had been somewhat self-conscious of my lack of clarity and direction and had construed a rational explanation for the benefit of giving others what I imagined they wanted to hear as well as giving myself a more concrete feeling of purpose. I was self-conscious because I believed and had been led to believe that I, like others, should be living out a planned, future oriented, and upward sloping linear trajectory of experience and direction for my life. Indeed, I even started to believe my rationalization a little myself, and certainly it fitted neatly into the somewhat contrived personal biography that I was gradually carving out of the rather discontinuous life I had lead thus far.

A combination of fortuitous circumstances and a little active career building on my part led me by 1991 to be working as a white-collar salaried worker at a semi-governmental organization in Tokyo. As much as is possible for an English man on a fixed term of employment, for two years I lived the life of a salaryman and commuted to work daily in Shinjuku from a one-room apartment on the east side of central Tokyo. I stayed at work often until very late at night and occasionally even came to work at weekends, for no extra salary. Although I did sometimes resent the sacrifices required of me by my employers, sacrifices that they never requested but which I was made aware were nevertheless required, I enjoyed my work and gained a sense of fulfilment from it. It was a challenge that I discovered I could rise to and which required creativity and effort. I believed I was making a positive contribution to human relations between Japan and other countries and, quite coincidentally, I learned how to use computers for the first time and felt that my understanding of Japan and Japanese people was becoming less deficient with each passing day.

Throughout that time I was not so much interested in getting and securing a permanent job with a regular salary. For I took it for granted that whatever happened I would always be able to find material support for myself. Instead I was more interested in finding something useful and stimulating to do, developing and using my abilities, making a positive contribution to others' lives, and living a vital, stimulating, and fulfilling life. For those two years I was able to do all these things and I was happy and grateful for the opportunity that, by a mixture of chance and design, had come my way.

After two years working back in Britain, trying to discover a role for myself, I returned to university to commence the long road to completing this book. I had always harboured a quiet desire to be an academic and, not having developed a long-term career with which I was satisfied, decided to give it a try. I wanted to combine my rather disconnected knowledge and experience and put it to good use. Moreover, and perhaps most importantly, I craved a return to the experience of work I had enjoyed in Tokyo. I felt, correctly as it turned out, that social research is something I would find to be valuable in and of itself, that it would be a difficult challenge, and that I would be able to achieve a feeling of fulfilment.

Had I convinced myself that I was interested in researching the sociology of contemporary Japan? Or was there a latent interest and desire of which I was only dimly aware at the time and of which I gradually became more aware as my experiences and knowledge of Japan and Japanese people deepened? How much was the path I took a series of considered and active decisions based on a coherent and consciously understood set of values and motivations, how much was it the product of a subliminal teleology, and how much was it a passive reaction to others' expectations and external circumstances, structures, and events? The precise answers to these questions are not apparent to me. Indeed, I would find great difficulty in searching for the memories, developing and connecting the strings that linked the disparate thoughts and events, and even finding the right language to describe exactly why I had done what I had. However, as well as being cast into a world of being compelled to decide, and take responsibility for, my own fate, I have been able to make considered decisions and experiment with the choices that have been available to me. Through that process I could learn to understand myself more completely, enhance and expand my abilities and knowledge, and find some fulfilment through expressing aspects of my inner self in substantive reality.

In keeping with the discussions on reflexivity and work consciousness in capitalist modernity that form part of the theoretical basis for this study, the above is not simply an exercise in introspective self-absorption but a serious expression of the principal assumptions and methodological approach of this investigation. For if an important aspect of this book is an investigation of the relationship between the modern Japanese salaryman's work consciousness and the institutions of capitalist modernity in Japan, then, in the interests of clarity and depth of understanding, it would seem appropriate that I should also include within it a discussion of the motivations and experiences that I, as a child of capitalist modernity who has lived and worked in Japan, bring to it. In addition, I believe that these reflections might facilitate for you the reader the opportunity for a richer or more well-rounded judgement of the suitability of my research method, the quality of the data collected in its execution, the depth of analysis brought to bear, and the validity of the conclusions developed therefrom. These discussions are, therefore, intended to assist in building an appreciation of the human as well as scientific bases of social research.

First principles

While we all suffer from the problem of physiological and cognitive limitations constraining our understanding of ourselves as well as our subjects, this crucial aspect of our work is rarely explored. All scholars inevitably rely on unavoidably flawed and subjective judgements in the development of their conclusions. However, it cannot be denied that these conclusions, and the methods and data that support them, may be considered valid.

I feel, therefore, that it is important that we demonstrate an awareness of our own shortcomings as well as our unique circumstances and motivations such that we can develop a research strategy and research conclusions that move towards a more authentic representation of both ourselves and our respondents. It is also important that we can confidently incorporate our own experiences and feelings into the research process, its analysis, and its conclusions so that we can enhance its quality, depth, and resonance. For all social research is as much an expression of the consciousness of the researcher as it is of the research subjects.

In addition, it is partly through self-examination that the researcher may become more receptive to the research subject as he or she attempts to provide meaningful responses to investigative methods and questions that are, more often than not, outside the realm of ordinary day-to-day experience. It is important to maintain that respondents, on the whole, do not consciously try to misinform the researcher as to the motives and causes for their own social behaviour. However they may not describe completely or clearly the experiences and thoughts that they have because, as human beings, they suffer from the very same limitations that restrict researchers themselves and, as laypersons, they may not be knowledgeable of the theoretical and intellectual world that surrounds the analysis and conclusions that may be derived from their responses.

Ordinarily I do not subscribe to theories of false consciousness, since they are almost invariably the product of an artificial separation from the realm of the subject on the part of the researcher, reserving for himself or herself clarity of thought and expression while condemning the respondent to ignorance and incoherence. However, upon consideration of my own circumstances it becomes impossible to avoid the conclusion that at least some of the respondents who contributed to this project may have been trying to construct and reconstruct meaning, rationality, and contiguity in their lives precisely to alleviate the anxieties that they experience from living in a world that they feel they can neither fully control nor fully understand and that may at times appear meaningless, irrational, and directionless. But this in itself, in the context of the theoretical discussions to come, is useful empirical data and indicates to us aspects of the social phenomena of capitalist modernity that we are trying to discover.

Finally, and to conclude these discussions on the personal foundations for this study, there is an insoluble and irreconcilable problem as to the nature of truth that is vital to our understanding of the research process and that is also highly relevant to our understanding of capitalist modernity. What is truth? Is it what is, is it what we want it to be, is it what we think should be, or is it simply what we perceive? Like Merleau-Ponty in his *Phenomenology of Perception* (1998 [1962]) I believe the answer to be an imprecise, irreducible, and indescribable combination of these. There is an external essence that we know to be true in itself and of which we have a basic and necessarily incomplete understanding. However, we can only understand what we can perceive from our own position of sensory focus. In order to reconcile what we perceive with what we want truth to be and what we think it should be, we end up constructing the parts that we cannot perceive using the flawed cognitive and intellectual processes of analysis, judgement, and imagination. These reconstructions we believe to be true yet they are, even if we do not want them to be, a compromise between what truth is, what we think it is, what we want it to be, and what we think it should be. Moreover, my perception of truth is merely mine and although its similarity to others' may be great it is never identical. This is *true* as much for the researcher as it is for the respondent and we must both be constantly aware of the dangers into which it can lead us, and allow these apparent weaknesses of the human condition to become positive advantages for further and deeper enlightenment of the research process and our understanding of human beings as self-constituting individual subjects embedded in social and institutional relations.

Overview and acknowledgements

The rest of this book is a theoretical discussion of a particular and admittedly rather narrow aspect of capitalist modernity as it is manifested in Japan, that takes as its empirical basis the relationship between the Japanese salaryman and the lifetime employment system in large corporations. Chapter one presents a research agenda and sketches out the theoretical and empirical rationales for this study as well as providing a description of the research method undertaken. Chapter two sets out the theoretical foundations for the project and provides a discussion of the principal academic literature that informs it. Chapter three is an analysis of the origins and institutional establishment of lifetime employment in large Japanese corporations and presents some empirical data in the form of respondents' recollections to inform a description of the post-war system as a transitional or intermediate institution in Japan's socio-economic development. Chapter four presents empirical data on the present-day structure of lifetime employment, its direction of development, and managerial approaches to these developments. Chapter five presents empirical data on the consciousness of contemporary Japanese salarymen towards lifetime employment. Both chapters four and five present the idea that Japanese society is gradually emerging into a new more intense, more dynamic, and more global phase in its capitalism and modernity. The final chapter provides a review and analysis of chapters three, four, and five in the light of the theoretical arguments presented in chapters one and two.

Through the six years it has taken me to complete first my PhD dissertation, and latterly this book, I have been fortunate enough to have received generous funding from the following organizations: The British government's Economic and Social Research Council (ESRC), the Japanese Ministry of Education (formerly Monbushō and now Monbukagakushō), and the Japan Foundation. Their financial assistance has enabled me to concentrate on my work and to produce a dissertation and now this book which, I hope, will be useful for them in their endeavours. In addition, I would like to express my sincere gratitude to each of them.

It remains for me to thank those who assisted and guided me in the process of producing this project. First, I would like to thank Dr Hiroko Tanaka and Professor Ian Neary of the University of Essex, both of whom were essential to getting me started on this project. Thanks must go to all of the staff and students of the University of Sheffield's School of East Asian Studies who have been instrumental in one way or another in helping me to achieve what I set out to do. The staff and students of the Institute of Social Science at the University of Tokyo, Dōshisha University in Kyoto, and the Faculty of Law at Niigata University have all been very generous in hosting me in Japan and among these I would like to thank Professors Abo and Tabata of Tokyo University, Professor Hattori of Dōshisha University (now at the University of Tokyo), and Professors Minamikata and Namazugoshi of Niigata University, all of whom were willing to take me on as either a foreign graduate student or employee and who contributed in numerous different ways to helping me live, study, and work in Japan. In particular, I would especially like to thank my PhD supervisor at Sheffield and now my colleague, Dr Harukiyo Hasegawa, who has been patient, understanding, and thoughtful. Always willing to listen to my ideas, he gently and painlessly guided me through to submitting the dissertation and then advised me on converting it to this book.

My respondents, the members of the four companies at which I researched, as well as other persons whose names I cannot mention, all deserve special credit and thanks for the efforts to which they went in helping me to understand their work and how they feel about it. I will never be able to repay the debt of gratitude I owe to them. Special thanks must also go to Stephanie Assmann, Daniel Baheta, Timothy Brierly, Dr Christopher Hood, Park Mi Jeong, Jarno Lyytinen, Hayakawa Mineko, David Porter, Philip Shetler-Jones, Michiko Yoshida,[1] Nicholas Henck, and Jutta Vogt who gave of their time to read my drafts, contribute in various other ways, and give me their criticisms and opinions. Many others also contributed ideas, discussion, criticism, and time to this project and I wish to thank them all here. Lastly, it is my duty to insist that all errors of text, fact, and judgement contained herein are entirely my own responsibility.

Glossary of terms and abbreviations

buchō	General manager/division chief
chōnan	Eldest son
furīta	Freelance temporary worker
gekkyū-tori	A pre-war term to refer to those who received, or took (*toru*), their salary (*kyūryō*) on a monthly (*getsu*) basis
hōkōnin	Business executives of the Mitsui House during the Tokugawa period
honne and *tatemae*	One's true feelings and one's public face
ie	Idealized traditional Japanese household
ikigai	That which makes life worth living
ippanshoku	Ordinary clerical career track for regular employees
kachō	Manager/section chief
kaisha	The Japanese firm
kakarichō	Assistant manager/assistant section chief
karōshi	Death from overwork
keieikazokushugi	Literally, managerial familism. It is a term used by Hazama (1997 [1964]) and refers to the pre-war managerial ideology
koshiben	A pre-war term to refer to those workers who carried their lunch-boxes (*bento*) to work tied around their waists
manga	Japanese-style comic books
mokuhyō kanri seido	System of management by objectives (MBO)
mura-shakai	Village society
nenkōjoretsu	Seniority-based pay and promotion
nenpōsei	Annual salary review system
nōryoku	Abilities
oyabun–kobun	Parent–child (relations)
salaryman	Usually a male white-collar university graduate employed by a large Japanese corporation as a regular employee under an implicit lifetime employment agreement
shakaijin	An adult member of society

shanai kōbosei	In-company system of advertising job vacancies
shikata ga nai	(Also *shiyō ga nai*) Loosely translated it means nothing can or could be done to alter the situation
shūsha	Company hunting
shūshoku	Job-hunting
sōgōshoku	General managerial career track for regular employees
teinen taishoku	Customary retirement age fixed by the corporation
uchi and *soto*	Inside and outside
ura and *omote*	Behind and front

Abbreviations

CSC	Chōgin Sōken Consarutingu
JIL	Japan Institute of Labour
MOW	Meaning of Work International Research Team
NKSKK	Nihongata Koyō Shisutemu Kenkyū Kai
NRKK	Nihon Rōdō Kenkyū Kikō
OECD	Organization of Economic Cooperation and Development
SKSH	Shakai Keizai Seisansei Honbu

1 Introduction

Researching Japanese capitalism and modernity

Modernity is as much a state of mind as it is a material condition. It can most neatly be understood as a transformative ethic that has as its engine pushing it forwards and outwards the positivistic and economistic rationalism that is capitalism. With capitalism as its engine, modernity seeks a progressive and linear transformation of the human experience into a rationally and reflexively ordered life-scape that can be proactively controlled and manipulated for the purposes of providing an ever more comfortable, fulfilling, liberating, challenging, and complex life for its human subjects.

Mediating the mental and the material aspects of modernity are the institutions and organizations which individuals and groups construct in order that they might express their consciousness through the process of creative adaptation. That is to say, institutions and organizations are the social mechanisms by which people not only create their environment out of the mental images they have developed but also accommodate themselves to the circumstances of their lives.

Moreover, because capitalism requires expansion if it is not to implode under the weight of its own internal contradictions, so capitalist modernity compulsively expands out from its centre in the West.[1] In so doing, it becomes both a globalizing and a totalitarian phenomenon. It is globalizing in the sense that it ceaselessly and ineluctably extends into previously untouched areas of the world and totalitarian in the sense that as it enters into and interacts with ever deeper and wider realms of the human consciousness it becomes a seductive and beguiling yet enforced and problematic liberation from traditionalism. Like a giant seismic sea wave it colonizes and envelops the future as well as the present and the past in its steady and irresistible advance across and around the earth. Yet, just as the advancing wave, by dint of the underwater terrain it encounters, must possess within it cross- and counter-currents, so capitalist modernity, as it spreads out from its epicentre, contains the capacity to mutate according to the character of the domains it confronts. Consequently, and initially at least, through the process of the globalization of capitalism, modernity becomes not a singular phenomenon but evolves to develop and exhibit a variety of forms according to the circumstances of its appearance and subsequent development in any particular region of the world.

Accordingly therefore, and paradoxically, an epiphenomenon of the globalizing tendency of capitalist modernity is that of the collision and perhaps hybridization, or even convergence of different versions of the modern. Thus, the ongoing transformative process of the destruction, reconstruction, and mutation of ever more complex versions may also have within it the capacity for capitalist modernity to evolve itself into a singular global phenomenon.

Work in capitalist modernity

Work is, with the possible exception of the family, the most important social institution of the modern world (MOW, 1987) and research in the sociology of work is thus central to an understanding of both capitalism and modernity.[2] For in circumstances where premodern ascribed social roles and relations have all but disappeared, life in modern capitalism compels all but the most resourceful to seek the satisfaction of their basic physiological needs through the wage relation. The exchange of labour for money, or paid employment, in a monetized society allows individuals to purchase food and shelter as well as provide security for themselves and their families. In addition, those who do not engage in regular paid employment in the formal economy must ordinarily, through the mediating role of either the state or the family, depend on people who are thus employed.

However, work in the modern world is not simply an instrumental means to physiological security. It is also indispensable to the achievement of a modern self-identity. The content of a person's work, the social and status relations external to the family determined and made possible by work, and the consumption and leisure opportunities opened up to an individual through the wage relation not only provide the principal means by which an individual can construct his or her identity, they are also the principal means by which a person's identity is unwittingly revealed as well as deliberately signalled to others. Furthermore, involvement in work may also provide an opportunity for individuals in mass society to experience feelings of liberation, fulfilment, and deep enjoyment through the activation and actualization of productive and creative abilities and impulses (Csikszentmihaly, 1988).

It is also important to recognize that few people are likely to be able, or perhaps even wish, to use work in employment as a vehicle for the satisfaction and expression of the full range of their needs, desires, and values. Examples of degrading conditions are legion and many are compelled by force of circumstance to struggle even to provide basic material comfort and security for themselves and their families. Boring or repetitive labour that requires little creative input is also unlikely to result in feelings of satisfaction or psychological enrichment. And here lies, of course, one of the basic predicaments of capitalist modernity. Although we are compelled by the ideologies of liberty and self-determination to create our own individual identities and biographies, and we are seduced by the fiction of each person having an equal chance to participate in the race to achieve success in this endeavour, the structural requirements and limitations of a modern capitalist political economy prevent or inhibit a significant proportion of the people of the world's advanced industrial democracies, not to mention the majority of those living in developing countries, from doing just that. Nevertheless, in the modern world, even at this impoverished level, as Jahoda (1982) observes, only work in paid employment, as opposed to unemployment, provides the categories of experience necessary for the maintenance of an individual's mental health and sense of well-being.

> [I]t imposes a time structure on the waking day; it enlarges the scope of social relations beyond the often emotionally highly charged family relations and those in the immediate neighbourhood; by virtue of the division of labour it demonstrates that the purposes and achievements of a collectivity transcend those for which an individual can aim; it assigns social status and clarifies personal identity; it requires regular activity.
>
> (Jahoda, 1982: 83)

Thus, capitalist modernity and, within it, the modern culture of work, are characterized by their tremendous transformative capacity, both through the visible changes that are wrought on the material environment by the industrial and commercial processes as well as by the invisible transmutation of consciousness that engenders and is engendered by the reflexive construction of an entirely different way of life. Modernity, through work as its core social element, defines itself in negation to the past and in its discovery of the future as a temporal territory to be colonized, constructed, and transformed. Thus, work, capitalism, and modernity are intimately bound together in a transformative embrace, each within the other, each acting on and reacting to the other. Without the institution of work, and in particular paid employment, modern life would be impossible in its present form.

Work values

If we can accept the proposition that modern life is inconceivable without a modern culture of work, asking why one would wish to research aspects of people's work values might seem, at first glance, to be unnecessary. Indeed, most research on the subject implicitly assumes an objective validity in examining work values without raising questions as to its underlying purpose.

The enormous interest shown by researchers in work values, attitudes, and dispositions has mainly been generated by the assumption that by studying the meanings and orientations that people bring to their work tasks we can in some measure predict economic and work-related behaviour (Furnham, 1997). Underlying this approach lies the assumption that some values might have a positive relationship to productivity while others might have a negative relationship. Thus, it might be possible to manipulate the work context to maximize the impact of positively related values in order that an economic benefit may accrue. Immediately, one is tempted to ask the question: for whose benefit is this assumed and predicted improvement in economic performance?

Even if this approach does indeed bring forth concrete and positive economic results, and these are shared equitably among all stakeholders in the enterprise, economic expansion per se is not supposed to be an end in itself. It is only important in so far as it provides the means by which people might lead longer, more comfortable, happier, and more fulfilled lives (Oswald, 1997). While the spectacular expansion in the material well-being of the peoples of the world's most technologically advanced industrial societies over the past 100 years or so has no precedent in the entire history of the human race, and this has been accompanied by real and measurable improvements in the standard of living of the majority of people in the developed world, can it be confidently asserted that personal happiness and fulfilment worldwide have increased in proportion to the advances in our material wealth? Notwithstanding the undoubted importance of the economic arena, are we not in danger, therefore, of confusing the means for living in the modern world with its ends?

It appears that much of the academic research on work values and related social phenomena is done with material enrichment in mind and sometimes therefore, by implication, places the interests of employees in a subordinate position to those of management and owners. In so doing it also subordinates all concerns to economic and political priorities, thus contributing to a devaluation and a corruption of the legitimate social, emotional, and psychological needs, desires, and values of all stakeholders as well as of the nobility of the institution of work itself. While economistic and managerial approaches can make a justifiable claim to seeking improvements in working conditions for all employees, and they may be considered a significant step forward from the harsh authoritarianism of Frederick Taylor's Scientific Management, they continue to be as manipulative and to deny employees the opportunity to be considered a stakeholder in the enterprise as well as denying all stakeholders the opportunity to satisfy interests that go beyond the merely mechanistic and material.

Interestingly, and aside from the above ethical issues, there is considerable debate even as to the validity of the assumption that sustainable productivity increases might be achieved by improvements in the working context and, thus, work satisfaction of employees. Intuitively it might be assumed that the relationship is in the direction of productivity but some research suggests that the causal relationship might be in the opposite direction. Reversing the presumed dependency, Paul, Robertson, and Herzberg (1969), as well as Locke and Latham (1990), found that satisfaction tends to increase as a result of high but attainable challenge and performance. Furthermore, Csikszentmihaly and Csikszentmihaly's edited volume (1988) points unequivocally to attainable challenge being the source of deep satisfaction in the process of task completion. Setting aside for a moment ideological and moral criticisms, even if, as Sagie, Elizur and Koslowsky (1996) suggest, the causal relationship is reciprocal rather than simply in the direction of satisfaction alone, the rational economic validity of economistic and managerial approaches is itself questionable.

Moving closer towards a humanistic explanation for this research, if work takes up approximately one-third of the waking hours of a mature adult for a period of, say, between 30 and 50 years, then it is perhaps trite to state that the quality of that experience will be of great importance to the participant. If education and preparation for the world of work, the impact of work on individuals' non-work activities and relationships, and the effects of work on the length and quality of life after retirement are also taken into consideration then the importance of the work experience becomes yet more significant. Likewise, when the unambiguous consequences for people's life chances of structural inequality are combined with an increasingly global and complex division of labour in society, great variation in people's experiences of work and its outcomes can produce feelings of envy, exclusion, and even hatred, loathing, and contempt, with all the associated social repercussions of such divisiveness.

Accordingly, the study of work values ceases to be merely an exercise in finding ever more devious mechanisms for extracting greater surplus value from employees and takes on quintessentially human, social, and even political, requirements of its own.

Institutions and organizations of employment

While the theory of personal agency suggests that people's experience of work depends on the demeanour they bring to their tasks, it is also clear that the institutions and organizations of employment influence the degree to which individuals can satisfy their needs and desires and realize their values. Thus, while it is important to study the ideologies and cultures of work in order that we might have a greater understanding of how people wish to live in modern society, it is also crucial that we study this aspect of social life in the context of the character and structure of the institutions and organizations that enable and constrain our ability to achieve our objectives.

In addition to providing a presumed basis for the prediction of economic behaviour, it has also been contended that work values might be a causal variable in organizational, institutional, and social change (MOW, 1987). It might be presumed, therefore, that the reverse is also true. For people not only develop meanings out of the work that they do but they also bring meaning to their work tasks and, thus, there should be a reciprocal relationship between change in both value systems and the circumstances in which those values are played out in social life. It might also be presupposed, therefore, that if structures are incompatible with or contradictory to those meanings, working people may take measures to alter the social or institutional constraints upon the realization of their needs, desires, and values to gain a greater degree of compatibility. Thus, in order to understand the process of organizational, institutional, and social change we must study the relationship between institutions and organizations and the ideologies of the individuals of which they are comprised.

A large body of research in psychology, sociology, and political economy has been steadily accumulating that advances the controversial opinion that governments and decision-makers in advanced capitalist democracies are attacking the wrong issues (Inglehart, 1990 and 1997; Oswald, 1997). In fact, it may not be an exaggeration to state that the principal goal of the governments of the capitalist democracies has become the achievement of continuous increases in the material standard of living of their peoples. The presupposition that dominates this strategy is to assume that the good life will more or less automatically follow from raising productivity and output. In addition, the principal aim of most capitalist enterprises, large corporations being the most enthusiastic advocates, is to achieve increases in revenues, profits, and market share more rapidly than their competitors. What is the philosophical foundation for such an ethos? Because, for employees, at least, the result of such government and corporate policies has been an apparently unrelenting intensification of the work process coupled to a progressively increasing insecurity within the work context that, combined together, produce ever greater feelings of anxiety among the producers of a nation's wealth (Sennett, 1998).

Perhaps there is something in the nature of our institutions and organizations that causes us as individuals to feel trapped within a self-regulating system that prevents us from realizing our nature as unique human beings embedded in a sustainable society. For as Max Weber contested in his best-known and most controversial work, *The Protestant Ethic and the Spirit of Capitalism*:

> Man is dominated by the making of money, by acquisition as the ultimate purpose of his life. Economic acquisition is no longer subordinated to man as the means for the satisfaction of his material needs . . . the care for external goods should only lie on the shoulders of the saint like a light cloak which can be thrown aside at any moment. But fate decreed that the cloak should become an iron cage.
>
> (Weber, 1976 [1904]: 53 and 181)

If correct, what does this say about the nature of industrial development, the institutional arrangements of market capitalism and liberal democracy, and their relationship with the human condition? Surely, if the course of capitalist development runs counter to, and the institutional arrangements of the modern political economy constrain or restrict the achievement of our goals, goals which may be as much determined by our essential humanity as they are by personal agency and structural conditions, then, should we not question the validity of and seek to reform our social, economic, and political institutions and organizations so that they facilitate the achievement of our ideals and aspirations? Research into the relationships between individuals and the institutions and organizations through which they channel their energies for the achievement of their hopes and ambitions, therefore, would seem to be an urgent priority.

Japan, the lifetime employment system, and the Japanese salaryman

Japan is an important challenge to Western assumptions about the nature of socio-economic development, its directions, and its possibilities. As the most technologically advanced and modern non-Western capitalist economy and representative polity, Japan offers a special opportunity to refine sociological theory and make it more generalizable than is possible through a concentration on Western individuals and institutions (Williams, 1996 and Clammer, 1997). For although the West was the first region of the world to experience modernity and industrial development, and Western capitalist expansion meant that all subsequent forms of modernity are derived in part as a consequence of contact with the West, the Japanese example shows that, although the West will influence and give colour to the Japanese experience, capitalist modernity is no longer a Western, but a global, phenomenon.

Nevertheless, although average material standards of living among the Japanese people have improved dramatically since Japan's virtual collapse in 1945, and even after more than a decade of economic stagnation Japan is still the world's premier industrial manufacturer and second largest capitalist economy, if one spends some time in Japan it is impossible to avoid the feeling that many Japanese people are not quite so sure that the progress their country has made is such an unqualified success. Many know that their country is wealthy but feel that they themselves are not. High prices for basic consumer necessities, cramped, distant, and shabby accommodation, a relative lack of social amenities, polluted cities, and overdeveloped rural areas are frequent and, in my opinion, justifiable complaints among many Japanese people. Further, after having achieved the lofty collective ambition of being accepted as a full and equal member of the club of the world's richest and most powerful nations, many Japanese now wonder where they should go from here (Nakanishi, 2000).

With a consensus on the need for fundamental reform taking shape, but as yet little agreement on how far it should proceed as well as what is to replace the existing system, it would seem to be an opportune moment to observe the characteristics of socio-economic change in Japan from the perspective of refining existing sociological theories.

Although it might reasonably be claimed that it is inappropriate to examine Japan's capitalism and modernity through the lens of Western theoretical approaches, this book challenges that assumption. For is it not the case that, while most theories of social and economic development that are generated by Western scholars come out of a Western historical and cultural milieu, there is an implicit message buried in the text of many of these theories that they can be applied worldwide? This book sets out to examine some of the most significant recent theories of modernity that have been developed in the West, or at least use a Western frame of reference, and applies them to the Japanese experience in order that the process might contribute towards making Western sociological theory sophisticated and sensitive enough genuinely to incorporate and describe both Western and non-Western experiences of capitalism and modernity. In so doing this book, I hope, does not make Japan artificially Western but, rather, makes Western sociology more global.

In Japan, working cultures and the institutions of employment are dominated by the lifetime employment system in large corporations. Although it is claimed a minority of the workforce is actually employed in this system[3] it dominates the employment horizon. It is the system to which the secondary and tertiary education systems are geared and into which they feed their most successful and diligent students (Takeuchi, 1997 and Yano, 1997). The normative power of the system is such that, even in the dual labour market that continues to characterize employment in Japan, small and medium-sized enterprises must organize their recruitment efforts around the cyclical and structural requirements of large corporations (Nomura, 1998) and even provide some of the trappings of long-term security and welfare corporatism to attract and retain scarce high-quality employees (Dore, Bounine-Cabalé, and Tapiola, 1989). In this context it might not be too bold to claim that the lifetime employment system in large corporations is the defining characteristic of the Japanese management system and can be regarded as the core institution of the Japanese firm. Within this system works the so-called salaryman, who can be defined for the purposes of this study as a male white-collar employee of a large corporation who is recruited upon or shortly after graduation from a four-year college course and who has an implicitly understood but not contractually guaranteed opportunity to remain either employed directly by the corporation, or at least in its care, until the mandatory retirement age. In this sense lifetime means for the working life of the employee. For one needs to bear in mind that the average life expectancy for Japanese men during the 1950s and 1960s, which is the time when the lifetime employment system took root across Japanese society, was not what it is today. In fact if a man could only reasonably expect to live until his late fifties or early sixties then working until, say, age 55 really was, to all intents and purposes, very nearly the entire adult life of the employee.

While it is simplistic and reductionist to speak in terms of stereotypes, to the Japanese people the salaryman is more than simply a man in a suit who commutes to work on the train every morning and returns to his family in the suburbs late in the evening after a long day working at his company and, perhaps, drinking with clients and colleagues in a city centre hostess bar. Although post-war stereotypes of masculinity in Japan are coming under increasing scrutiny and criticism (Roberson and Suzuki, 2003), the salaryman remains the principal normative embodiment of Japan's post-war economic success and, as such, he is a cultural icon and ideological model. Salarymen appear as lead protagonists in virtually all Japanese television soap operas and romantic dramas and whole series of *manga* comic strips, such as *Sararīman Kintarō* and *Kachō Shima Kōsaku*,[4] are devoted to life as a white-collar male employee in a Japanese corporation.

The peculiarly Japanese term 'salaryman' was being used even as far back as 1925 when Yoshida Tatsuaki published his book *Sararīman-Ron* ('Theory of the salaryman') and by 1929 the salaryman had achieved his status as a cultural figure in the hit song *Koi no Maru Biru*, which celebrated the symbolic construction of the Marunouchi Building opposite Tokyo Station.[5] However, it was during Japan's high-growth period in particular that the salaryman became one of Japan's best-known and most well-loved cultural icons. From the achievement of sustained and rapid economic expansion and material abundance, through the urbanization of society and nuclearization of the family, to the hedonistic orgy of consumption in the late 1980s 'Bubble Economy' and the consequences of its collapse in the early 1990s, the salaryman has been a central figure in virtually every aspect of Japan's post-war socio-economic development. Further, in this present period of restructuring of the organizations and institutions of the Japanese political economy, it is possibly the salaryman who is bearing the heaviest burden (Kameyama, 1995). Thus, we clearly cannot avoid him, his values, and the institutions of his employment if we seek to find some answers as to the nature of Japan's experience of capitalism and modernity.[6]

Research methodology

Social science now depends almost entirely for the philosophical foundations of its methodology and method on the legitimacy of the scientific method as developed by the natural sciences. There can be little doubt that quantitative and qualitative studies of various kinds that follow the hypothetico-deductive model as explained by Karl Popper (1972 [1959]) have revealed much about our social world and have enabled people from all walks of life to benefit from the decisions made and actions taken as a result of the dissemination of the knowledge acquired.

Nevertheless, it is also clear that this model, although conceptually ideal, is rarely adhered to in its entirety by even natural scientists themselves in the day-to-day practice of their research (McNeill, 1989). It has long been known that while much science is set out as if it were conducted in a coolly and logically consistent manner, imagination and intuition as well as accident and plain luck all play a crucial role in the discovery and dissemination of knowledge. More importantly, the precise order of hypothesis construction, empirical data collection, and further hypothesis development as a theoretical model remains just that, particularly in the domain of social research.

Yet it is comparatively infrequently that scientists actually discuss these aspects of their research and report on them in the formal presentation of their work. This is also true in the social sciences, as Joy Hendry (1999) points out in her illuminating book on the practicalities of research. A description of a nine-month anthropological fieldwork trip to Japan, the book emphasizes the role of chance in the acquisition of knowledge and also demonstrates how moments of insight can be embedded in a mass of everyday activity that may not be directly involved in or related to the actual process of empirical data collection.

The process of writing and presenting research also has a direct and perceptible influence on the development of conclusions and hypotheses since it is at this stage that the researcher has to reconcile and organize into a rational and digestible package often contradictory, confusing, and disparate ideas and data. Consequently, flashes of inspiration and fortuitous circumstances cannot be confined to or eliminated from any part of the research process in a temporal sense and can occur at any time, often without warning in the dead of night.

Although this book quite deliberately and reasonably clearly displays certain subjective leanings on my part, with the hypothetico-deductive model in mind I have pursued a programme of research which has, on occasion over the six years it has taken to research and publish, deviated from the mechanical process that the method dictates but which has not deviated from its underlying philosophical principle. That is to say, I have allowed flashes of inspiration to guide my thoughts, I have allowed blind luck to assist me in accessing respondents and resources, and I have allowed the process of writing itself to lead me in directions that I had not previously anticipated. However, I have also understood that the principal basis of my research has been to try to disprove the hypothesis that the Japanese lifetime employment system and the principal work values of the Japanese salaryman were changing in response both to the globalization of market capitalism and the achievement of material affluence.

In this sense, therefore, this research has both failed and succeeded. For, as the coming chapters will show, genuine change rather than mere adjustment may be appearing in the Japanese socio-economy, both in an institutional sense towards greater flexibility and fluidity of employment structures, and in a subjective sense towards greater self-determination by and individuation of the Japanese salaryman.

Nevertheless, what this book also shows is that very long-term employment at a single organization has not disappeared in Japan and neither has the affective relationship between the corporate community and the salaryman as an individual. Rather, present developments signal a progressive and gradual intensification of forces already present in the macro-economy coupled to an attenuation of many of the structures, relationships, cultures, and ideologies that have hitherto given Japanese people some of their sense of identity and belonging.

Research strategy

Through personal contacts and introductions kindly provided for me I was able to conduct interviews and obtain documentary data from four Japanese corporations of more than 1,000 employees, each of which is listed on the first section of the Tokyo Stock Exchange.[7] The companies are from different business sectors, they occupy different competitive environments, and all four have a reputation for not being pioneers in their sectors, thus being perhaps a stricter test of claims that the lifetime employment system is collapsing and Japan is converging on Western, or Anglo-American forms of industrial organization and social life.

The first, Company A,[8] is an optical and associated high-technology electronic products manufacturer currently employing approximately 5,000 regular employees. The second, Company B, is an automotive components manufacturer also employing some 5,000 employees. The third, Company C, is a non-bank financial services company employing approximately 11,000 people and the fourth, Company D, is a regional utility of approximately 18,000 employees.

The method of access and circumstances of data collection were different for each company and depended on my relationship with it, thus making direct comparisons difficult but not altogether impossible. I had been introduced to the first company during my MA course in Japanese Studies at the University of Essex. I approached it directly and requested to research there a second time. I was granted the request after an interview. For the second company, I was introduced to a director of the company by an academic contact at the University of Tokyo, where I was based at the time, and my request to research there was granted, again after an interview. For the third company I asked a personal contact to introduce me and make a formal request on my behalf. I knew my contact had high-level links with the company and, after a few weeks of negotiations, I was granted my request. I was introduced to the last company by my PhD supervisor at the University of Sheffield.

I interviewed between 15 and 30 male university graduate white-collar employees of all ages and ranks at each company. I also interviewed at least one senior personnel manager and one senior union official from each company. All formal interviews took place on company premises and were, apart from a handful of occasions where my respondent insisted on speaking English, conducted in Japanese. In all interviews with employees only the respondent and myself were present with confidentiality being guaranteed to all. In personnel department and union interviews there was often more than one representative from the company or union present, though at no time did I feel that this fact alone impeded my ability to gain information.

Each interview with the company employees lasted more than 30 minutes and some were as long as two hours. Given the resource and opportunity constraints that I was under I used focused interviews comprising questions related to the interviewee's family and educational background, application and entry into the company, progress through the company, attitudes to the employment system, work values and, finally, hopes for the future. Each interview with the personnel and union officers related to the formal and informal systems of recruitment, training, promotion, pay, rotation and labour–management relations at each company. In addition, I requested documentation regarding these issues. At each company I spent at least one week in interviews and data collection, although at Company D I was able to spend one month researching as well as stay throughout that time in a company dormitory for single male employees. In addition, since the first set of interviews conducted in the autumn of 1998 I was fortunate to be able to visit each company again in the summer of 2001 and interview personnel managers and a small selection of employees.

At each company I had an intermediary, or gatekeeper, to negotiate through. This person arranged interviews, collected data that I requested of him, and often related personal opinions and anecdotes regarding various issues to do with his company and its external institutional and social environment. Grönning (1997) describes how gatekeeper relations in overt requests to research at Japanese corporations can be difficult and obstruct the collection of accurate data but she also explains how attempts by the researcher to gain covert access are fraught with operational, theoretical, and ethical difficulties. Both Grönning's and my solution is to recognize the necessity of making compromises to maintain good relations and to try to minimize the pernicious effects of such problems by devising additional research methods that check or validate the data obtained in overt, often company-controlled, research situations. Thus, in addition to the more formal company-arranged interviews, I was able to arrange meetings with company employees independently of the gatekeeper. These more informal interviews were mostly conducted over food and drink in local restaurants and other locations off company premises.

I did not always get answers to my questions or the documentary evidence that I asked for and I occasionally met with a polite but firm refusal. However, I tried at all times to be open and friendly with all my respondents and not to appear to judge any of their answers. I tried to make them feel as comfortable as possible with me as a foreigner and sometimes rather inarticulate Japanese speaker and, on the whole I am pleased with the results. On only very few occasions did I feel awkward or sense that the respondent felt uneasy with me or that the respondent may not have been telling me what he believed to be true at the time.

In addition to the above in-company field research I collected newspaper and magazine cuttings from the late 1960s, mid-1970s and late 1990s[9] and conducted background interviews at related organizations such as the Japan Federation of Employers' Organizations (Nikkeiren),[10] the Japan Institute of Labour (Nihon Rōdō Kenkyū Kikō), and the Japanese Electrical, Electronic, and Information Union (Denki Rengō). Moreover, through living in Japan for approximately two years during the period of data collection and writing up the original dissertation I have been fortunate enough to meet or be introduced to a great variety of people and institutions who have been kind enough to grant me time for interviews as well as give me valuable documentation, information, and advice.

Finally, although all research of this nature is in large measure a rationalized reconstruction of partial recollections coupled with incomplete documentary evidence, it does give us clues to the circumstances, feelings, thoughts, and values that motivate behaviour as well as an insight into the cultural and ideological orientation of the subject as well as the biographer. This is also true for autobiographical accounts, for individuals, when describing the circumstances of their own lives and the bases of their own behaviour, often seek to persuade themselves in addition to the listener or reader of the rational foundations of their own behaviour. It is in the nature of the modern condition that not only do people wish and expect to be able to determine or influence their future careers, lifestyles, and identities, but they wish to be seen to be in rational and reflexive control of their lives, even if the actual circumstances of their internally generated decisions and reactions to external circumstances, may not actually possess a strongly and intrinsically rational dynamic of self-determination. Thus, in terms of my research objectives in exploring the nature of Japan's modernity, it is appropriate that importance is placed on what respondents actually say but consideration is also given for the cognitive and emotional bases for those statements. The following chapters, I hope and believe, will show that this has been done such that this book proves to be an original, deep, and sympathetic, though not uncritical, examination of one of the most central and defining aspects of capitalist modernity in contemporary Japan.

2 Japanese capitalism and modernity in theoretical perspective

What does capitalist modernity look and feel like? Is there a family likeness that can be discerned when comparing different versions of the modern at different times and in different regions of the world?

Erwin Scheuch (1998) found 11 different definitions for modernity and concluded that the criteria for defining the term are so complex and controversial that it is hopeless to attempt to derive a statement that expresses all its features. Indeed, such a statement would be unavoidably reductionist and, in its tendency to generalize, would obscure and glaze over the unique properties that each expression of modernity possesses. To conclude from Scheuch's work, scholars should perhaps focus on selecting the identifying features that catch, or exemplify and describe, some of its structural and cultural universals. In making such an attempt, therefore, we should study both the macro- and micro-features of social life in combination.

The most obvious and striking of the common features of capitalist modernity might be the physical manifestations of the technological developments that have taken place over the previous 150 years or so. For example, developments in transportation and communications systems have transformed all aspects of our lives and it is not unusual in Los Angeles, Osaka, or Birmingham, for example, for people to commute daily to work and back over a cumulative distance of more than 100 miles. Air travel, telephone, and other electronic communications media mean that one can instantaneously do business with people living on the other side of the earth. Even intimate personal relationships can be conducted for extended periods using these means.

However, there is no disputing that an intercontinental working and personal life is still relatively uncommon and the majority of people might consider such lifestyles to be as remote from their own spheres of experience as those of the aristocracy in earlier times. Perhaps the élite members of the international political economy are indeed the new aristocracy in that not only do they appear to conduct their lives in a sort of inaccessible and glamorous stratosphere of unattainable wealth, they also possess the capability to radically alter other people's destinies through the ostensibly incontestable power of their decisions.

Nevertheless, the working and living arrangements of the majority also are conducted in quite radically different ways to the premodern world. Work is performed in locations distinct, both geographically and culturally, from the home, and the modern and international division of labour has resulted in a complex global matrix of social, economic, political, and cultural differentiation that goes beyond ascribed social hierarchies and ancient geographical boundaries. The inside of our homes, too, has changed to the extent that our private lives are also conducted in radically different conditions. Indeed, the concept of a private life itself is a distinctly modern idea and a comparatively recent phenomenon.

Thus, the material conditions of life in modern society have been transformed out of all recognition in the comparatively short period since the first railway lines were laid and the first factories built. More importantly, however, the physical presence of these modern arrangements has implications deeper than simply making life cleaner, more comfortable, and more convenient. They have consequences for the way we perceive the contexts and meanings of our lives and how we construct strategies for coping with and living in modern society.

In a very general sense, the shift from a comparatively stable and predominantly agricultural society composed of tight communities of extended families within a rigidly ascribed social hierarchy to a permanently transforming mass urban society of small households consisting of an assortment of shifting relationships within an open political economy that enforces the ideology of self-determination is a no less significant development within the transformation to modern society. Consequently, it is also the emotional, spiritual, and psychological aspects of modern society that have transcended traditional or feudal cultures and ideologies and which define us as who we are today. In a deeper sense too, the material and the psychological worlds cannot readily be disentangled. The means to travel easily, cheaply, and regularly over greater distances expands our choice of where we work, consume, play, and build relationships and this has consequences for our conception of the limits to our psychological and emotional growth and the definition and fulfilment of our aspirations and capabilities.

Within the process of becoming a modern developed society and its globalization are there discernible differences between societies that are the product of historical and cultural circumstances and which give rise to different versions of modernity? Even if discernibly different versions can indeed be identified between societies or even between different sections of one society,[1] is it not the case that a consequence of the globalization of economy and society is that of a singular global capitalist modernity gradually emerging out of fragmentation and particularity? While a single brief statement encapsulating all aspects of the modern is too much to ask for and, more to the point, in its extreme generality is also not very informative, perhaps a longer and more detailed examination of a single feature of capitalist modernity might reveal to us both universals and particulars and, thus, be of more concrete use in augmenting our understanding of the complexity of the world in which we live.

A theory for modernity and the individual

While economists have tended to focus on material processes it is one of the tasks for sociologists to examine the relationships between individuals and the institutions and organizations that constitute modern society. Investigations of and reflections on the quality of this nexus will enable us to understand more completely the contingencies inherent in constructions of the modern self and how modern organizations, institutions, and societies develop out of the dynamic interface between individuals, culture, capitalism, modernity, and globalization.

Probably the most influential treatise on modernity in the 1990s is that of the British sociologist Anthony Giddens. The first of his two principal books on the subject, *The Consequences of Modernity* (1990), provides us with a theoretical statement of the nature of modernity at the level of institutions and his second, *Modernity and Self-Identity* (1991), does the same at the level of the individual. In sketching out a preliminary definition of the contours of modernity Giddens states:

> As a first approximation . . . 'modernity' refers to modes of social life or organization which emerged in Europe from about the seventeenth century onwards and which subsequently became more or less worldwide in their influence.
>
> (Giddens, 1990: 1)

Explaining further, he states that although continuities might remain with premodern modes of existence, in a general sense modernity represents a fundamental discontinuity with previous periods in human history and is characterized most clearly by the sheer pace of change and its breadth of scope (ibid.: 6). Therefore, modernity sets itself up as a negation of the stability and continuity of the traditional order through the appropriation of reflexively ordered incoming knowledge and rationality and the establishment of the modern transformative order.

> Inherent in the idea of modernity is a contrast with tradition . . . The routinization of daily life has no intrinsic connections with the past at all, save in so far as 'what was done before' happens to coincide with what can be defended in a principled way in the light of incoming knowledge. To sanction a practice because it is traditional will not do; tradition can be justified, but only in the light of knowledge which is not itself authenticated by tradition . . . this means that, even in the most modernized of modern societies, tradition continues to play a role. But . . . justified tradition is tradition in sham clothing and receives its identity only from the reflexivity of the modern.
>
> (ibid.: 36–8)

However, for Giddens, modernity is not an embracing of the new for its own sake, but the presumption of wholesale reflexivity, including reflection on the nature of reflection itself. Accordingly, the outcome is a feeling of unending uncertainty arising from the designation of all knowledge, relationships, and institutions as being permanently provisional, or in a constant state of potential revision.

Modern life, therefore, comes to be characterized by what Zygmunt Bauman (1995) calls an 'endemic indeterminism'. The more people are attracted by the possibilities of self-determination and self-construction that open out as a result of the gradual collapse of the traditional order, the more they actively and reflexively attempt to reconstruct and control their social world in the light of rationally revealed but permanently provisional knowledge. Consequently, this mode of life inevitably introduces the elements of trust and risk. Trust because automatic and unthinking, or non-reflexive, reliance on traditional modes of life is impossible in modern life and people must depend on, or trust, rational expert systems and unfamiliar persons for even the simplest of life tasks. Risk because, 'No matter how well a system is designed and no matter how efficient its operators, the consequences of its introduction and functioning, in the context of the operation of other systems and of human activity in general, cannot be wholly predicted' (Giddens, 1990: 153).

In these circumstances of what Giddens (1990, 1991) calls a 'reflexive', 'radicalized', or 'high' modernity appear the institutionalization of doubt as well as fundamental problems of ontological security and existential anxiety, which in turn result in the potential for a feeling of personal meaninglessness. Ontological security refers to the confidence that people have in the constancy of their own identity and surroundings and, therefore, central to an understanding of modernity is an appreciation of the psychological problems arising out of the collapse of certainty in traditional systems of knowledge about the world and traditional orders of hierarchical and external ascription. The resolution to this psychic problem of the disembedding from traditional structures requires what Giddens (1991: 9) calls a 'reflexive project of the self' to generate programmes of self-discovery, self-mastery, and self-actualization for which the individual is solely responsible.

Thus, Giddens (1991) goes on to explain, the search for and the discovery of self impact on us all and invite individuals to actively intervene in and transform their internal and external worlds through future-oriented life-planning and the acting out and continuously reflexive revision of those plans in social life. And it is here that the notion of lifestyle assumes a particular significance as individuals are forced to negotiate choices which are increasingly important in the construction and constitution of self-identity. Life-planning also presupposes individualized risk calculation through contact with rationally constructed systems of expert knowledge, where people choose their own career paths or obtain, for example, personalized health services. In this way the institutional reflexivity of modernity individualizes the participant as it penetrates into and transforms the core of the self. For the ideology of modernity is characterized by the belief that one's individual self-identity is no longer externally determined or shared with others through being staked out by the traditional order but must be individually explored, constructed, and transformed as part of the reflexive process that connects the personal, the institutional, and the social.

A person with a stable sense of self-identity must acquire a feeling of possessing a rational biographical continuity that can be grasped reflexively and communicated to others. Consequently, identity comes to be found in the capacity to maintain a sense of narrative and strategic life- and career-planning achieves a crucial role. An intrinsic part of the construction of this rationally contiguous biography is the reflexive monitoring of action, or the deliberate connection of motives, actions, and results in an endlessly repeating cycle that moves through ever more challenging, more absorbing, and more vivid thresholds of experience. Motives are the 'well-springs of action' (Giddens, 1991: 63), which are themselves connected to the construction of identity through the acting out of one's strategic life-plans. Further, the moral thread connecting motives and identity through life-planning is the principle of authenticity, or being true to oneself. Thus, Giddens argues, if successfully achieved, the end result of connecting motives, actions, and results by the thread of authenticity through ever deeper and more complex experience thresholds and life-stages is a rich feeling of what Abraham Maslow (1987 [1954]) referred to as 'peak experiences' and 'self-actualization' or what Csikszentmihaly (1988) calls 'optimal experience' or 'flow'.

But motives do not exist as discrete psychological units (Giddens, 1990). They are an underlying state of feeling and imply a cognitive anticipation of a state of affairs to be realized in the future. This brings us to another important aspect of modernity that Giddens, among others, takes up. Modernity is oriented to the future whereas tradition is oriented to the past. In addition to reflexively preserving existing structures of power and learned dependency, traditional systems gear themselves non-reflexively to protecting the meaning and legacy of the past through the repetition, for its own sake, of both custom and the life-cycle of the generations. However, in Giddens's schema, the possibilities inherent in modernity open up a linear consciousness towards time, or the lifespan, where the future becomes a territory, or a vista, to be colonized in the present through reflexive and strategic life-planning. Life becomes full of the possibilities of realizing one's authentic self in the future through the actualization in self-determined experience of one's true nature. Modernity is thus a profound change in the temporal structure of human experience. Time, self, and life are to be mastered. Central to the ideology of modernity, therefore, is the process of individuation and self-determination whereby the individual's biography becomes a reflexively planned and rationally contiguous story consisting of on-going and purposive growth and transformation culminating, ideally, in the psychological end-state of authentic self-actualization.

It is in this process of individuation, subjectification, and self-construction of identity that the characteristics of modernity are most clearly identifiable. For at the base of modern conceptions of life is the principle of reflexive rationalism which, like a rust, corrodes the supporting structures of the edifice of the traditional order. We are left with little to substitute for the certainties of the past and are condemned to be free to determine our own nature and, thus, our own destiny. Out of the ambiguous void created by the retreat of ascription and withdrawal from the cyclical rhythms of tradition emerges the image of an individually planned and determined, and continuously reconstructed linear trajectory of personal identity and biography.

Giddens's description of identity and modernity is, perhaps, a little optimistic as he does not draw a clear enough boundary between the unilateral construction and determination of modern institutions and ideologies that élites undertake for themselves and then thrust upon a somewhat unwilling and dependent mass society. Bauman (1995) is a little more realistic. For him the endemic indeterminism of modernity leads to a desire by the masses for a new level of stability. However, the restlessness of modernity and the pace and scope of change are characterized by the search for an order which cannot be secured. The ideology of identity construction is experienced as a reactionary urge to fill the void created by the disappearance of the certainties of the premodern period. Thus, Bauman explains, individuality as expressed in the compulsive need to construct one's own identity is experienced as the modern predicament as well as a modern liberation.

Who am I? Where shall I live? What shall I do with my life? These are all, for the majority of those of us who live in modern society, fundamentally problems to be solved rather than opportunities to be celebrated and exploited. Bauman goes on to explain this idea more explicitly through a periodization of experience. Initially it was the élites who cast themselves into the choosing mode and the masses were spared it, with the consequent development of a relationship of domination and dependency. The two responses to the modern identity crisis were, thus, the individuation of self-determination and the communalism of fictive or contrived collectives such as the nation, the corporation, and the union. Now it appears, however, that the globalization of market capitalism is tearing up the cultural foundations of even these communities in its push towards the polar opposites of hybridization and individuation.

Moreover, not only has the ideology of identity choice been forced upon the majority to some extent against their will, the ideology itself is a fiction that can only fully be realized by the few. For is it not the case that while the dependent have been forced to subscribe to the ideology of modern identity construction, most are prevented from achieving full participation in the modern world by the very forces of modernity and globalization that were supposed to release them from the chains of the *ancien régime*? Maximum flexibility for self-construction of identity for the élites in the developed world necessitates at least some inflexibility for the masses and those in the developing world. That is to say, the élites require the masses to accept and believe in the ideology of choice in order that cynicism and disillusionment do not collapse the edifice of modern self-determination from within. The structural conditions enforced by competition in market capitalism require that, even if the majority fully subscribes to the ideal of limitless self-construction, many are condemned eventually to feel that they have, in one way or another, failed. Into this arena enter the media conglomerates sponsored by the trans-national corporations through their proxy, the advertising and marketing industries, and one can see the gradual and inconspicuous, but nevertheless unplanned, formation of a new and global mode of ideological subjugation of the many by the few. As John Clammer (1997) so perceptively asks, in capitalist modernity has seduction, therefore, replaced traditional forms of repression as the principal form of domination and manipulation of the many by the few?

Tradition and the self in Japanese modernity

How does Japanese modernity fit into this schema? For if there are questions as to the suitability of Western constructs for explaining the Japanese experience, these need to be asked and the answers incorporated into a working theory that then needs to be looked at in the light of empirical investigations. Two areas of difference are important in the context of these discussions. The first is the problem of the incorporation of tradition into Japanese capitalism and modernity, and the second is the concept of the relational and dependent self in Japanese society. For if modernity equates in essential measure to the withering away of tradition and Japan actively incorporates real and not sham tradition into the fabric of its development then can Japan confidently be called a modern society? Second, if individual reflexive self-construction is central to the ideology of modern society and the Japanese self depends to a large extent on external structures for its realization in social relations then, again, can Japanese society be considered truly modern?

Tradition

Giddens's work on modernity, a little unfairly in my view, suffers from the accusation that it is ethnocentric. In his two theoretical examinations of the particularities of Japanese modernity Clammer (1995 and 2001) throws up a challenge to what he refers to as the 'universalist pretentions' (1995) of Giddens's rendering. The central thesis of Clammer's work is that Japanese modernity exhibits quite different characteristics to those which exist in the West and that Japan, as a non-Western though materially developed society, is a unique and powerful challenge to the preoccupations and epistemology of much conventional sociological and cultural thinking.

Clammer sees the maintenance and management of tradition as an essential ingredient of Japanese modernity and criticizes what he calls Giddens's 'unargued assumption' that modernity is fundamentally a post-traditional order. Concurring with Maruyama (1965) that modernization is disruptive for the individual in that he or she is emancipated from traditional bonds, Clammer contends that Japanese modernization has perhaps proceeded more quickly and more successfully precisely because tradition was incorporated into the development effort. In Maruyama's view, for example, the incorporation of the traditional paternalistic family, or *ie*, ideology into the modern business organization and the national polity has been a comparative advantage in Japan's modernization. Giddens's reply might be that a strategy of using tradition in a rational and purposive manner is simply 'sham tradition'. However, it cannot be denied, first, that in order for the strategy to work, rank and file employees had to subscribe to the ideologies of managerial familism and welfare corporatism in a more or less uncritical and received manner and, second, that managerial familism itself was invented as, and then became, a tradition and has been more or less preserved until today, against powerful rational arguments for its abandonment.

Andrew Gordon's (1998a) historical examination of the invention and use of industrial paternalism as a traditional ideology describes well the seductive capabilities of various élite groups in achieving and maintaining dominance through appealing to the communal sympathies of the masses. Nevertheless, although managerial, union, and government leaders actively and purposively incorporated traditional structures into their construction of the modern Japanese corporation in the interests of furthering Japan's modernization project (Gordon, 1998a and Vlastos, 1998), many rank and file employees certainly internalized a genuine belief that their corporation was, and perhaps is, a traditional structure incorporating an authentically Japanese traditional ideology.

Moreover, there are arguments to suggest that the incorporation of the *ie* ideology into the corporate system was not solely the result of a strategy devised by Japanese management to nail down scarce and unreliable skilled labour to a single workplace, as in Hazama's (1997 [1964]) and others' view, but was probably also an emotional and subconscious attempt by the employees themselves to cope with a rapidly changing and confusing environment by the application of previously acquired experience, knowledge, and culture through a process of 'cultural modelling' (Ashkenazi, 1996). This seizure, transference, and then adaptation of a practice or ideology from a previous social milieu are valuable for the sake of efficiency and organizational strength because of their familiarity. But they are not simply employed in a reflexive manner for rational economistic reasons but also in a reactive or defensive and unconscious or instinctive manner in order to establish zones of comfort in response to confusing and unfamiliar developments in the external environment. For as Eric Hobsbawm (1983) states, one of the purposes underlying the invention of tradition is to establish a suitable link with the past for the sake of preserving familiarity in continuity and, thus, this invention occurs most often during periods of rapid and profound transition.

In a general sense, of course, all tradition is invented but the more important questions surely are: by whom was it invented, when, for what purposes, and what were its effects (Vlastos, 1998)? No doubt there were instrumental and forward-looking objectives involved on both sides of the labour–management divide at the time that managerial and national familism were invented as traditional ideologies in Japan. However, there were also on both sides, and continue to be, powerful emotional and backward-looking reasons for holding onto familiar cultures and ideologies at a time of confusion, insecurity, and profound material transformation. Does this indicate, therefore, that genuinely traditional systems can become re-embedded into modern Japanese culture, thus partially overcoming Giddens's somewhat restricted interpretation of the meaning and role of tradition in modernity?

The Japanese relational self

Again in Clammer's descriptions of Japanese modernity (1995, 1997, and 2001), the emphasis in modern Japanese life hitherto has been on the social nexus rather than on developing the individual. For Clammer, the Japanese self, while reflexive, is also relational, which leads to a greater closure of social life. That is to say, risks are greatly moderated by ongoing relations of interdependency leading to less personal autonomy and less discourse about authenticity and self-actualization. Such a society, although possessing a deep sense of practical reason in the application of technological developments to the problems of everyday life, emphasizes the particularistic, personal, and emotional as normative guides to behaviour over and above the universalistic philosophical reason and individualistic rationalism of the West. Clammer (1997) claims that Japanese society is thus more realistic in its understanding of the human condition but that it is also profoundly utopian in character in its search for a genuinely humane solution to the dehumanizing and alienating potentialities inherent in modern urbanism and capitalism.

Loiskandl (1998) goes further to contend that if the Japanese psyche 'knew an original sin it would probably be that of individualism'. For Loiskandl, Japanese thought is based on 'trans-rationality' where the search for beauty and harmony can be equated with the Western search for rationality. More weight is given to group consensus in decision-making and the Japanese prototype for the ethical person is one with a strong sense of loyalty to others rather than the lonely, angst-ridden, philosophical hero possessed of intellectually derived universalistic ethical principles. Further, while Western ethics concerns itself with the Socratic dictum of the 'unexamined life', the Japanese system proposes a sacredness of experience and aesthetics that transcends the rationalistic surgical scalpel of Western reflexive analysis (Clammer, 1995 and Loiskandl, 1998). Again, according to this critique, the Japanese have been able to transmit, adapt, and use to their advantage value orientations from an earlier era.

Clammer's description of the shifting, contextual, and relational Japanese self is not new and has by now become one of the standard interpretations of Japanese social psychology. For example, Hamaguchi Eshun (1982) contended that the basic principle underlying Japanese society is that of *kan-jinshugi* or 'relationalism'. Hamaguchi's Japanese society is neither the society of individualism nor that of complete communitarianism. However, he does appear to lean towards the communitarian in his descriptions of the priorities of the Japanese self. He describes a society of interconnectedness between the self and the collective where the location of the most significant part of the self is in the area between interrelated selves that can be called society or community.

After having lived in Japan for more than eight years now, it is hard for me to accept completely these descriptions of the modern Japanese relational self. On the contrary, rather than basing one's understanding solely on cultural schematics, it may be possible also to explain aspects of contemporary Japanese social relations and social action by supplementing them with the analytical tools of modern political economy. Japanese society often appears to me to be relational, emotional, and flexible if one possesses power and status, if one is rich, or if one is able and prepared voluntarily to subscribe and conform to others' expectations and the singular normative model for living. It can sometimes be frustratingly and disappointingly uniform, procedure-bound, unsympathetic, and inflexible for the weak and vulnerable, the poor, or the distinctive. By way of example, Plath's (1983) edited volume of life-course studies of various Japanese individuals and groups challenges the generally accepted view of the Japanese submerged self and leaves one with the feeling that the group works best for those who have the task of making decisions that have consequences for others. In both Skinner's (1983) and Noguchi's (1983) essays in the same volume, the ideal career path that is set down in the ideology of the group-centred corporation is seldom realized in practice. Uncertainty and anxiety are extremely high for those individuals who are at the mercy of senior managers and central government bureaucrats who often manipulate the system to ensure continued security for themselves and their cadres at the expense of loyal, hard-working, and expectant company employees' interests.

Despite these reservations, Clammer makes a valuable and important contribution to our understanding of the social and cultural dynamics of Japanese capitalism and modernity and correctly identifies in Japanese conceptions of the self an important challenge to Western epistemologies. For if identity lies at the centre of conceptions of the modern, and if Japanese identities possess substantially different characteristics from modern capitalist Western societies because of their possessing a more significant relational basis, then the challenge that Japanese society poses to sociologists of capitalist modernity is indeed a powerful and intriguing one.[2]

However, it may also be the case that, as a result of the achievement of material affluence and the external pressures arising from the process of economic globalization, the Japanese self is itself undergoing a profound transformation of the sort that renders standard interpretations obsolete. It is Clammer himself who, in his second study on contemporary Japanese society

(1997), hints strongly at this possibility. If this process is occurring, how can we include it in terms both of our understanding of the Japanese self and of our understanding of capitalist modernity as a global social phenomenon?

Before discussing contemporary social change and recent developments in the relationship between self and society in Japan, we must first examine the historical circumstances of the emergence and evolution of modernity in the West and its later appearance and development in Japan. Through this approach it is possible to demonstrate that the Japanese experience has been historically distinctive and that this may have influenced the formation and character of contemporary Japanese capitalism and modernity.

Modernization in Europe and Japan

It is now widely agreed among historians and sociologists that the fulcrum around which the transformation from a medieval to a modern society in Europe turned was the twin cultural revolutions of the Renaissance and the Reformation. Although debates continue as to how far back the roots of this transformation lie, it was not until the seventeenth century that these revolutions had overcome religious and political suppression enough that its spread could confidently be asserted as heralding a sea change in human consciousness.

This thesis was first put forward forcefully by the German sociologist Max Weber (1976 [1904]). Although Weber's work remains controversial, his main contribution to sociology was in making a causal link between cultural values and the organization and development of society or, more specifically, between ascetic and reflexive rationalism and the rise of modern bureaucratic capitalism. Weber fully posited that cultural values mark out the parameters for social and economic development. As a part of this general theory he specifically attributes the rise of modern capitalism in Europe to an elective affinity between it and the Protestant ethic. He goes on to expand this idea into a general hypothesis on the rationalization and bureaucratization of all areas of social, economic, and political life and the enslavement of all participants within what he called 'the iron cage' of rationality, regardless of whether they continue to, or ever did, believe in the religious principle of predestination. Towards the end of the book he describes it thus:

> The puritan wanted to work in a calling; we are forced to do so. For when asceticism was carried out of monastic cells into everyday life, and began to dominate worldly morality, it did its part in building the tremendous cosmos of the modern economic order . . . Victorious capitalism, since it rests on mechanical foundations, needs its support no longer . . . The idea of duty in one's calling prowls about in our lives like the ghost of dead religious beliefs.

> (Weber, 1976 [1904]: 181–2)

This was a revolution in consciousness originating from below in the subversive religious teachings of Martin Luther and John Calvin. Nevertheless, Weber was careful to describe that the subsequent emergence and expansion of capitalism was an unintended consequence of a specific religious and cultural orientation to the material world.

Beginning with and occurring alongside these cultural changes there were philosophical developments that provided the intellectual conditions for the growth of reason, secularization, and instrumental rationality and that formed the foundations of the enlightenment, modern science, and the birth of modern capitalism. The culmination of this firmly placed humankind at the centre of the human imagination for the first time since classical antiquity and caused Europe to pass through a series of social, political, and economic revolutions that rooted themselves in social mobility, industrial development, capitalist markets, rational bureaucracy, the consolidation of the nation state, and liberal democracy, and ultimately fostered a conception of the modern person as an essentially autonomous and reflexive individual. The seedbed of Western capitalist modernity, therefore, was a transformation of consciousness; the belief that at the centre of the universe stands the individual and that the individual has the capability to guide, if not determine, his own destiny.

Japan's development into a modern capitalist society, however, followed quite a different path and this leads us to contemplate the possibility that Japan's modernity, as a result, may exhibit some different qualities from those which exist in Western societies. Tominaga (1990 and 1998) posits the quixotic idea that Japanese society followed precisely the reverse path of modernization to that of Western Europe and that this has resulted in social life in Japan possessing quite different characteristics. Below is a brief summary of his thesis.

When Japan was confronted by the superior military power of the West in the middle of the nineteenth century, the course of action chosen by the Japanese élites, after much internal debate and some strife, was to agree to Western demands to open up to trade and embark upon a defensive and reactive policy of rapid national strengthening through industrial development, or what Maruyama (1965) called 'purposive modernization'. Contrary to conditions in Western Europe, economic modernization in Japan did not occur from below in an ad hoc manner as a result of the activities of reflexive, proactive, and autonomous individuals who were steeped in the cultural, social, and political transformations of the Reformation and beyond. Economic modernization was imported into Japan from the West and methodically enforced by the new Meiji government precisely because Japan's new élites did not want Japan to become like the West in a spiritual and cultural sense.

Tominaga accepts the basic Weberian proposition and, further, divides the social system into the four Parsonian[3] components, or sub-systems, of economy, politics, society, and culture. According to this schema, European modernization occurred with a modernization of the cultural sub-system first and then progressively through that of society, politics, and the economy. However, Tominaga contends that Japan, because of the peculiar circumstances of its seclusion and enforced opening, modernized along the reverse path. Not only was economic modernization a policy instituted first in a deliberate manner by the new Meiji government, the people of Japan were emotionally and culturally somewhat unprepared for the requirements of the industrial age in terms of their semi-feudal consciousness, and were educated and persuaded by the new regime to accommodate to economic modernization and then to embrace it. Tominaga then goes on to explain how the process of modernization in Japan encompassed the political and then the social sub-systems through the tumultuous events of the twentieth century. However, he also suggests that if cultural modernization means the rationalization of religious thought, because religion is the foundation of culture, then Japanese society has yet to achieve cultural modernization because there never has been a functional equivalent of any real significance to the Protestant Reformation in the Japanese religious system.

Given the enormous changes that had been proceeding throughout late Tokugawa society, it is difficult wholeheartedly to accept Tominaga's contention that Japanese economic modernization could have taken hold so comprehensively and so rapidly upon such a *tabula rasa*. The logic of Tokugawa development meant that there were powerful forces building up in Japan even before the arrival of Commodore Perry's Black Ships. For example, Thomas C. Smith's (1959) scholarly account of agricultural change in the Tokugawa period shows clearly how the steadily increasing power of agricultural markets caused a gradual hiving off of economic rationality from the social sphere such that he feels able to claim:

> These changes, however, were of great importance for Japanese history, perhaps justifying comparison with the agricultural revolution in Europe . . . their central feature was a shift from cooperative to individual farming.
>
> This change is easier to describe than explain, but if one of its causes may be singled out as especially important, it must be the growth of the market, with all that implies about changes in men's ways and ideas. More than any other influence the market lifted economic life in the village out of the context of traditional social groupings. Economic exchange . . . became increasingly independent of social organization and created values of its own.
>
> . . . Thus the power of status, traditionally defined, was greatly reduced, and new routes were opened to social position and political power.
>
> (Smith, 1959: ix–x)

Tominaga's interpretation of the order of European development, while admittedly schematic, could also perhaps, take greater account of the role of structural developments that presaged the emergence of capitalism, particularly in England, and the overlap and interweaving of the cultural, social, political, and economic forces at work throughout Europe even before, but certainly after, the Renaissance and Reformation. These changes included, for example, the dislocations following the series of plagues in the mid- to late fourteenth century that provided the impetus for gradual but dramatic changes in European social life.[4] For example, the earlier appearance of industrial capitalism in England owes much to structural social, economic, and political developments over the whole period of the Middle Ages. It is important to recognize, therefore, that the Renaissance and Reformation were not just a new beginning in Europe but were, like any period of great historical change, as much a culmination of the processes that preceded them as they were the start of an altogether new construction of reality.

Tominaga's thesis, as a broadly schematic representation, is sound in so far as it identifies the crucial differences between the historical development of European and Japanese capitalism and modernity. However, it is a little too neat in its explanation. The structural interplay of social, economic, political, and cultural forces and their weaving in and out of each other through history in a complex process of mutual cause and effect were more complete, long ranging, and significant than Tominaga accepts. Further, and perhaps most significantly, the cultural logic of contemporary capitalist modernity itself may be categorically different from earlier incarnations and, as it globalizes and hybridizes both the institutions and individuals that make up society, are we not witnessing, therefore, the emergence throughout the developed world of a new global hybrid form of capitalist modernity?

The self and modern society in the West and in Japan

There is a powerful ideology existent in the West that individual purposive action to control and manipulate the external world is possible and, even, that it is morally correct. Active intervention by individuals to substantiate in their social world the future-oriented mental images they have created about themselves has achieved the power of a normative value in society. In this cultural milieu, therefore, life is lived from the inside out. That is to say, and speaking in only the broadest theoretical and most schematic sense, transformations and developments in the inner world of cognitive experience precede transformations and developments in the external material and institutional environment.

In direct contrast to the West, it is said that Japanese people believe the self to be deeply embedded in social relationships (Lebra, 1976; Hamaguchi, 1982; Markus and Kitayama, 1991). So much is this apparently so that there is little confidence in the power of the individual to devise and execute his or her own destiny, especially if those plans run counter to prevailing normative conditions. Of course, Japanese people are possessed with self-consciousness and an understanding of the self as a distinct biological entity, but there is also a real recognition of, or assumption about, the deep interdependency of selves in society which is less powerful, though by no means absent, in the West. But this leads the Japanese to a greater accommodation with existing reality rather than an active attempt to mould the external world. The expressions *shikata ga nai* or *shiyō ga nai* (loosely translated: nothing can or could be done to alter the situation) are uttered by Japanese people with such regularity that this alone convinces me that Japanese people feel more heavily constrained in their actions by external conditions and relationships. Dichotomies such as *ura* and *omote* (behind and front), *uchi* and *soto* (inside and outside), or *honne* and *tatemae* (one's true feelings and one's public face) and so on also indicate that there are sharper distinctions in the Japanese mind between the inner and outer consciousness. The outer consciousness is more dependent on, and determined by, semi-ascribed social roles and relations and the inner consciousness is where free rein is given to one's own thoughts. However, according to the customs of proper social discourse and behaviour, this inner world should not normally be displayed to the outside world for fear of disturbing the emotional, moral, and aesthetic imperatives of proper social behaviour, or because they are felt to be mostly unrealizable in practice due to the limitations placed on the individual by a complex and hierarchically arranged web of social relations.

This comparative lack of faith in the power of the individual successfully to act out his or her mental maps in the external or material world is, perhaps, both a direct consequence and an indication of the direction of the process of Japan's modernization. As has already been discussed, modernization was largely thrust upon the Japanese people from without and from above, and the process of modernization began with transformations in the external and material worlds, not the inner world of the self as it did in the West. In this representation it is possible that the Japanese self has yet to experience a cultural transformation that places the individual at the heart of the Japanese world-view. As a result, Japanese social life remains deeply conservative, and transformative developments appear to be accepted in a manner akin to a defensive and reluctant retreat from the traditional and premodern. In this schema, then, life is lived from the outside in. In other words, transformations and developments in the external material and institutional environment precede transformations and developments in the inner world of cognitive experience.

In a very basic sense, Marxist analysis presents material transformations as the source of cultural change and Weberian analysis the reverse. Undoubtedly, day-to-day social life in any society involves an interpenetration of both material and ideological processes. Not only did both Marx and Weber understand and stress this, neither thesis is a complete explanation for the differences between Japanese and Western societies. However, a difference can be observed in a generalized social consensus, or belief, as to the relationship between, and the roles of, the individual and larger social groups. The Western ideology of the modern self is based on a linear approach to time and stresses the individual's moral responsibility for the realization of his or her authentic nature as an autonomous, independent, and distinctive adult in an open society. The Japanese world-view has hitherto been founded in a cyclical approach to time and sees the mature ethical adult, or *shakaijin*, as voluntarily becoming embedded in and adapting to social relations that require negotiation for the realization of a dependent, communal, and common nature within a comparatively closed social structure. Naturally, this is a very schematic description but nevertheless, we can, at this stage, qualify Western societies as being broadly progressive, philosophical, and idealistic, and Japanese society as being broadly conservative, practical, and realistic.

Contemporary social change, globalization, and convergence

The American political scientist Ronald Inglehart (1990 and 1997) posits the interesting idea that a profound generational culture shift in value systems is taking place across the whole of the developed world. Basing his theories in Abraham Maslow's theory of needs,[5] Inglehart describes the basic outline of his thesis thus:

> as a result of the rapid economic development and the expansion of the welfare state that followed World War II, the formative experiences of the younger birth cohorts in most industrialized societies differed from those of older cohorts in fundamental ways that were leading them to develop different value priorities . . . the historically unprecedented degree of economic security experienced by the postwar generation . . . was leading to a gradual shift from 'materialist' values (emphasizing economic security above all) toward 'Postmaterialist' priorities (emphasizing self-expression and the quality of life).
>
> (Inglehart, 1997: 4)

Marshalling an impressive range of empirical data, Inglehart builds a controversial thesis that there is a dialectical relationship of cause and effect between economic development and cultural change and that, therefore, the interrelationship between economic growth and cultural change is predictable in a general sense. He divides contemporary society into two phases; the modern, where material values take precedence and where the core project is economic growth, and the postmodern, where postmaterialist values are paramount and where the core project is individual well-being (ibid.: 75–6).

In this analysis, there appears to be a threshold beyond which economic growth brings diminishing returns in terms of subjective well-being. Once beyond this people begin to place greater emphasis on lifestyle, self-expression, and other quality of life concerns in an effort to increase their personal happiness. For example, in the sphere of work there appears to be a shift away from maximizing one's income and employment security towards a growing insistence on meaningful and rewarding work (ibid.: 44). People, thus, begin to spend more time thinking about the meanings and purposes of their lives and their work, the means by which they may achieve satisfaction, fulfilment, and self-actualization, and the consistency of fit between their beliefs and aspirations and their substantive expression.

With specific reference to Japan, Inglehart has been criticized by Flanagan (1982) on a number of points that not only throw up questions about Japan's place in his basic framework as a non-Western but developed society, but also, as a result, question the very basis of his thesis. Flanagan's 'functional constraints' approach differs from Inglehart's Maslovian needs theory-based approach in the following way.

> The functional constraints approach starts with the assumption that every state of human civilization is accompanied by a 'consciousness' that reflects the underlying material technological realities of the human condition. Social values impose functional constraints on the 'state of nature' drive for self-actualization for the purpose of maximizing the individual's life-chances within a particular socioeconomic environment. A society's norms, then, are a response to the question 'what attitudes and behaviour patterns will best ensure the survival and well-being of the individual and the community in this socioeconomic context?'
>
> (Flanagan, 1982: 407)

Thus, Flanagan goes on to say, austerity, frugality, pietism, conformity, and deference are the prevailing normative values in agrarian societies because they are characterized by scarcity as their principal functional constraint. However, industrialization causes a change in socio-economic conditions from 'insecurity, interdependence, and scarcity to those of economic and physical guarantees, self-sufficiency and affluence' (ibid.: 408) which alters the conditions for individual success and thus permits changes in values in the direction of weaker moral constraints, or a move from authoritarianism to libertarianism. Flanagan interprets Inglehart's theory as associating value change with a decrease in acquisitive and materialist values but argues that value change is more correctly interpreted as being associated with a decline in inhibiting authoritarian values which themselves are derived from the basic material condition of scarcity.

Inglehart defends himself (1982 and 1990) by attributing the apparent difference between the structures of Japan's and Western countries' value systems to Japan's comparatively recent and rapid industrialization. Thus, he argues, premodern, modern, and postmodern value systems have come to exist simultaneously within the same society and give off a confusing and often misleading picture. For example, Inglehart cites Japan's cooperative premodern wet-rice culture as a cause of Japanese society's apparently groupish tendencies but states also that this is waning with industrialization, urbanization, and affluence.

While both scholars attempt to justify their theories with historical and cultural evidence, their arguments are perhaps ahistorical and acultural in the sense that they do not delve sufficiently into the cultural and philosophical foundations of premodern life in either Europe or Japan (the United States possessing a modernist transformative ethic from its inception as a Western society). In addition, they do not account fully for cultural contingencies in the formation of a world-view and the behaviours derived therefrom. Flanagan implicitly assumes that agrarian societies would possess a libertarian self-actualizing dynamic were it not for the 'functional constraints' of economic scarcity and Inglehart also assumes that premodern societies would have a similar post-materialist dynamic were it not for economic scarcity and insecurity. This assumption that the self has a basic, or essential, self-actualizing dynamic that may be repressed by external political or economic conditions neglects to ask the question as to whether the self is also historically and culturally contingent (Casey, 1995) or if human development itself possesses an evolutionary teleology that points towards growth, complexity, and differentiation (Csikszentmihaly, 1988 and Inghilleri, 1999). It also neglects to ask the question as to whether the self is a singularity or whether individuals possess multiple selves that are contingent upon immediate circumstances and relationships as much as they are by the formative experiences of youth (Rosenberger, 1992).

Certainly the early medieval and agrarian European world-view saw the self as a part of God's universe and absolutely dependent on God, through the Church and its temporal representatives in the form of kings, princes, and priests. God, not humankind, was at the centre of this universe (Tawney, 1975 [1922]). The idea that the self could possess a self-directed will on earth independent from God's grace was virtually absent from the early medieval European mind. The closest one might come to recognizing a self-actualizing dynamic at that time was in the renunciation of sins and faith in heavenly salvation after one's death. Those few medieval humanists who did exist had to study the texts of classical antiquity in secret, often in their Arabic translation, and when discovered were customarily either banished beyond Christendom or simply tortured and executed as heretics. The humanistic current that remained through the medieval period was thus very much an underground movement that did not reach its fruition until the late Middle Ages and the Renaissance.

In the premodern and modern periods, the Japanese experience and world-view suggest that the individual may not possess so much a self-actualizing dynamic but a desire, or need, to contribute to the ongoing preservation and success of the group, while subordinating personal concerns to social aesthetics. Inglehart refers to these social values as a hangover from Japan's recent agrarian past, though this is a speculative assertion that is difficult to prove.

Furthermore, far from attributing value change in Japanese or any other society to the impact of Westernization or even cultural imperialism, both Inglehart and Flanagan, as well as others, adopt an acultural posture by flatly rejecting this thesis and asserting that it emphasizes superficial concerns and ignores the core process. Inglehart writes, 'Wearing Western clothing was not crucial; industrialization was' (1997: 24), while Flanagan states,

> We are not arguing the case for cultural convergence here . . . We do find, however, a number of value dimensions along which a quite pronounced degree of change has been taking place in postwar Japan which parallel, though perhaps lag behind, the direction of change in the West.
>
> (Flanagan, 1982: 440)

This is the area where Inglehart's thesis is both very persuasive and vulnerable to criticism. Powerful because the idea of a path-dependent developmental process is not new and is supported by a number of scholars, but vulnerable because he appears to ignore the globalizing tendencies of Western capitalist modernity. As Daniel Bell describes in *The Cultural Contradictions of Capitalism* (1996 [1976]), capitalism requires that all people become simultaneously both consumers and producers of its products. Extrapolating from Bell's idea, in an age when the capitalist process is intensifying and globalizing at an unprecedented rate, capitalism makes demands on our time, as well as our mental capabilities, to the extent that we may become slaves to the process rather than its masters. In this sense, alongside other intellectual and cognitive developments, the globalization of Western capitalism comes to condition even the basis of culture itself.

Capitalist expansion and industrial development are intimately bound together with modernization and all possess a globalizing dynamic which itself has transformative consequences for the basic characteristics of these processes. Nevertheless, it is also inescapable that, for all the optimistic globalism of the transnational élites, all three processes originated in and are dominated, if not controlled, by the West. For better or worse, they are all also perceived by many, if not most, non-Western people as essentially Western phenomena that penetrate into and disrupt their ways of life from the outside, but that are at the same time impossible to resist. Notwithstanding, globalization and Westernization can also be forces for good in pushing back the frontiers of ignorance, oppression, and exploitation and are often, therefore, welcomed for these reasons by the very people who subsequently and unwittingly become ensnared in newer, subtler, or more seductive modes of domination and dependence. The value changes that occur within modernization, therefore, cannot be so neatly disentangled from globalization and Westernization and thrown at the feet of industrialization. We must, in addition, take account of these processes that envelop, squeeze together, and then subsequently export and hybridize the process that Inglehart describes.

Moreover, while the preponderant weight of media and commercial interests lie in the West, indeed, in the United States, and the word globalization is often somewhat misused as a synonym for the expansion of the American economic and cultural system, globalization does not equate with either Westernization or Americanization. Looked at positively, it is a process of hybridization that allows for a plurality of cultural, institutional, and organizational forms to exist within a mélange that allows individuals and groups to choose the forms most suited to their particular needs, and use a variety of them simultaneously, while caring little for where they first originated (Pieterse, 1995).

However, this is perhaps not a sufficient explanation since particularism, in the form of, for example, strong ethnic or national identities, appears to be itself a product of globalization and contact with the other (Robertson, 1995). Thus, Robertson uses the Japanese business term 'glocalization' to describe the process whereby there is progressively greater differentiation within an increasingly global consciousness or, in other words, a simultaneous interpenetration of the global and the local. For Robertson, it is the contemporaneous expansion within society of the local and the global and the interpenetration of particularism and universalism.

Quoting the Japanese business guru Kenichi Ohmae (1995a), Giddens (1999) is more blunt: 'The era of the nation state is over. Nations . . . have become mere "fictions".' Giddens goes on to emphasize that globalization, while assumed by many to be purely an economic phenomenon, incorporates virtually every aspect of our lives. It is in addition intensely political, social, and cultural. For Giddens, globalization is only partly Westernization since it also involves a decentring from the West as non-Western cultural systems seek to be and are incorporated into the global system. He uses the reverse colonization of Los Angeles by Latin Americans as an example of this point.

In a similar vein J. S. Eades (2000), using Manuel Castels's trilogy *The Information Age* as a guide, presents us first with a working definition of globalization as that of 'the world economy: the increasing dominance of the multinational companies at the expense of the nation state, the speeding up of capital flows both within and across international boundaries, and the consequent movement of labor across the globe.' He then adds a cultural dimension to this economic definition by describing globalization as 'the global diffusion and "creolization" of cultural forms and meanings, manifested in phenomena such as the McDonaldization of eating habits, the proliferation of theme parks, or the popularity of international brand name goods.'

Perhaps, however, neither Giddens nor Robertson nor Eades gives enough consideration to the relative weight that Westernization and Americanization play within the multi-directional process of globalization and, moreover, the feeling and perception, rightly or wrongly, among most non-Western peoples that globalization has come to mean the colonization of their life-space by the expansion of Western (read Anglo-American) capitalist modernity. For although globalization has been a more or less permanent feature of human development, it is only in the contemporary period that it has accelerated, widened, deepened, and intensified to the extent that no one can now avoid its consequences. Those who live outside the core networks and processes of global capitalism are coming to feel that they are being compelled to capitulate to, and collude with, non-native forms of social and economic life merely to protect some vestige of the meaning that their previous existence had given them from further dilution by the tendency towards rationalization and commercialization that is generated by the expansion of Western modernity and the globalization of Western market capitalism.

Nevertheless, the British political philosopher John Gray (1998) argues against any form of convergence, homogenization, or hybridization as consequences of globalization since, he reasons, if economic systems are predominantly built upon, and predicated by, culture then as capitalism spreads across the earth it will come to be incorporated into differentiated systems of belief and, thus, take on forms specific to the cultures into which it is absorbed. Globalization, therefore, in Gray's view, leads to precisely the reverse of convergence, or an increasing proliferation of differentiated capitalisms as capitalism expands into previously untouched regions of the world.

Gray uses the Japanese example to propose his idea that global capitalisms will proliferate and strengthen themselves and that the Anglo-American version is merely one singularity among many. However, his arguments appear to be based upon popular though outmoded beliefs about the strength and stability of the Japanese economic system as well as somewhat stale assumptions about the history of Japanese modernization and the traditionalist cultural and ideological roots of Japanese economic organizations. Even so he does feel forced to concede that the Japanese system may have to change, but does so without giving the reader much idea as to the sources of such change or any indication as to what kind of system may thus develop (Gray, 1998: 174). Further, and more tellingly, he does not give enough consideration to the notion that culture is a dynamic system that is produced, reproduced, and modified on a daily basis by its participants as they encounter and adapt to changing circumstances. He therefore neglects to explore the question of how the nature of a particular version of capitalism might change if the culture upon which it is based evolves or develops in the direction of the dominant cultural model, in this case the Anglo-American system.

Bauman (1998) also argues against global homogenization but from an entirely different perspective. For him globalization leads to a hierarchy of mobility between what he calls 'tourists' and 'vagabonds'. That is to say, global capital needs flexible and compliant governments, weak labourers, and credulous consumers in order to reproduce itself and expand and these it gets. For the primary criterion that global capital requires before investing and locating in a particular area is the conditions in which it can sell up and leave whenever circumstances become inconvenient or uncomfortable. Shareholders become the new absentee landlords, demanding flexibility and deregulation as they move themselves and their capital around the world, without consequences for themselves and virtually without opposition, to wherever they can achieve maximum return on their speculative investments. This deprives the 'other', or labour, of its gripping or resistant nature, thus polarizing a hybridizing global society into élite global 'tourists', who can come and go as they please, and local 'vagabonds', who remain and depend almost for their very existence on the apparently capricious decisions of the transnational élites.

Similarly, Ulrich Beck (2000) argues that the globalization of American forms of capitalism and work organization is leading not to the 'new civil society' that he argues for but, instead, a 'Brazilianization' of work where instabilities and insecurities mount for the masses while, and because, the neoliberal American economic model continues to dominate and expand.

Writing nearly 30 years earlier, the renowned British scholar of Japanese society and political economy Ronald Dore (1973) concluded from his empirical investigations at English Electric in Britain and Hitachi in Japan that, because of what he called the 'late development effect', Japan had been able in some measure to leap ahead of the United Kingdom, and by implication the United States too, into a more advanced or more modern form of industrial organization upon which henceforth the UK would converge. A key aspect of this ability to leap ahead, Dore claimed, was the development of the so-called lifetime employment system which, according to his theory, had come into being precisely as a result of Japan's late development. The implications of Dore's work, therefore, were profound because they implied strongly that the incorporation of Western technology into the traditional Japanese ethos had indeed been successful, so much so that Japan had been able to develop significant comparative advantages and efficiencies in production management. His work also implied that, while systemic convergence is a product of the globalization or intensification of competition, it is by no means a given that this is a one-way process flowing inexorably out from the West. Importantly he alerted us to the idea that Japan is also a globalizer and an exporter of culturally-based economic and social systems.

Since that time there has without doubt been a certain Japanization of US and British management and production systems. Lean production as practised by the Toyota Motor Corporation has been studied extensively by many scholars and practitioners for any aspects that might be transportable to the West. Abo's (1994) book on the hybridization of American production systems around the Japanese model emphasizes this point simply by its very choice of subject matter. However, more recently and in other industrial and business sectors there have been studies on the subject of global convergence and hybridization that focus on Japan and some of these have come to the opposite of Dore's original conclusion. For example, Malcolm's (2001) examination of the consequences for the Japanese financial services industry of the 'Big Bang' regulatory reforms argues for what he calls an 'awkward convergence'. He concludes that the Japanese system is gradually and reluctantly converging on the predominant Anglo-American system, but that it has managed to retain some distinctive features of its own.

Although Dore has now somewhat reversed his thesis (Dore, 2000), maintaining that the Japanese system, while it remains strong and distinctive, is now under tremendous pressure to converge towards the Anglo-American model, his two theses combined have very powerful implications for the relationship between globalization and the development of capitalism and modernity. For if Japan can successfully compete against the most powerful economies of the West and Western societies feel in turn that they must ratchet up their response and defeat the Japanese challenge, then the Japanese may, again, feel that they have to respond in kind. In this scenario we have the makings of a continuously accelerating and intensifying cycle of catch-up and counter catch-up, with all of the attendant consequences for individual employees and their families that Beck (2000) describes.

Conclusion

At the start of a new century it is tempting to look optimistically forward to new beginnings. This is even more so when one's present circumstances are not in accord with one's desires and expectations. The Western calendar is a comparatively recent adoption for the Japanese people yet they too are looking tentatively forward in such a manner to a new beginning for their society and economy. Mired in a stubborn, structurally induced stagnation, there is a consensus emerging among the Japanese people that the only solution is a drastic restructuring of economic and social systems and the creation of a more vigorous and dynamic economy and society. Government and industry appear to be taking some bold steps for a national culture that suffers from the accusation of being risk averse (Hofstede, 1984). Moreover, both academic and media reports suggest that a sea change is taking place in the orientation of younger people towards a more vital and fluid individualism that, in addition to the undoubted social orientation of the Japanese self, places the reflexive construction of one's personal life-scape at the core of modern Japanese culture (Nitto, 1993; Herbig and Borstorff, 1995; Ohmae, 1995b; Economic Planning Agency, 1996; Clammer, 1997; and Sugimura, 1997).

There is little doubt, also, that the organization-oriented ideology of welfare corporatism itself is under extreme strain, partly as a result of external pressures to the system resulting from the apparently irresistible forces of economic globalization and partly as a result of the changing orientations of the Japanese people themselves. Is it not reasonable to suggest, therefore, that if work is the principal means by which individuals in modern society are able to substantiate themselves, then active career planning and management have become vital tools for Japanese people for the achievement of self-actualization and an authentic self-identity? Would it not, therefore, be reasonable to suggest that, now that material security and stability have been more or less assured, complex and dynamic labour markets and work organizations as well as an open institutional framework and a tolerant culture would be essential if self-actualization and authentication are to become a possibility? For without the opportunity to make the experiments in living that such an institutional framework facilitates, people might be unable to develop their abilities and experiences to the extent that they are able to understand themselves deeply enough to make the mature decisions that are necessary to being able to construct an authentic identity and experience the state of self-actualization (Se, 1999). Would it not also be possible that, in a society such as Japan, where labour markets and institutions have the reputation of being rigid and closed, there might exist an incompatibility between the ideals of modern Japanese individuals and the structure of modern social life in Japan as well as an incompatibility between our academic understanding of the concept of modernity and its substantive expression in Japan?

Further, and attempting to provide a link between how individuals' lives unfold and wider social and economic developments, within the process of the collision of differing forms of modernity is it not probable that, first, some kind of convergence among developed societies is indeed taking place, not just of capitalist systems of production or in the material aspects of people's daily lives but also in the forms of consciousness that develop in order to engage with the new and global forms of social life that are taking shape around us? As the preponderant power of the Anglo-American political economy comes to dominate an increasingly global capitalist modernity is it not possible that such a convergence of economic and social forms might come to be coloured mainly, but not exclusively, by Anglo-American forms of capitalist modernity? But because competition itself has now become entrenched at the heart of capitalist modernity as a normative condition, is it not also the case that the globalization of capitalist modernity is creating a self-regulating and independent system whereby corporations, and indeed whole societies, defensively compete against each other to achieve a state of ascendancy while, at the same time, serving to accelerate and intensify the capitalist process itself, to the eventual detriment of the individuals who feel compelled to live and work within such a system?

3 Lifetime employment in post-war Japan

In 1958 the American industrial sociologist James Abegglen was the first Western observer to describe the post-war paradigm of the Japanese firm to the Western world in his book *The Japanese Factory: Aspects of its Social Organization*. He described the 'critical difference' between Japanese and American industrial organization as an implicit and non-contractual agreement between employer and employee to membership of the organization for the whole working life of the employee. The basis of this arrangement was 'a system of shared obligation' that took 'the place of the economic basis of employment' (Abegglen, 1958: 17). He described the agreement thus.

> At whatever level of organization in the Japanese factory, the worker commits himself on entrance to the company for the remainder of his working career. The company will not discharge him even temporarily except in the most extreme circumstances. He will not quit the company for industrial employment elsewhere. He is a member of the company in a way resembling that in which persons are members of families, fraternal organizations, and other intimate and personal groups in the United States.
>
> (ibid.: 11)

Without fully investigating the specific nature of the invention and role of tradition in social and economic organization, Abegglen assumed that the culture of welfare paternalism that had developed within the Japanese firm had evolved organically out of Japan's pre-industrial values. To be sure, Abegglen also recognized the economically rational appeal to management of maintaining the lifetime employment system but concluded that such justifications for its existence 'might be seen more accurately as a rationalization of a system rather than as an explanation of a real cause of a system of job relations' (ibid.: 16). However, he predicted that, although the corporate system itself was at that time socially and economically consistent, there was a potential for incompatibility between it and the economic and social changes that might derive in future from further macro-economic expansion and technological development that, he argued at the time, threatened to steer the Japanese corporate system towards a convergence with the American model.

In 1973 Abegglen updated his thesis to argue more forcefully that the life-time employment system 'taps first the very basic motives involved in group-centred, non-contractual, and hierarchy-oriented society' (Abegglen, 1973: 30). His conclusion was that tradition may not always be a barrier to economic growth and moreover, in the particular circumstances surrounding Japan's case, could actually facilitate and enhance it and was a comparative advantage in Japan's economic development. According to Abegglen, the pattern of employment reinforced a pre-existing emotional identification between employer and employee that leads to personal, family, and corporate success being 'inextricably enmeshed' in what Abegglen was later to call a 'partnership of fate' (Abegglen, 1973 and Abegglen and Stalk, 1985). In this second volume he identified the now famous 'Three Pillars' of the Japanese management system as lifetime employment, seniority-based pay and promo-tion, and enterprise unionism (Abegglen, 1973).

Importantly, Abegglen claimed that though the suggestion that Japan's employment situation is changing is a recurring one and that 'some change has occurred at the margins of the system . . . it is not changing in any basic or extensive way' (ibid.: 47–8). He predicted, however, perhaps fortuitously, that patterns of employment would be transformed as basic social relations and value priorities changed with the growing internationalization and afflu-ence that Japanese society was increasingly experiencing.

> As the society changes, and it is changing, under the impact of affluence, increased leisure, a much altered pattern of family life and a greatly increased interaction with other nations, so patterns of relations in the workplace will change. Changes in the employment system will arise from these more basic social changes, and will reflect in the future as to date the characteristics of the broader society.
>
> (ibid.: 49)

Twenty-eight years after his first book, and at the pinnacle of Japan's indus-trial ascendancy, Abegglen, in collaboration with George Stalk Jr, produced his insider's guide to competing against the Japanese challenge, *Kaisha: The Japanese Corporation* (Abegglen and Stalk, 1985). Again, he repeated his claim that the comparative advantage of the Japanese corporation lay in its high level of social integration around the lifetime employment system which itself, he argued, is rooted in Japan's premodern Confucian values and the view of the traditional Japanese family as a model for nation and organi-zation.

In its sophisticated resolution of the needs, desires, and values of both employer and employee the system was proving to be more durable than even Abegglen had previously anticipated. He described the system for the employee as a trade-off between the opportunities for high reward and long-term security and in this case the Japanese company employee appeared to prefer the latter. Moreover, although he theorized about Japanese young people's greater propensity to take risks with their employment, in the conclusion to the volume Abegglen predicted that, 'dramatic changes in the internal structure of the kaisha appear unlikely' (Abegglen and Stalk, 1985: 286). This change in consciousness among young people, therefore, would lead to a gradual abandonment of the seniority-based pay and promotion systems but the core lifetime employment system would remain.

The period covered by Abegglen's three volumes is the one in which most observers of Japan consider to have existed the post-war model of the Japanese corporation. For the years between 1945 and 1958 were mostly taken up with the allied occupation, the urgent task of reconstruction, and the labour struggles of the early 1950s that sought to define the post-war labour–management settlement. Moreover, shortly after 1985 came the onset of the asset price inflation referred to subsequently as the 'Bubble Economy' and its collapse into deflationary stagnation.

Abegglen correctly identified lifetime employment as the defining institutional characteristic of the Japanese corporation as a distinctive bureaucratic capitalist organizational type. He also correctly identified the source of its durability as lying in the complex constellation of both employers' and employees' interests in the institutionalization of employment at a single organization for the whole working life of the employee. Nevertheless, Abegglen did not investigate closely the employee needs, desires, and expectations that he declared to be so well satisfied by the system.

Thus, in order to establish a model with which to compare contemporary developments we must not only look to the structural dimensions of the post-war lifetime employment system but also try to unravel the nature of the employees' values that existed under that regime. For if we are to attempt to make some judgements as to how Japan's experience of capitalist modernity is unfolding by an analysis of this particular aspect of Japanese social and economic life then it is appropriate to draw a base line against which we can compare contemporary developments.

Consequently, this chapter explores the principal cultural and ideological characteristics of lifetime employment from the point of view of both management and employee and will present the paradigm of the post-war Japanese company as a transitional institution that sits between the semi-feudalism of early nineteenth-century Japan and an emerging global hybrid modernity that is taking shape around us today. That is to say, the post-war model of the Japanese firm is one which fuses together both a modern economic rationale and what Robert E. Cole (1978) refers to as a 'recrystallization . . . of norms and structures' that were operative in premodern Japanese society. In other words, even within the rational bureaucratic economic organization that is the modern corporation, some features of the Japanese firm, acting in the manner of a social adhesive, were crucial to its operations but were idealized and instrumentalized reconstructions of premodern patterns of thought. For the most part, employees readily accepted and actively adopted the underlying principles of a paternalistic and semi-ascriptive hierarchy operating within a closed and cyclical social system in a received and uncritical manner that is quite unlike the reflexive ideology of high modernity that Giddens describes. Such a complex interweaving of fictive premodern social and modern economic attributes allows us to borrow Loiskandl's (1998) concept of trans-rationality as well as Ashkenazi's (1996) theory of cultural modelling and characterize the Japanese lifetime employment system as a transitional institution in the history of the development of capitalist modernity in Japan.

The origins and establishment of the Japanese lifetime employment system

The origins of the system

It is generally agreed among historians of Japan's corporations that the lifetime employment system had crystallized by the late 1950s amid the circumstances surrounding Japan's emergence from the chaos and destruction of the Second World War. Nevertheless, its origins can be traced in various ways back to the period prior to the war. According to Chimoto (1986 and 1989) a prototype for the lifetime employment system, at least for white-collar administrative and managerial employees in private business, can even be found in the system of *hōkōnin* employed by the Mitsui House during the later Edo period and its conversion into a more economically rational and bureaucratic system of long-term employment of administrative businessmen after the Meiji Restoration.

This system of business employees who had completed a minimum of ten years of apprentice-type training was used to nurture and develop long-term continuous service among a small coterie of talented individuals. In order to retain these high-quality employees, in addition to granting long-term continuous employment, regular salaries and reward bonuses were paid which were considerably more than the pocket money received by lower grades and which increased 'the higher one was promoted and the longer one worked in continuous service' (Chimoto, 1989). Further, a retirement lump sum payment was paid, calculated according to the position attained and number of years of service and, again, considerably more than the payment accorded to lower grade personnel. These incentives became entrenched and were bureaucratized in the Mitsui House and other similar businesses such as Sumitomo and Mitsubishi (Chimoto, 1989) during the Meiji period as increasingly these enterprises were forced to compete with the expanding national bureaucracy and government-owned enterprises to attract imperial university graduates as well as to retain and nurture talented home-grown employees.

Nevertheless, we should caution against assuming a smooth take-up and transition from the practices adopted by the Mitsui House for their managerial employees in the Edo period to a generalized system of permanent employment after 1945. Unlike in the post-war system, the Mitsui-type system was only possible through the rigorous weeding out by management of the majority of workers during the period of apprenticeship. More importantly, from the point of view of the employees, the primary purpose for persons wishing to become *hōkōnin* during the Edo period was neither in order to serve the merchant family for the whole of their lives nor to secure their income and become enmeshed in a closed community of company members but, conversely, to receive the training and finances necessary to be able to leave the organization and set up business on their own. Significantly, the majority of commercial and industrial entrepreneurs during the Meiji and early Taisho periods either ignored older business conventions or actively sought to have them abolished in order to further their own interests, more often than not at the expense of employment security (Chimoto, 1986). Thus, although conditions were different in governmental institutions and government-owned corporations, the early period of Japan's economic modernization is perhaps more appropriately characterized by what Hazama refers to as 'the period when the logic of capital manifested itself in its most naked form' (Hazama, 1997 [1964]: 24).[1] Even though long-term employment existed prior to the Second World War, there was little if any commitment by management to lifetime employment as a normative social condition for core male employees in the sense that it existed after the war.

Although long-term continuous employment had already existed for élite administrative staff in the government bureaucracy and at some large enterprises and trading houses since at least the Meiji period (Kinmonth, 1981 and Hazama, 1997 [1964]), long-term continuous employment at a single enterprise appeared for skilled manufacturing workers only in the 1920s as a management response mainly to technological developments. Cheng and Kalleberg (1997) found that employment retention rates for both blue- and white-collar employees began a secular increase from the 1920s onwards and fell only in the 1930s and 1940s because of the government's military requirements. Thus, Nishinarita calls the early inter-war years 'the period of establishment of Japanese fundamental labor–employer relations' (Nishinarita, 1995: 18) and it was not until production workers were brought into the employment system that we may begin to think of it as resembling that which crystallized in the post-war era.

One of the most authoritative and convincing accounts of the prewar period of Japanese industrial relations is that of Hazama in his classic work *The History of Labour Management in Japan* (1997 [1964]). This is a sociological examination of the Japanese firm as a structural microcosm of Japan's transition to modernity, and thus it is an appropriate point of reference to turn to here. In it Hazama puts forward the proposition that Japan could not have grown so rapidly and so continuously, given the dire working conditions existent at the time, if there had not been in place an ideology of employment with which workers could readily identify and which possessed an internally and culturally consistent legitimacy. According to Hazama (1997 [1964]) it is to the ideology of managerial familism, or *keieikazokushugi*, that we can attribute the motivation of workers to contribute to the growth of the enterprise and their willingness to cooperate among themselves and with management.

Management in heavy industrial enterprises, with the active support of the government, modelled the logic of managerial familism on their interpretation of the traditional *ie* ideology. It was a reinterpretation of a premodern patriarchal and paternalistic ideology that was introduced by management to stabilize and retain a skilled workforce and gain a return on long-term investment in training male employees to operate the complex machinery that was being introduced particularly in heavy and process industries. Within this ideology, for example, class relations were seductively explained in terms of the status relations of parent and child in the premodern Japanese family, or *oyabun–kobun* relations. Yet, at the same time, management was studying and successfully implementing Western, or Fordist, industrial and production philosophies and practices. Hazama reasoned, therefore, that what has come to be termed Japanese-style management had grown out of the instrumental weaving together of Japan's societal foundations and overseas influences (Hazama, 1997 [1964]: 12). He also argued that the traditional logic of the *ie* itself facilitated the transition to a modern economy because it had been primarily a unit for the protection, growth, and intergenerational transmission of familial wealth and that, consequently, the calculation of economic and social interest predominated over, but did not exclude, love. Here, therefore, we can see the process of cultural modelling at work, as well as a reflexive reinterpretation by management of a premodern received logic of social legitimation for the purpose of securing the implementation and development of an instrumentally rational and modern system of production. For, notwithstanding the fact that, for a large proportion of the twentieth century, Japanese management successfully implemented Western Taylorist practices in production and managed to adapt these to Japan's peculiar developmental conditions (Tsutsui, 1998), the familistic ideologies that management were able to construct both within and around the corporation, even though fictive, were understood by a large proportion of Japanese employees as authentically and traditionally Japanese.

The establishment of the lifetime employment system

The wartime period itself also served to presage the entrenchment of the lifetime employment system and it is worth describing here how this came about because the government's motives point to one of the defining characteristics of the Japanese firm. This characteristic is what Ronald Dore (1973) calls the 'organizational orientation' of management and employee, or the very real sense of ownership and membership of, and absorption into, the corporate body that employees and management come to feel through long-term participation in a socio-economic community that is dedicated to survivability and expansion for the purposes of long-term employment security and, its corollary, steady and predictable income growth and status achievement.

As part of its wartime mobilization measures the government sought to stabilize production and minimize social dislocation through the implementation of a rigid regulatory regime (Okazaki, 1994). One policy was to stabilize and restrict labour flows and to reduce shareholder power in order to orient firms to production, and a series of measures were introduced with the 1938 National Mobilization Law being the most symbolic. The following describes succinctly the employment system that emerged out of the wartime regulatory framework:

> The wartime regime is characterized by labor practices based on the seniority system and lifetime employment . . . Along with the custom of long-term, stable employment that took root in society, [the] wage system formed the basis of the labor practice seen today, whereby greater importance is attached to length of service than to productivity or performance.
> (Miura, 2000)

Nevertheless, it is not until the post-war formation of enterprise unions that the lifetime employment system can be said to have fully taken root as a normative social contract. Initially Japanese industrial relations were characterized by conflict as the newly formed unions struggled to assert themselves and to challenge the philosophical basis of Japan's emerging capitalism (Hasegawa, 1993). Both Gordon (1998b) and Kumazawa (1996a) show in their examinations of post-war labour relations how it is out of this conflict that the character of a corporate-centred society emerged and reached its ascendancy in the 1960s. They argue that what unions achieved was perhaps not the best scenario that they could have hoped for, but they did not lose. Unions achieved their most pressing goals of employment security, material affluence, and equal status between white- and blue-collar workers. However, this was gained at the expense of employees losing direct control over the direction of their careers and lives. That is to say, unions ceded to management the right to manage the corporation through unilateral control over the allocation of labour in the interests of long-term organizational survivability and expansion.

Thus, out of the wartime government measures to create 'production communities' not beholden to shareholders (Sugayama, 1995) and the democratization of the Occupation reforms, including the break-up of family-owned enterprises (Fruin, 1983), came demands by the recently legalized unions for recognition by management of workers' basic economic and security needs. Autonomous and powerful labour unions campaigned vigorously for a system of long-term full employment which guaranteed a living wage (Nomura, 1998) and this demand was founded on normative societal expectations of personal circumstances based on the employee's age as a marker for his stage in life. The resulting dynamic growth-oriented compromise lay in a system that came to be labelled 'welfare corporatism'.[2] For the, albeit re-invented, pre-war ideology of familistic hierarchical ascription was no longer automatically accepted by employees in Japan's new egalitarian democracy and there came with this developments in the ideology of management. The basic long-term economic and security needs of labour were conceded by management in return for the securing of the right and responsibility to promote the long-term survivability and growth of the corporation on behalf of all employees. It is the establishment of this compromise that formed the basis of what Hasegawa (1993) calls the 'cooperative' and, later, 'compliant' labour management relations that are so characteristic of Japan's post-war economic development.

Nevertheless, even if we acknowledge that the post-war Japanese political economy could be represented as possessing a modern, path-oriented, rational, developmentalist consciousness in an economic sense, we cannot readily characterize Japan at that time as being resolutely modern in a social or cultural sense. Union demands represented a desire for the achievement and maintenance of material stability and security within a heavily ascriptive and closed fictive community of mutual dependence. By way of example, Takezawa's (1995) study of Japanese corporate employees' work consciousness between 1960 and 1990 clearly shows not only a strong preference for material security and stability in 1960 and in 1976 but that this preference had, in comparison to others, become less pronounced by 1990. This post-war consciousness was founded in the notion of needs expectations according to one's life-stage which might itself be labelled an intermediate, or transitional, consciousness that lies between premodern conceptions of an externally ascribed life-cycle and the extreme fluidity of high-modern representations of the self-constructed and individualized life-span.

It is important not to forget that, compared with the material abundance of Tokyo at the beginning of the twenty-first century, life in Japan in the early post-war period was difficult even for the salaried middle classes. In his description of life in Tokyo in the early 1950s, *City Life in Japan*, Ronald Dore graphically depicts the material conditions of the time.

> O is a policeman, 39 years old, the son of a carpenter . . . The five of them (two parents and three children) live in one 'four-and-a-half-mat' room, that is, a room about nine feet square with one large recessed cupboard to contain the bedding, which is rolled up and stored away in the daytime . . . The O family can rarely afford meat, but they have fish four or five times a week, though generally the least expensive salted salmon . . .
>
> One sink with a single cold water tap, and one lavatory are shared with three other families . . . There are no baths, but Mrs. O takes the children to the bath-house every other day and Mr. O goes regularly once a week.
>
> (Dore, 1999 [1958]: 29–31)

In such conditions it was imperative for men first to safeguard employment for themselves and from there to secure and protect their own and their families' basic material needs. If they were fortunate, they could invest in some of life's luxuries such as a refrigerator, but nowhere in Dore's book can one find evidence of a widespread desire for authentic self-actualization through reflexive self-development. In support of this contention, in 1955 Jean Stoetzel concluded in his empirical investigation of the attitudes of Japanese youth that economic difficulties weighed heavily even on young people's minds in the early 1950s and, further, that security and standard of living were considered by young people to be the most important conditions for happiness by those who thought that health alone was not enough (Stoetzel, 1955). It should come as no surprise, therefore, that unions fought their struggles on the issues of securing long-term employment, a living wage based on personal circumstances, and equal status between blue- and white-collar company members. In short this was a mass ideology based on what might be termed the ethic of democratic materialism, or an insistence on the achievement of equality of outcome for all.

The lifetime employment system in the 1960s and 1970s

What evidence do we have for the claim that the post-war model of the Japanese lifetime employment system is a transitional institution in Japan's capitalist modernity? What aspects of the system will reveal most to us about the quality of its institutions? How can we most easily describe its characteristics?

The principal characteristics of the lifetime employment system

Beginning with a brief but illuminating examination of management's construction of the culture and ideology of the post-war Japanese corporation and doing so by looking at an internal company magazine from the 1960s, it is not difficult to detect managerial attempts to actively and instrumentally construct a culture of, first, sacrificial duty to the organization, and second, its corollary of self-fulfilment for the individual by the living out of semi-ascribed roles through absorption within a closed corporate community.

In the May 1967 issue of Company C's in-house magazine is reprinted, and of course subsequently distributed to all company members, the Company President's address at the entrance ceremony for the year's new high-school and university graduate recruits. Interestingly, although the tone of the address and the advice it contains are highly paternal in nature, in the opening messages the President claims to be speaking to the audience, 'not from the position of parent but from the heart',[3] thus recognizing implicitly and emphasizing the underlying and ordinarily paternalistic character of management while attempting to distance himself from it for this occasion. He then goes on to urge employees, first, to take care of their health and consult the company medical service if they have any difficulties in this regard; second, to learn and adopt the company character through actual experience; third, to continue to study through learning by doing; and fourth, to develop and nurture good personal relations with other company members in order to facilitate and smooth the working environment as well as make their own working life happier.

Reading through the speech and examining the text, as well as attempting to grasp what the company president was trying to communicate, I felt that he perceived the company neither as a strictly familistic enterprise, nor as a purely economic collaboration between self-interested individuals, but as something in-between. He was welcoming the new members not into a family but into a mutually supportive membership of, and journey through, a communal hierarchy of interdependent men and women, a hierarchy that possesses a life, a quality, a continuity, and a long-term dynamic of its own, founded on lifetime employment and distinct from, but intimately involved with, wider society.[4] It is a self-contained unit, or social world, with its own history, customs, relationships, and systems and these must not only be learned, they must be deeply internalized if the individual is to realize his or her role as a fully integrated member of the organization and achieve a happy and fulfilling working life. This speech, therefore, was an exhortation to new members to enmesh themselves in the corporate community and become loyal, devoted, and organization-oriented company men and women. In the following closing remarks, in addition to referring frequently to very long-term employment in various ways, he calls on the new employees to deeply internalize the corporate ethos.

> This company was established in the year Meiji 20 and in a year or two we will be celebrating the 80th anniversary year of the establishment of the company. So, in our more than 70 years of long history we have established a company character. This company character cannot be described simply in one or two words but please come to understand it through actual experience . . .
>
> But, I would like you all to understand that this character does not remain the same forever. It changes with the entry every year of hundreds of new graduates and as every year a new set of graduates enters and passes up through the company. Thus it is not fixed but something that changes gradually. So, at the same time as absorbing the long history of this company, if there is something good that you can add then please contribute it from now on.
>
> The following is a little abstract but, once one enters the company, life is no longer like it was as a student and it changes forever. Relations between people, relations between colleagues, as well as human relations with the huge number of *sempai*, are complicated in various ways, I think . . . Living in this world is extremely complicated and there are many things that cannot logically be explained . . . One needs to understand that life in the company is not a breeze. Please do not try to avoid this thought and believe that by working hard you can advance and overcome. If you properly deal with your difficulties then you will exceed yourself . . . I believe those people who think that this can be done

without difficulty will fail during the long life they will spend in the company.

(President, Company C, *In-company Magazine*, May 1967: 2–3)

It is difficult to judge to what extent speeches are genuine expressions of the deep-seated beliefs of their speakers as well as how much of their content is internalized and subsequently acted upon. Notwithstanding, through the working life of the employee these ceremonies, and others like them, deliberately serve to construct, reconstruct, and reinforce the affective foundations of the corporation. They provide a forum for management, over and above the practical day-to-day mechanics of administering corporate expansion, to communicate to employees its ideologies and visions.

The above excerpt is fairly typical of speeches made at company ceremonies and it would be very easy to judge in hindsight that the company president was merely attempting to manipulate the impressionable young minds of the new entrants but, if one does then the following questions must necessarily come out of such an interpretation. Why did he choose the particular ideological constructions adopted in such a method of manipulation and why has there been so little resistance to the ongoing construction of what have often been termed oppressive and totalitarian ideologies (Kamata, 1983 and Kumazawa, 1996a and b)?

To be sure, the speech was a conscious attempt to inculcate corporate ideologies. In addition, explanations for the pre-war period certainly hold for post-war Japan too, in that there was and is an apparent contradiction between some employees' outward observance and their inner acceptance of corporate ideologies and this was, perhaps, a consequence of their desire simply to get on in life. Conversely, Hazama's contention that Japan and its corporations could never have grown so rapidly and so continuously had corporate ideologies not been internalized by at least some employees holds as much for post-war Japan as it does for the pre-war period about which he was writing. Moreover, there is considerable anthropological and sociological research that can be used as evidence to suggest that these ideologies were indeed internalized by a large proportion of employees (Cole, 1971; Rohlen, 1974; Clark, 1979; Dore, 1987; Sugimura, 1997, and Tao, 1998).

What can be most clearly discerned about the 1960s personnel system is that it almost entirely revolved around a semi-ascriptive hierarchy of seniority that was principally determined by the number of years of continuous service that each employee had attained. This method of hierarchical determination itself, because of the nature of recruitment at regular intervals of employees on graduation from school and university and the perceived need to pay a living wage commensurate with the employee's stage in life, was effectively reduced down to age and educational background becoming the basis of personnel administration. Much of the academic literature on the system indeed confirms this in presenting the foundations of the 1950s and 1960s age-based pay and promotion system as a normative expectation that the employee's personal expenses would rise as he married, had children, and then sent his children to school and perhaps college (Nakamura and Nitta, 1995 and Nishinarita, 1998). Indeed, the reverse is also true in that such structures placed constraints on people's behavioural parameters and helped to mould the life-course among Japan's salaried middle classes and their families into a standardized and normative system of patterned dependence on the organizational community.

Although there was an understanding that long-term on-the-job training and rotation systems required employees to spend a minimum number of years in various related positions in order to develop the breadth and depth of skills necessary for progression to management, and this placed structural limits upon the speed of promotion, the system worked in practice as a method for advancement for the whole cohort up through the corporation and it was only when employees reached management grades that merit came to be included as a consideration for placement and promotion.[5] A practical consequence of this structure was that age and educational background were the principal determinants of the rewards obtained as a result of promotion through the system, that all the attributes of the system were implemented under the basic, but always implicit, assumption that the employee would work at the company until the retirement age and, finally, that the employee could rely on the company even in retirement because he would be paid a retirement bonus based on the length of his service. In the following excerpt from his explanation of the employment system, the Personnel Manager at Company A explains the practical application of that system from the point of view of management.

> 1960, at that time if you ask what kind of era it was then it was the period of rapid economic growth . . . At that time at our company the style of dealing with workers and the pay system was age based . . . it was based on the principle of seniority. The company's system, or the personnel system, was based on the ranking system. Our training was based on improving and developing human resources and we used a cycle where employees were moved from one position to another and that way we could develop the employee. It was based on that way of thinking . . . so . . . we trained the employees over a long period.
>
> Concretely, how was this done? Well . . . combining OJT, on-the-job training, and Off-JT . . . While being made to do the work the employee was made to learn how to do it. So, that traditional system of job rotation . . . not so much one speciality but various experiences to give a wide range of abilities . . . in that way we could develop the employees. That's completely different to Britain isn't it? . . .
>
> For wages . . . It wasn't a job related salary system. The structure was basically one based on ranking but . . . in the end continuous service. Seniority, and age and so on were extremely important. Abilities and so on were not really included . . . instead academic record, if one graduated

from university for instance, improved wages . . . but it was a system based on the thinking that those who entered at the same time and occupied similar positions would get similar wages. It was a system with regular increments in pay according to age and so on.

Retirement payments were also calculated more on the length of service than on other factors . . . it was based on a fixed retirement age. Continuous service was extremely important.

As far as lifetime employment was concerned . . . There wasn't very much movement between companies and so there wasn't really an economics-style labour market in existence. About that, loyalty to the company thus increased among us. So . . . recruitment at regular intervals was an important part of the system.

(Personnel Manager, Company A)

Reinforcing this view, below, are excerpts from an interview with the Director of Corporate Information Services at Company B, who joined his company in 1961.

At that time, once you entered the company, for ten years you would do various jobs and then become *kakarichō* [assistant manager] and then after 15 years *kachō* [section manager]. Mostly that was the progression. At that time the Japanese economy had no problems and so, as long as you didn't say that you couldn't do the work or something like that, then the company grew and so the organization did too . . . and so more or less everyone would become *kachō* and then *buchō* [general manager], but of course not company president! For a long time every company in Japan was like that and were growing bigger.

. . . It is often said that a characteristic of the Japanese system is lifetime employment. However, I said earlier that I had never heard the company make that promise but I think it [lifetime employment] exists in the company. The effect of Japan's economic growth has been the existence of it, even though there has never been a contract to that effect.

. . . Until now another characteristic of the system has been seniority-based promotion. That is to say, as people got older so they were promoted. Within those conditions work was decided. It was expected that know-how developed and grew with the time that people spent in the company and so more than years of service, in actuality it was age that determined the system.

. . . Why were wages determined by age? That is because after the war Japan was very poor and so wages were determined by age and the older one was the more one was paid. Living costs were high and so it wasn't so much how long one had been at the company but how old one was. So, realistically, those that had reached their fifties or so, their children were becoming independent and so their living costs were lower and they were paid a little less. At that time, the retirement age was 55 and there were none, except directors and so on, that remained past 55. There was a direct link between living costs and age.

(Director, Company B)

A number of important points derive from the above statements and the first is that the maintenance of a personnel management system based on lifetime employment was dependent to a large extent on the performance of the Japanese economy as a whole as well as the individual corporation. The period of high-speed growth of the late 1950s and 1960s thus provided the economic framework within which the lifetime employment and personnel systems could function in a state where all its internal attributes were in a state of 'organic compatibility' (Hasegawa, 1996).

Second, unlike in the Anglo-American system, the recruitment and personnel management systems were not based on a system of job functions or specific tasks but arranged around the acquisition by all employees of a broad range of skills within a ranked hierarchy. Employees were, on the whole, not recruited on the basis of any specific or previously acquired skills or knowledge, excepting those gained by nearly everyone who had progressed through secondary or tertiary education. Once inside the organization neither wages nor career advancement were based on specific functional capabilities nor the acquisition of specialized skills and abilities other than those nearly all employees were required to possess in order to progress to the next rank. Thus employees did not consider themselves to be, say, marketing, law, or finance careerists first and company members second. Instead they felt themselves to be simply and completely company members and they possessed the expectation that so long as they could fulfil the requirements of the personnel management and training systems in gaining the required set of capabilities within a specific, though not unusually fast or slow, period of time, could complete their immediate work tasks to the satisfaction of supervisors, and, importantly, did nothing drastically wrong, they could be promoted to the next level along with their colleagues from the same cohort.

Third, the employment system consciously mirrored and, in addition, served in a seductive manner to reinforce a semi-ascriptive life-cycle for the salaryman. It was fundamentally a closed and cyclical system, at least in terms of the passage of the generations, which, under a high-growth regime, allowed for phased entry on graduation and exit on retirement and, thus, was a self-contained community. Job content and personnel movement were determined by the personnel department in consultation with the employee's immediate superior according to the long-range allocative requirements of management with precious little input from the employee himself as to where or when he would like to be posted. It allowed for almost no mid-career entry and early exit resulted, except in extremely rare cases, in a drop in status as well as income.[6] Salary levels within the cohort varied little according to ability and productivity, thus resulting in externally controlled status achievement becoming the defining criterion for signalling success to others within and without the company as well as to oneself. Moreover, the strength and effectiveness of the system can be revealed in its normative power to introduce semi-ascriptive structural rigidities into social systems external to the corporation such as in education, the urban family, and external labour markets (Takeuchi, 1997; Yano, 1997; Nomura, 1998).[7]

Systemic and ideological compatibility

The above discussion leads us to another aspect or consequence of this semi-ascribed hierarchical life-stage-oriented approach to the salaryman's career. Economically rational and reflexive self-determination of a future-oriented, authentic, linear career path and life-span within a continuously flexible range of possibilities simply was not available as a realistic possibility even to the graduates of Japan's most élite educational institutions and, thus, was not within the realms of most people's consciousness as they grew up and worked throughout most of the post-war period.

In such an environment, most people followed, and were expected to follow, a line of least resistance through the education system and on into the corporate employment system. They voluntarily and enthusiastically did what they felt was expected of them, as well as what they believed to be possible within the realm of their perceptions from among the limited range of options available. Thus, externally ascribed role-fulfilment as a social, corporate, and familial duty was a strong normative motivation towards achieving, securing, and maintaining material stability and security for oneself and one's family through contributing to corporate expansion.

However, we must be careful not to cast pejorative interpretations on the functional, cultural, and ideological characteristics of the employment system since, for the most part, this appears to have been a positive, expected, and willing acceptance of the roles that were ascribed to employees by the educational and corporate systems and the majority almost unthinkingly sought security and stability within the confines of that structure. There was a complete acceptance of the institutional arrangements of the system itself and a deep level of trust in the motivations and capabilities of management to act in the interests of all employees. In addition, challenges to its existence and structural composition were almost non-existent after the achievement of the labour–management compromise of the late 1950s. A series of quotations follows from interviews with employees who joined their companies in the 1960s and early 1970s that in one way or another serve to emphasize the above points.

The first quotation is from a director of Company D and he makes particular emphasis of the rigidity or even non-existence at that time in Japan of a labour market for salarymen at first rank companies as well as his acceptance of what he refers to as the 'Japanese tradition' of lifetime employment and his apparent rejection of even the thought of leaving the company to go elsewhere. Moreover, the tone of the excerpt does not convey any frustration about having to work within such a structure but, on the contrary, a matter-of-fact acceptance of it.

Q: When you joined did you want to stay until the retirement age?

A: Yes, at that time, as well as now. That kind of Japanese tradition was strong at that time and, especially I didn't think at all of giving up. Even if I had wanted to give up, realistically, I couldn't have given up. That is to say, the labour market . . . now it is becoming fluid but . . . it wasn't a time when it was easy to change company even if you wanted to do so. So, even if I gave up at [the company], where would I go? If I looked for work with bad conditions at small and medium-sized companies I could have found some but . . . at first rank companies I couldn't. It was that kind of era.

(Director, Company D)

The next respondent, a Director of Company B, describes his desire for material security and bears out the above respondent's matter-of-fact acceptance of the structure of lifetime employment and what it offers. He also makes an interesting comparison between his experiences in Japan and the USA. He compares the contractual, occupational, and market orientation of the United States with the implicit, affective, and organizational orientation of the Japanese firm. The former focuses on particular tasks and individual skills while the latter de-emphasizes the role of the individual in favour of the total outcome.

Q: When you joined did you want to stay until the retirement age?

A: I can't confirm that I clearly felt that I would definitely stay until the retirement age. Probably. Also those people around me didn't feel that they would definitely stay until that time but . . . one thing is that when one entered a big company one knew that one could expect a feeling of security. Also, big companies operated annual salary increases and the welfare systems were of a high standard. When I joined, as I said, I decided for economic reasons to find a job and at that time I did it because I wanted security . . .

Q: So, did the company promise you that you could stay as a regular employee until the retirement age?

A: No. Not at all. For example, I have experience working at the American subsidiary, and if there is work the company needs people to do then they go out and find them if they cannot find them from within the company. That person can do the job properly and they make a contract. But in Japan, in my experience I have never seen the company make a contract with a regular employee. Of course, when one enters the company there is a letter of appointment from the company to the employee and there are other papers concerning salary and so on but I have never had a contract. And I have also never seen a contract or a promise from the company saying that they will employ someone, say, for the next 30 or 35 years. But, at that time when I was in my twenties, those salarymen who were in their fifties or so had for the most part spent 30 or so years in the company and there were quite a lot of them around. So, I thought that if I worked diligently then that would probably happen to me. But I didn't expect it, if that is what you are asking.

Q: During the 1960s, how did you think about things such as self-fulfilment and so on?

A: At that time, I didn't think about self-fulfilment as an individual. I simply entered the company . . . I didn't enter the company to do anything in particular . . . it was a big and famous company that offered security and was well regarded in society. So, in my twenties I thought it was normal to work hard and I didn't think that I should try to make myself appealing to anyone for any particular reasons. I just wanted to work hard . . . At that time, people worked for the company organization and not for oneself as an individual. It was expected at that time that the individual did not work for himself but for the organization. So, I didn't think in any other way really.

(Director, Company B)

The following respondent states more clearly and more emphatically the relationship between the employee and company as being an affective 'partnership of fate' but, significantly, he also describes how individuals with different talents, tastes, and values did, even under the circumstances of the 1960s and 1970s, have a range of options in their career choice, even if these choices could for the most part only be acted upon at the point of entry into full-time work.

Q: When you joined did you want to stay until the retirement age?

A: At that time I did. It was 25 years ago and, of course, Japanese companies' employment structure operated lifetime employment and seniority pay and promotion. Everything branched out from there. I didn't know of anything else. Naturally, when I entered I thought I would be here for the rest of my life . . .

Q: So, since joining and up till now what has been the most important to you in your work?

A: At that time there were . . . banks, trading companies and so on and most of the people from my university went into them. Few went into manufacturers . . . well the salary was high but . . . I had no interest at all in joining a bank.

Q: Why?

A: The work wasn't interesting, I thought. It's not like now when there are lots of different types of work in banking . . . As far as work is concerned if things are being made where I am and then sold and after-sales service is being provided . . . it is deeply interesting, I think. Banks . . . well, they just deal with money and so as far as self-development is concerned well . . . it's better to work at a manufacturer . . .

Q: For whom are you working, do you think?

A: . . . When I was working overseas my feeling of working for the company's benefit was extremely strong. When I talk about the company of course I mean the profits of the whole company but also I mean for my superiors and my colleagues. When I was young I felt that very strongly.

Q: Do you think the company's future is your future?

A: Yes. A partnership of fate. I had that sense. Nowadays most people are quite different but . . .

(Manager, Company A)

The last respondent in this section supports the opinion that job-changing was severely restricted but qualifies this by stating that, should an employee have been disappointed with his choice of company or feel that he does not fit the company atmosphere, there were opportunities early on in his career to rectify that mistake. Most importantly, however, this respondent shows clearly, first, that employment security and lifetime employment do not preclude having an interesting and satisfying career and, second, the deep interconnectedness between security and fulfilment. That is to say, security provides the foundation upon which fulfilment can be achieved and this has long been a normative social expectation in Japan, so much so that there is a common idiomatic expression to that effect.

Q: When you joined did you want to stay until the retirement age?

A: Half and half, I think. That is to say, in Japan the custom, or trend, was to enter the company and work until retirement age. With my father that happened too and so I too, half and half, thought if there were no problems that I would enter a company and stay there until the retirement age. But one enters without knowing much about the company and the type of work and so I didn't really know whether it was really suited to me. I didn't have that confidence. So I sort of had the feeling that if it hadn't suited me then I probably would have changed. But, mostly, I thought, if there weren't any problems, then I would probably work at [the company] until the retirement age.

Q: If you had wanted to change when would have been best?

A: Well, in my personal opinion, within five years of entering the company.

Q: So why didn't you change up till now?

A: Well, when I finished the initial training that I received immediately after entry I belonged to the [financial service] division. It is a very active division and young people are given a lot of authority and opportunity. So the first year or so I didn't really understand it, but in the second year I felt that it was a great challenge. So it was interesting.

Q: Was a feeling of security important, do you think?

A: It was important yes.

Q: Was it the most important thing?

A: Whether it was the most important or not is a very difficult question, I think, but for me the most important thing to think about is that you can't change your family. You can change your company, you can change the type of work, or business sector, I think. So, with your family at home and if you really feel that you dislike your work then you can change it.

Q: So maybe, psychological aspects are more important than material aspects, do you think?

A: Well, that's an extremely difficult question. For me, if I don't have economic security then it has an effect on me psychologically. There's a Japanese expression you may know and it says that if you can eat enough today then it is the first step to being rich tomorrow. So, economic security is very important I think. If you have that foundation you can then do the work you like.

(General Manager, Company C)

What the above quotations reveal, in addition to providing much qualitative supporting evidence for the structures and cultures discussed above, is that, beyond simply emphasizing its economic rationality, a more nuanced and sympathetic understanding of the lifetime employment system and how it meshed with people's lives in the post-war years needs to be considered. Two aspects of the system stand out, therefore, to counterbalance an overly structured and economistic interpretation of the post-war system. The first is that, even in the 1960s and 1970s, people felt that real alternatives did exist in their choice of career and they considered and acted on them. Following on from this, the second is that work and a long-term career within a corporate community were emotionally important to these men and gave meaning and consistency to their lives.

When looking for employment the expression *shūshoku* was and is customarily used by final year high-school and university students. A direct translation into English renders it as job-hunting, or more precisely occupation search, but this is a misnomer. On the whole, and in contrast to the US and the UK, soon-to-graduate Japanese students did not and do not look for a job or an occupation, if that is interpreted as a specific task, trade, or profession unless they are going into vocational careers such as medicine. Instead they look for an organization within which they can develop their lives and careers. What students are really doing is *shūsha*, or company-hunting.[8] Even in the 1960s and 1970s, when the number and variety of companies were much less than today, there was a real choice of career available if one sees the process of job-hunting in this light.[9]

Within the normative standard of the post-war employment system, because this choice is so important to people's subsequent lives, students have typically gone to great lengths to search for the company that most conforms to their perceived long-term needs, desires, values, and expectations. Moreover, entry into and progress through the company gave the new employee a sense not of having to perform a specific task but of joining and being absorbed into a community where the individual's contribution is primarily for the long-term benefit of the whole, with personal benefits arising as a natural but secondary consequence of the growth produced by this collective effort. According to this understanding of the individual's roles, duties, and expectations, self-actualization is possible within the context of a growth-oriented production community and a paternalistic and semi-ascriptive hierarchy, if one takes the standpoint of the employee who internalizes corporate ideologies and identifies his own interests and goals with those of the organization in a corporate partnership of fate.[10]

It is perhaps appropriate here to introduce the concept of *mura-shakai*, or village society.[11] Although the analogy must not be taken too far or too literally, most Japanese consider themselves at most periods during their lives to be absorbed into and part of various closed functional and culture-specific groups and organizations, or communities. These communities are not unlike idealized constructions of the premodern village, in that events such as entry into the corporation and promotion to management, or birth and coming of age, are marked by various customs and ceremonies signifying to oneself and the rest of the group one's role and status. Moreover, it is extremely difficult to be accepted as a member of a competing group or organization if one either decides to leave or one is expelled for transgressing the normative behavioural codes too seriously or too often. Thus, it becomes important for the individual to become absorbed into the group by internalizing its behavioural standards and cultural dynamics in order that he can secure his place, gain the trust, respect, and liking of his colleagues and superiors, and thence progress up through the hierarchy.

In addition to possessing a basic instrumental loyalty, therefore, the individual voluntarily and even deliberately develops and internalizes an affective loyalty to the group or organization. This pattern of long-term affective membership of distinct and singular social entities is, of course, a long way from the open-ended, individualistic, and economistic ideology underlying labour relations in Anglo-American market capitalism today. Bruce Feiler vividly and engagingly captures the spirit of this process in his description of his arrival at and entry into the organization where he was to spend a year, 'As a newcomer in Japan, I would be welcomed into my office as I was welcomed into this world: with a bare body and a fresh bath' (Feiler, 1991: 2).

Once absorbed into the corporation the actual content of the work that salarymen were expected to perform was, for the most part, not contrary either to their desires and values or to their expectations. Indeed, before entering most salarymen had little inkling of the particular work tasks they would be assigned and, once inside, were often not overly bothered by whether the work accorded with their personal interests. Rather, they were more intent on feeling that they were a useful member of the corporate community and consequently were prepared to do almost anything they were assigned if it meant that their contribution would enhance the survivability of the whole. Many salarymen did, somewhat coincidentally, find the work interesting, challenging, and valuable, and gained satisfaction from it. Making a valid and verifiably important contribution to the organization as well as overcoming the steadily increasing difficulty and challenge that came from slowly rising up through the corporation were stimulating and fulfilling experiences, so long as they were viewed from a standpoint of achieving individual fulfilment as a secondary consequence of accepting one's status and duties within the existing corporate hierarchy.

However, this sense of fulfilment cannot be seen in the same light as the individualistic and somewhat self-absorbed preoccupations that Giddens and other Western scholars describe about people in their own societies. A limitless and unbounded biographical trajectory of personal growth and authentic self-actualization it was not. However, the structural limits that existed were not experienced as preventive encumbrances but rather either neutrally as existent facts to be negotiated or even positively as markers denoting the boundaries of the corporate zone of comfort and stability beyond which it was potentially unsafe and even self-destructive to proceed. It must be understood that, in the social, economic, and political context of Japan's post-war developmentalist ethic, an ideology of self-directed fulfilment and individualistic realization of one's authentic personality would have been considered, to repeat Loiskandl's (1998) description, close to committing the equivalent of 'original sin' because it would have been considered a violation of the social aesthetics of trans-rationality. As the above responses show, although real career choices, at least in the sense of choosing a company and its business sector, were available, to subordinate or put aside one's own personal, and perhaps selfish, work desires in order to be a salaryman who is an integral member of the corporate community was a positive value for many people at that time. [12]

Flexibility and adjustment

The above arguments demonstrate that, in terms of the schema for modernity laid out in chapters one and two, the paradigm of the post-war Japanese lifetime employment system in large corporations is a transitional institution in Japan's modern development and the work orientation of the core male white-collar employees is indicative of a trans-rational consciousness. Nevertheless, the lifetime employment system has never been a static phenomenon but has continuously evolved and adjusted according to circumstance and, moreover, it possesses great flexibility in its ability to weather external pressures and yet retain its primary purpose of providing lifetime employment.

Turning once again to the work of Ronald Dore, in a collaborative effort written for the OECD he wrote that, even in the late 1980s, 'The system seems to be of undiminished strength' (Dore, Bounine-Cabalé, and Tapiola, 1989: 26). Both in this book and in his own *Flexible Rigidities: Industrial Policy and Structural Adjustment in the Japanese Economy 1970–1980* (1986), he readily concedes, however, that the employment system had been undergoing internal adjustment as a result of macro-economic pressures resulting, in part, from the very success of the system itself as Japan gained its place among the top rank of world economic powers. Dore's contention was that, instead of the type of numerical employment adjustments that American and British firms practised in their reactions to external economic pressures, the Japanese firm was able to protect and maintain the principle of lifetime employment for core company members through a phased response of ever increasing urgency from product diversification through recruitment freezes, scheduled retirement, internal redeployment, transfers to subsidiaries, laying-off of temporary and part-time employees and so on. Lastly, 'the final and least attractive alternative is to break the implicit lifetime employment commitment' (Dore, Bounine-Cabalé, and Tapiola, 1989: 32). Thus, the Japanese firm is able to combine various forms of numerical flexibility with the functional flexibility of work process adjustment and employee redeployment to create long-term adaptability to external economic pressures while protecting the principle of lifetime employment for the core permanent workforce.

As early as 1958 James Abegglen had been questioning the long-term survivability and the apparent rigidity of the lifetime employment system and questions as to its durability have been raised repeatedly since then (Cole, 1971; Rohlen, 1979 or Whittaker, 1990), sometimes with barely concealed glee at the prospect of the impending collapse of the Japanese economic Goliath (McCune, 1990 or Robson, 1994). To be sure, the system has produced some unedifying effects, such as excessive competition for promotion, poor treatment of peripheral workers (Kamata, 1983; Chalmers, 1989), colonization of the upper echelons of affiliated companies' career ladders (Skinner, 1983) or the critical social problem of *karōshi*, death from overwork. More recently, there has been a marked increase in suicides by men who are either overworked to the point of mental exhaustion or who have suffered the humiliation and ignominy of not being able to fulfil their social obligation as male providers for their families because of being restructured out of the corporation or, even, the company going bankrupt.

By way of a lighthearted example that illustrates some of the extraordinary lengths to which employees have been prepared, and expected by their colleagues and superiors, to go in their efforts to conform to and succeed within the system, an article on salarymen from the weekly magazine *Shūkan Asahi* (5 July 1974) relates the story of a man who, while acting as a coordinator for a golfing party, was hit squarely on the head by a golf ball. In clear difficulty, he felt that he should stoically grin and bear the pain and humiliation, not only because his task was to secure a much needed commercial bank loan from his guests, but also because he wanted to preserve a harmonious atmosphere with his colleagues and with the bank in order to gain a promotion. Although he collapsed after he arrived home at the end of the day, he managed to gain his promotion.[13] The article then goes on to make the absurd claim that pressures were becoming so great that workers could not even afford to be unfaithful to their wives for fear of their boss discovering the indiscretion and having it damage their chances for promotion!

Although such articles might provide a little much needed levity for over-stressed salarymen, their dark humour simultaneously indicates and conceals a more significant development. That is the long-term progressive intensification of pressures on the Japanese firm, the employment system, and the salaryman who works within it. These pressures are a product both of short-term shocks and, more significantly, structural changes in the Japanese socio-economic and political environment. They include the oil crises of the 1970s, drastic realignments of the yen's trading range, increasing competition as a result of the internationalization of the Japanese economy and economic globalization, liberalization of government regulations in domestic markets, the falling birth rate and rapid ageing of the labour force, a steadily rising proportion of university graduates in the labour force, an increasing proportion of women wishing to participate in the labour force on an equal basis with men, and changing values among younger Japanese workers.

Even as early as 1967 newspaper articles were stressing the perceived need for companies to pay greater attention to merit and ability in their personnel administration systems and were highlighting examples of changes that appeared to signal a more economically rational approach to pay and promotion in response to a changing external environment. However, what is also revealing about the content of these articles is that at this stage there appeared to be no immediate threat to the principle of permanent employment; any changes that were occurring to the system, as Abegglen and others concluded, were happening at the periphery. Moreover, many accounts at that time, as well as now, reported on corporations' *intention* to alter their systems rather than providing much solid evidence of *actual* change.

A series of articles published in March 1967 in the *Nihon Keizai Shimbun* called 'Sararīman jidai' ('Age of the salaryman') serves well to illustrate the above points. For example, an article entitled 'Hiromaru "senmonshoku seido"',[14] ('Specialist system gaining ground') deals with a Nihon Nōritsu Kyōkai[15] survey that claimed more than half of all companies listed on the first section of the Tokyo Stock Exchange had already, or were *considering* introducing, a specialist career promotion track. It was reported that companies were doing so because of liberalization of labour markets for technicians, the need to computerize production, and the rapid increase in the number of university graduates entering the labour force. Yet, only seven days previously the same column, in an article entitled 'Sekinin kaihi kono nanbutsu taiji'[16] ('Getting rid of the difficult problem of responsibility avoidance') the newspaper had berated Japanese corporations and salarymen for continuing to foster *kotonakareshugi* (the principle of adhering rigidly to established procedure [against rational arguments for change]) by preserving the seniority-based pay and promotion systems.

There is no escaping the feeling that Japanese managers and employees believed themselves to be under both gradually intensifying external pressure derived from the long-term developments outlined above and, in particular, the effects of the comparatively short-term but significant oil shocks. However, it is also impossible to avoid the feeling that these developments, at least until the 1990s, had little effect on the employment practices of large corporations other than that of gradually and almost imperceptibly raising the importance of economically rational merit-based systems of evaluation for pay and promotion. For example, in the late 1960s and early 1970s many companies for the first time introduced management by objectives (MBO) systems of motivation and evaluation. Known in Japan by a variety of names, the most common of which is *mokuhyō kanri seido*, these systems are designed to respond to the increasing desire of employees to have their needs and desires reflected in the content of their work and the increasing requirements of personnel departments to motivate and incentivize employees by devising quantifiable goal-oriented systems of personnel management backed up by evaluations of the employee's level of achievement.[17] Yet an article in the *Nihon Keizai Shimbun* in April 1974 concluded that, based on data obtained from the Ministry of Labour's survey on wage structures, there had been little change in the Japanese managerial custom of *nenkōjoretsu gakurekijūshi*, or educational background weighted seniority-based pay and promotion.[18]

Lastly, press articles from that era and field-work interviews both give the distinct impression that the 1970s and 1980s, when various negative effects began to coalesce together, were the beginning of a watershed for Japanese corporations and salarymen in their consciousness. Below, the Personnel Manager of Company A explains how he understands the context surrounding and the extent of adjustments to the system in his company during the period.

In the early 1970s there was the oil shock and from that time the environment gradually changed and worsened. Also the ageing of society progressed and the number of administrative posts declined . . . and white-collarization also progressed and so because of that a system based only on age had to be changed.

. . . [At that time] there were very few university graduates and with the expansion in higher education there were many more university graduates and . . . so we began to base the treatment of employees on their abilities . . . If you ask what kind of abilities then it is the employee grade that is used as the basis.

. . . The [pay and promotion] system we have now is pretty much the same as that one. There have been a few adjustments such as more emphasis on ability since then but . . . the basic system is more or less the same and about 50 per cent is now based on ability and 50 per cent on age. That's the kind of system we adopted, I believe . . . So that was the system, ability plus age.

. . . But, how is the ability element increased? The basic principle is not at all clear. That is to say, it is not the job but the person's ability and that is very vague and impossible to accurately evaluate, at least difficult to evaluate. That's a very difficult thing to do but nevertheless we continued to try to increase the ability-based elements and reduce the importance of age-based elements. So we gradually moved around to that type of system.

As far as the retirement system is concerned we introduced a retirement system based on years of service but with other things added. Mid-career recruitment and the fluidization of the labour market affected it because the number of university graduates was increasing and so that means there were more people changing jobs . . . not as much as now, but still it was happening. Those with a short period of continuous service could not receive very much and we wanted to increase the amount they received by a little.

(Personnel Manager, Company A)

The following passage is taken from an interview with the General Secretary of the same company's labour union and is his summary of how and why labour management relations evolved in the post-war period. It confirms and demonstrates that the principal union demand was for long-term material security for all members and, although he concurs that was the principal employee need, by 1965 lifetime employment had become so well established that the union did not feel any need to campaign on this issue and could concentrate its energies on trying to gain real increases in living standards for its members. Once again, the interview shows how labour management relations and union activities gradually adjusted to changing circumstances from the 1960s and through the 1970s and 1980s.

> *A:* At [the company] there are two unions. Our [company's] labour union was set up in January 1965 . . . there was originally another union set up before that time as the company was set up again after the war. Its background was in the Communist Party and there were a lot of strikes which had a great effect on production, and the company nearly went bust. Various volunteers realized that this could not go on and so they set up another union. This was in 1965. Many years after the original union was set up it broke the agreement with the company and so we set up a formal agreement with the company to represent the workers and thus became the official union. So, we don't try to obstruct the company's production and we leave the management of the company to the company and we have a basic stance of cooperating with the company.

> *Q:* At that time, from 1965 till now, what have been your most important activities and demands?

> *A:* Our activities can be classified by three pillars . . . in the Showa 40s, or the 1960s and 1970s these were our most important aspects of working conditions and the most important was wages, then the reduction of working hours, and welfare. From the 1970s we concentrated more on events, mutual aid, and services that the union could provide. From the 1990s and into the next century we will concentrate on these things. We don't participate in management like they do in Germany but, as far as management is concerned, we provide advice and proposals and so on. This role is growing, I think.

> *Q:* In the 1960s and 1970s, was the most important thing the provision of security for union members?

> *A:* Yes, we wanted to secure living standards and this was an important objective since at that time living standards were quite hard and there was inflation every year and so we tried hard to gain annual increases in salary. This was the most important topic.

> *Q:* So, was lifetime employment taken as a matter of course then?

> *A:* Yes. Lifetime employment, even now it is very much taken for granted.
>
> (General Secretary, Company A Labour Union)

The two quotations above emphasize what James Malcolm (2001) refers to as 'the gradualist approach' to reform that Japanese political and managerial élites almost invariably choose for themselves and, by implication, the next respondent supports this idea since he feels that decisive reforms began to appear in his company only after the comparatively sudden change in the growth regime from high to low growth that was brought about at the time of the bursting of the Bubble Economy in 1989–90. Hasegawa and Hook (1998) confirm this interpretation in their edited collection on Japanese business management in the 1990s.

> Looking at it, the biggest change happened during the Bubble . . . From the 1960s till that time it didn't really change at all. From 1990 things began to change. I have that feeling. Why do I say that? The Japanese economy had progressed continuously and until that point we increased the number of our regional offices and the number of employees year by year and work increased year by year too. From now we will not experience that kind of growth. People have all the things they need because they are now wealthy and so [the company]'s income, just like most other companies', will not increase steadily like it did in the past.
>
> In the past people entered and expected to be treated in the same way as before, but from now it will change quite a lot I think. In the future, basically . . . well in the past we just recruited using university connections in the company. *Sempai* would be dispatched to the universities to recruit good candidates. From now on we won't do that . . . More than deciding on the basis of the name of the university we will think about their qualities and why they want to work at this company.
>
> (Personnel Manager, Company C, age late forties)

Next, the General Secretary of Company B's Workers' Union, Tokyo Branch, explains his impression of white-collar employees' consciousness at that time. Like some of the above interviewees, in his opinion decisive change began to appear in employee consciousness only comparatively recently. His explanation, moreover, confirms many of the arguments already discussed regarding the internalization by company members of a communal ideology of work within the corporation. He describes a deep level of connection that employees may have felt between themselves and their companies but, in slight contrast to some of the previous employees' recollections, he stresses the instrumental nature of this connection and how, in addition to being an affective attachment, this relationship might be born out of individuals' personal material needs and their desire for status recognition. Further, he also hints that the previously strong organization orientation of the salaryman may now be weakening in favour of one that focuses more on the recognition of achievement in one's work tasks.

> *A:*   White-collar workers in the 1960s and 1970s were happy if they

could help develop the company. They were happy if the company was successful . . .

Q: Did people in the past put the company's success in front of their own?

A: Yes. If the company succeeded it would become bigger and its social prestige would increase and those people would feel that their own value had increased, I think.

Q: Did those people not think too much about their own development and realization, do you think?

A: Well . . . that's difficult. They thought that their development and realization lay in being promoted within the company.

Q: So, the meaning of self-development and self-realization is gradually coming to change, is it?

A: Yes. Before, promotion was one's development and it signified success but now it's having one's work recognized. Gaining a higher position is not so important. Of course, one needs to be promoted if one wants to do that kind of work but being promoted is not the objective so much as the work itself.

Q: Did people in the 1960s place security over self-development, do you think?

A: Well . . . people thought about their own development and self-realization but for them the development of the company and their own development were one and the same thing. 'If the company develops then I develop' was the way of thinking, I think. So, on the contrary, those in the 1960s and 1970s didn't think that if one develops oneself then the company cannot but develop. Instead they thought they would be part of one company from when they looked for a job until the retirement age. Also, they thought that whatever work they did, if they didn't get to become section or department head then they could not be well regarded in society. From those two things one can conclude, I think, raising one's family depends on the development of the company and that will lead to oneself being more highly regarded. So, if one didn't develop oneself that was OK, they thought. They thought that the only way to develop was to develop the company.

(General Secretary, Tokyo Branch, Company B Workers' Union)

Lastly, in the following interview, we can see how the stresses occurring in the 1970s' external environment very directly affected individual salarymen. We can understand from this account confirmation of Dore's contention that the system possessed flexibilities within an outward appearance of rigidity. Using his own experiences as an example, this respondent describes very clearly the stresses that Japanese companies began to feel when the macro-economic and political environment began to change from the 1970s. In addition, he shows that not all Japanese salarymen conformed so readily to a normative understanding of company as community. Some, even at that time, possessed a more self-directed, but by no means self-indulgent, desire for individual achievement in their work.

A: As far as this interview is concerned I am a rare and, I think, interesting case. I am a mid-career recruit. Until university I was [here] and on graduation I joined a manufacturer, [a shipbuilding company]. I was in their research department. About 12 years ago, when I was around 39, I returned [to this city] and joined [this company] . . .

When I was at university it was just at the end of the period of high-speed economic growth . . . Against this background I graduated and I was influenced by the atmosphere of heavy and automobile industries, and I wondered what plan I should create for myself. I continued at university and did a Master's degree, so I actually left university in 1973 . . .

Originally I thought about [other large heavy industrial companies and manufacturers], all located here, but I thought I would like to work [elsewhere] as I had lived here from birth until leaving university.

Q: When you joined did you want to stay until the retirement age?

A: Yes. At that time it was normal, there was no feeling of restructuring like there is today. I wanted to work there until the end. My father was also a salaryman and worked at the same place until his retirement and I thought that I would like to follow the same route . . .

Q: So, why did you leave [the shipbuilding company]?

A: The period I joined was at the peak of the shipbuilding industry. After that was the Nixon and oil shocks. The yen began to rise against the dollar from a level of 360 yen to the dollar. Before that Japan was able to export a lot, but after that things changed and export competition intensified. After the two oil shocks orders for tankers dropped rapidly . . . From then on South Korea began to gain market share and the yen continued to rise and competition became much tougher. It was a really tough time, structural recession caused heavy industrial enterprises great difficulties. We tried lots of new things, but the company shrank in size anyway.

Q: Were you laid off or did you decide to leave on your own accord?

A: No it wasn't like that at all. We didn't feel at all that the company was forcing us out. I decided for myself. I felt somewhat lost, that my life-plan had collapsed. I wanted to continue to use my specialty rather than take on a new role. So I had to think again about what to do.

Q: So, you joined [this company]?

A: Yes. At that time I knew someone in the company and I had a chat with him. He knew a lot about the structure of the industry and invited me to join the company. I had thought seriously and wanted to continue in my specialty and looked for a place where I could do so. I was offered a possibility to do so here at [this company].

(Chief Research Editor, Company D)

Turning now to Hasegawa's (1996) idea of 'organic' and 'contrived compatibility', he posits the theory that the post-oil-shock period in Japan was one when the organic confluence of interests achieved in the internal and external corporate environments during the 1960s was being challenged by subsequently slower growth and pressures resulting from increasingly severe international competition. These pressures had forced modifications in the Japanese management system and Hasegawa concluded that the evolving system, while remaining true to its origins in a fundamental sense, could be described as being an artificial, or 'contrived compatibility', between the interests of labour and management as both sought to preserve a system under great pressure through the introduction of rationalization measures.

While management and employees understood that fundamental changes were occurring in the external environment, the system possessed the flexibility necessary to preserve its basic character, albeit with some adjustments. Importantly, Mari Sako (1997) poses the simple proposition that the stability of the Japanese employment system rests on both the desire of the company to offer security and the desire of the employee to take it. In the 1960s and early 1970s it appears that both sides of the labour–management divide held that desire. But by the 1970s stresses in the system had built up to the extent that management found it necessary to introduce rationalization measures to personnel administration, not because they wished to weaken the system but because, in the face of circumstances that appeared to be conspiring against them, they wished to preserve it.

The lifetime employment system as a transitional institution

Recollections by employees, managers, and union leaders were used as the principal empirical data for this chapter because these memories display both evidence for a particular ideology situated in the past and something about the present-day world-view and way of thinking of the respondents. Interviewees told how their needs and expectations on entering their companies were both economically rational in desiring security and stability at a time of material uncertainty, as well as socially located in a transitional environment, in that most followed a line of least resistance into and through education and employment in a non-reflexive and received but positive manner. The evidence shows how the employment system itself was given a fictive pre-modern legitimacy by management in order to embed employees into the organization and encourage them to work towards mutual material gain and social advancement. This fictive traditionalism can be seen, for example, in the seniority-based pay and promotion systems that came to take on the trappings of a new system of received hierarchical ascription based on educational achievement and age.

However, interestingly, respondents on the whole appear not to have reflexively sought to reconstruct, in the present, rationalized biographies out of their past motives and experiences. Older employees are even now comfortable with, and even proud of, having accepted and lived within a comparatively received and ascriptive social milieu that stressed a lifetime of duty to, dependence on, and absorption into the corporate community as the source of individual and group fulfilment and realization. Respondents did not express reticence at the prospect of an admission of this kind, stating matter-of-factly how they now believe they felt at that time.

This issue of the contribution of memory to this research project, as well as to qualitative sociological research in general, is crucial. In addition to providing us with important and context-rich data about how people understood their lives and the institutional arrangements of their past, how people remember, and how they forget, their experience of external reality also give us an interesting and important entry point into how they perceive, configure, and represent those memories in the present.[19] Most respondents, while stating that this was how life and work was for them, and that they willingly subscribed to and participated in such a society because they felt it was right and proper to do so, at the same time implied that this way of thinking and way of life were located in the past. In this sense, they implied that contemporary Japan is a different society from what it was.

This chapter was not an attempt to describe in great detail the actual institutional arrangements of employment in post-war Japan, for this has been done exhaustively elsewhere, but to present how people felt at the time about the circumstances of their employment, how they related to and negotiated their path through them, and what we can conclude from this about the cultures and ideologies of employment at that time in terms of our theoretical understanding of the development of capitalist modernity as it is expressed in the Japanese experience. More significant than the actual circumstances of life and the events that unfolded therefrom is how people felt about and understood these things as they experienced them, and how people feel about and understand their past lives in relation to their present circumstances, feelings, and perceptions. For how actors perceive their circumstances in terms of their systems of needs, desires, and values is considerably more important as a source of motivation for behaviour than actual circumstances as academic scholars might understand them.

This book starts from the assumption that economic systems, while possessing their own powerful dynamic, are necessarily embedded in social structures and systems of social relations which themselves are derived from the basic values of the society in which actors dwell. Although Alfred D. Chandler Jr's (1980) groundbreaking research on the origins of the American management system suggests that organizational structures follow from the particular economic strategies pursued by management and that these are, in substantial measure, an adaptive response to external economic conditions and technological contingencies, external conditions and management decisions themselves must also be embedded in social and cultural values. For when faced with a set of options from which to choose, the actor will decide on the course that most conforms to his or her priorities and objectives. As much as they come from external exigency or immediate economic need, these priorities and objectives emanate from the core values and experiences of the individual as well as those of the human group, or organization, of which the actor is an integral part. Thus, it cannot be denied that strategy itself, in part, must necessarily also be a product of the cultures and values that managers bring to organizational decision-making. Further, it can be assumed that management decisions, to a greater or lesser extent, must also be responsive to the needs and desires of other stakeholders, including employees, and that these too, if we continue this line of argument, must necessarily reflect in some measure the principal value systems of the actors involved.

Returning to Hazama's study in historical sociology (1997 [1964]), I believe that it is in the area of social embedding that the importance of my research reveals itself. For while Hazama concedes indirectly that the introduction of the ideology of managerial familism was a conscious and rational decision made by management with the encouragement of a government eager to promote its version of national familism, its long-term effects, as well as those of its post-war incarnation in industrial paternalism and welfare corporatism, reveal it to us as a transitional institution in the history of Japan's modern development. Further, explicit references to livelihood guarantees, complex systems of welfare for the paternalistic care of employees, and so on, encouraged employees to see the company as a community that possessed tight relations of dependence not unlike idealized recollections of the organic family and village communities which many employees had only recently left. Long-term employment thus became synonymous with membership of, and absorption into, the organizational community, or village, and it became difficult, if not impossible, to distinguish the psychological and emotional division between instrumental and affective loyalty. The Japanese company had become what Nakane (1972) famously referred to as a 'fictive kin group'.

The ideology of managerial familism, while starting out as a calculated managerial imposition was, in addition, a product of cultural modelling and became in the course of the developments of the twentieth century a genuinely affective relationship between management, employee, corporation, and even nation, to the extent that it ceased to be meaningful or important to the various groups of stakeholders of Japan's large corporations how the 'tradition' had originally come about. To be sure, rational economic imperatives and needs remained important to both management and employees, but to all intents and purposes the ideological basis of the corporation was received and non-reflexively traditional. As such, therefore, it would be difficult to term this a 'modern' organization.

When we come to survey the post-war period, it is important to note that, while it is difficult to locate the underlying values of the post-war system as being directly derived from even the pre-war managerial familism that Hazama describes, it is also difficult to dispute that the system had come to possess an identity which Japanese people themselves believe is distinctly, essentially, and traditionally Japanese. This identity is most easily described as a belief that a corporate community based within and around a non-reflexive social system of hierarchical semi-ascription and affective communitarian and paternalistic relations of trust and dependency is at one and the same time both modern and traditional. It possesses a modern identity in the sense that it is a capitalist organization for the long-term pecuniary advantage of all stakeholders, and it is traditional in the sense that, whatever the real origins of these corporate values, both management and employees have come to believe, for the most part, that the organization is embedded in an essential Japaneseness that is located in Japanese people's affective and idealized images of premodern social relations. Thus, through the process of cultural modelling, in order to satisfy modern instrumental and economic needs, the system plays a role as an intermediate or transitional social institution that provides the psychological and emotional requirements of coping with and succeeding in the drastic and wrenching transformations to the premodern world-view that economic modernization inevitably engenders.

4 Re-fabricating lifetime employment relations

To what extent and in what ways is the contemporary structure of the lifetime employment system changing? Why is it changing? What do such changes signify in terms of the development of Japan's capitalism and modernity?

In her book *Work, Self and Society After Industrialism* (1995), Catherine Casey presents us with a critical analysis of workplace developments at a US multinational company. She describes how management manipulates employees to conform to a deliberately but defensively constructed corporate 'designer culture'. That is to say, in addition to extracting the surplus labour from employees' instrumental energies, capital seeks to penetrate the employees' inner consciousness so that their intrinsic energies and motivations are directed into providing productivity gains and, presumably, profits for management and shareholders. However, Casey opines that this is at the expense of employees developing an individual self-consciousness that is authentic to their own personalities and capabilities as well as their own needs, desires, and values.

Accordingly, Casey wishes to persuade us that we are living through a transitional phase in the development of capitalism, between the materiality and solidity of industrialism and an as yet unnamed era dominated by symbolism, discourse, and flux. She theorizes that, as the self is multiple, fluid, and historically and culturally contingent, employees are easily steered into colluding with, and capitulating to, managerial power. Her description is of a corporate dystopia in which culture becomes a simulated yet resolutely defensive response to the demands of a decentred or diffuse, and thus unchallengeable and irresistible, economic globalization. Because it mitigates against the achievement of authenticity, it produces a chronically anxious and narcissistic employee self that is unable even to locate the source of its anxiety, let alone confront and overcome it.

How are Japanese managers coping with and responding to the intensification of global competition? Are they, too, engaged in a policy of designing the needs, desires, and values of their employees in a defensive struggle to maintain and enhance their competitiveness?

The contemporary structure of lifetime employment

Arguments that the Japanese lifetime employment system is on the point of a fundamental structural transformation are not new and yet its enduring survivability has confounded such prophets now for more than a quarter of a century. Writing approximately 30 years ago, Ujigawa and Uemura (1970) proposed just such a development in their book *Sararīman Kakumei* ('Salary-man revolution'). Interestingly, their assertions parallel many of the arguments of today's observers. Predicting the effects of corporate rationalization on the salaryman, they argued that creativity would become increasingly important and they advised salarymen to become more autonomous and reduce their commitment to the company because, they believed, the lifetime employment principle would in future be offered only to a small coterie of élite specialist employees.

A substantial proportion of these works have predicted that the Japanese management and employment systems would gradually converge on Anglo-American forms of capitalist organization as the exigencies of economic modernization and globalization become more powerful and those of tradition and culture fade (for example, Cole, 1971 and Beck and Beck, 1994). Nevertheless, it has also been frequently asserted that cultural differences present an insurmountable barrier to, or at least places limits upon, the convergence of economic systems because, so the argument goes, society and culture are historically and geographically contingent and economies are rooted in society, culture, and custom (for example, Clark, 1979 and Eisenstadt 1998). But, what if a new set of economic, social, and political dynamics appears which presages, or even simply appears to presage, the convergence of culture? And what if a new set of technical arrangements appears that challenges our notions of time and distance? For, if one first accepts the Weberian proposition that institutions and organizations are rooted in culture and, second, that the globalization of Western capitalist modernity is becoming an existent fact around the world and in Japan, then surely institutional and organizational convergence cannot be far behind.

Research on the Japanese lifetime employment system has for some time presented the observer with a confusing picture and virtually all possible shades of opinion are represented in the academic and popular literature. These range from those who believe the system may actually be continuing to strengthen (Okazaki, 1996), through those who assert that present developments represent adjustments within the pre-existing paradigm (Whittaker, 1990; Sato, 1997b; and Benson, 1998), to those who argue that the system may be on the point of drastic change (Lincoln and Nakata, 1997), or is in the midst of change (Beck and Beck, 1994), or those who assert that the system has changed so dramatically that it no longer even exists (Takahashi, 1997).

More recently, in his introduction to a group of articles on atypical and irregular labour[1] in *Social Science Japan Journal*, Suehiro (2001) claims that 'a rapid increase in various forms of employment outside the regular worker (*sei-shain*) model' is contributing to a 'collapse in lifetime employment'. Yet, a year earlier, Ronald Dore (2000) had presented the argument that the structure of employment is not yet changing in any fundamental way but that there is an ideological battle being waged between those neo-liberals inspired by the 1990s success of US-style capitalism and the conservative old guard who wish to preserve Japanese-style consensus capitalism. Further, Kato (2001) found that there is little evidence of any widespread decline in job retention among male regular employees in large corporations and Matsuzuka (2002) found that in the period 1982–97 job retention had increased among regular employees, mainly because of a combination of lifetime employment and the ageing of the labour force. Kato adds, however, that employment adjustment is being carried out on the margins of the system and to the detriment of employment security among younger people, female and older male employees. Matsuzuka speculates that present and future developments in the culture of employment may presage more substantive changes to its structure.

In addition to disagreement on the actual structure and extent of lifetime employment, there has also been a similar amount of scrutiny of its dependent attributes, such as phased recruitment at or shortly after graduation of entire cohorts, the structure of long-term career development (training, personnel movement, and promotion), the reward structure (wages, welfare benefits, and pensions), and the structure of retirement from the organization.

Clearly the issue is contentious and it appears necessary not only to investigate further the empirical structure of regular employment in large Japanese corporations but also to make efforts to understand some of the ideological and cultural mechanisms that underpin it. Thus, this chapter first presents data from a variety of secondary sources that investigate the current state of the system of lifetime employment and then presents primary empirical data for the purpose of examining the contemporary qualitative texture of lifetime employment from the perspective of management. In the next chapter we will examine some of these issues from the perspective of employees.

Lifetime employment

Taking first the core issue of managerial approaches to the normative legitimacy of very long-term employment security, and looking at some recent research from Japan that is fairly typical of economistic and quantitative approaches to the question of lifetime employment, Nakata and Takehiro (2002) use firm level panel data sets to make the theoretically important claim that Japanese leading companies' employment policies 'reflect basic economic principles' and that they make adjustments to employment levels according to 'fluctuations in economic conditions and the relative price of labor' (ibid.: 17). By implication the paper argues that corporate management pays little attention, if it ever did, to normative societal expectations of permanent employment.

Based on the assumption that any employment reduction of more than

5 per cent in a single year would be 'very unlikely' and a 10 per cent or more reduction 'inconceivable' (ibid.: 4) under a system that precludes laying off employees except under circumstances of near bankruptcy, Nakata and Takehiro found that reductions of more than 5 per cent were 'not uncommon' (ibid.: 5) and that reductions of more than 10 per cent had occurred in the 25-year period for which they have data.

Looking more closely, however, out of 12 companies surveyed in the automobile sector,[2] three (two of these from the Nissan group) accounted for 80 per cent of the number of occasions when employment reduction measures resulted in a greater than 5 per cent fall in the workforce. By contrast, of the other companies in the sample, four had no occasion in the 25-year period to reduce their employment levels by more than 5 per cent, four had done so only once, and one had done so twice. Further, the article does not provide details of whether the employee totals used include temporary or part-time workers, what age the employees were who lost their jobs, and where these employees went after leaving the organization. When thinking sociologically these are important issues to raise since many scholars recognize that voluntary early retirement as well as transfer to an affiliated company should not be regarded as equivalent to an involuntary lay-off into the external labour market. For in cases of both early retirement and transfer, basic financial security or employment are still taken into consideration by the firm and, thus, quite characteristic of the Japanese industrial system, the boundaries of the firm should be seen, in this context, as encompassing those of affiliated organizations (Sato, 1997a and 1997b, and NRKK, 2000).

Investigating further, and looking at Nakata and Takehiro's data from department stores[3] and supermarkets,[4] much higher levels of employment adjustment than in the automotive sector can indeed be observed. As with automotive companies, these predominantly came at times of exceptional difficulty; either shortly after the oil shock of the mid-1970s or during the mid-1990s when dramatic falls in domestic consumption and the effects of the collapse of the real-estate and stock investment bubble of the late 1980s were beginning to bite more deeply. These circumstances required exceptional measures, particularly in the retail sector which, because of its exposure to private consumption levels as well as urban real-estate price fluctuations, has proved to be one of the most vulnerable to the structural difficulties exposed by the collapse of the Bubble Economy.[5] Moreover, the data shows much higher maximum proportions of female workers in department stores (62.39 per cent) and supermarkets (51.75 per cent) than in automotive manufacturers (11.94 per cent), which perhaps explains the greater ease of use of numerical flexibility in the retail sector and, conversely, of a concentration on functional flexibility in the automotive sector.

When we look at length of service and average ages for the industries covered by Nakata and Takehiro's study and deduce the average age of entry, a number of interesting patterns emerge. Figure 4.1 indicates that very long-term employment stability and security for men in all three sectors appears to

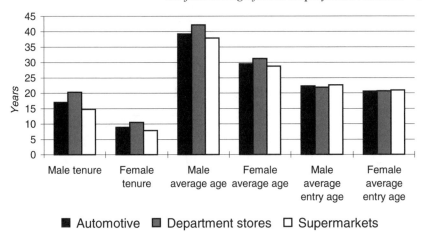

Figure 4.1 Average tenures, ages, and ages of entry by gender in the Japanese automotive and retail sectors.

Source: Nakata and Takehiro, 2002 (average age of entry my calculation).

be strong. In addition, entry is concentrated uniformly and in the standard
manner very early in employees' careers, being at or shortly after graduation
from senior high school or university.[6] Interestingly, in all three industries
the average age for women is approximately ten years less than that for men,
indicating once more that, in addition to women having a greater propensity
to leave employment for marriage and childbirth, female employment may
be being used by management as a protective buffer for male employment
stability.

From the point of view of labour economics, Nakata and Takehiro certainly present a good case for stating that Japanese management in the three
industries covered is very mindful of their firms' economic circumstances and
that labour costs are one of the most important factors that weigh on managers' minds when they make their decisions, but it also appears that long-
term employment security and stability for male regular employees is more
than purely a market-based and economically rational arrangement. In this
way it is important to remind ourselves that the normative culture of long-
term employment does not prevent the firm from possessing an instrumental
economic rationality. In fact, its economic rationality has been shown to be
one of the principal reasons for its enduring survivability. However, neither
should we also assume that any organization that remains economically effective, and whose institutional arrangements are compatible with prevailing
social and cultural norms, is necessarily prevented from continuing to exist
simply because it operates at a lower than optimum level of economic efficiency (North, 1990).

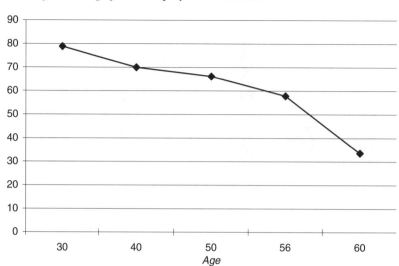

Figure 4.2 Percentage by age of white-collar male regular employees remaining with
their original employer.

Source: NKSKK, 1995.

Among quantitative surveys of the Japanese management and employment systems probably the largest and most comprehensive are those of the
Nihongata Koyō Shisutemu Kenkyū Kai (NKSKK, 1995), Chōgin Sōken
Consarutingu (CSC, 1998), Nihon Rōdō Kenkyū Kikō (NRKK, 2000), and
Shakai Keizai Seisansei Honbu (SKSH, 2000 and 2001a)[7] and it is worth
looking at these first if we wish to understand some of the contemporary
manifestations of the lifetime employment system. Compiling data from both
the first and second halves of Japan's decade or so of economic stagnation,
together these research efforts present a detailed picture of the actual state of
employment restructuring in Japanese industry as well as, and perhaps more
importantly, the attitudes of management and employees towards the issues
that face them.

NKSKK used data collected from the management of 515 large corporations listed on the first section of the Tokyo Stock Exchange and from 4,063
mostly male white-collar employees (78.3 per cent university graduates) of
the same companies. On the issue of employment retention, Figure 4.2 shows
average retention levels by age of white-collar male employees recruited on
graduation from university over the whole sample. The graph reveals that
employee retention is high across all age groups but that it is by no means
true that all employees remain until the fixed retirement age.[8] Nevertheless,
judging from this sample, more than half of all male white-collar employees
in large corporations recruited on graduation from university remain at
their original company until their mid-fifties whereupon, presumably to make

way for advancing cohorts, a number are either transferred to affiliates or retired.

Looking at the whole labour force, in a 1996 OECD study (quoted in Economic Planning Agency, 1999: 292) the average length of service in Japan differed little from that of France and Germany yet differed substantially from the USA, UK, and Canada. In Japan the average length of service actually increased by one year to 11.3 years in the period 1985–95. Germany showed 10.8 years and France 10.4 years in 1995 while the USA, UK, and Canada showed 7.4, 8.3 and 7.9 years respectively.

However, in the NKSKK (1995) study, employee retention rates for Japanese male white-collar university graduates were considerably higher than figures for the whole labour force cited in the above OECD report. Of the 4,063 respondents 3,281 (80.6 per cent) stated they had never changed employer and of those who had changed their employer, 12.7 per cent had done so only once, 3.7 per cent had done so twice, and only 2.5 per cent had done so three or more times. Put another way, between 93 and 94 per cent of employees, of an average age of 38.9 years and with an average length of tenure of 15.2 years, were either working at their original employer or had only changed employer once, most probably in the early years of their careers.

Yet it appears from the NKSKK research either that management retains employees beyond what might be considered economic self-interest or there are structural reasons, such as legal restrictions,[9] that prevent management from laying off workers into the external labour market. When asked whether they felt their company possessed an excess of white-collar university graduates over the age of 40, 11.1 per cent of managerial respondents said they had many excess employees, 37.1 per cent said they had some, 41.6 per cent said that there were not many, while only 9.3 per cent said that they had none (NKSKK, 1995).

The idea that lifetime employment continues to be more than simply an economic relationship can be more readily understood when methods for dealing with these excess middle-aged and older white-collar employees are analysed. As can be seen from Figure 4.3, which shows the various measures companies use to deal with their excess middle-aged employees, even during the most severe recession since the Second World War, large Japanese corporations rarely resort to mass lay-offs into the external labour market when pursuing employment restructuring. This, of course, is in marked contrast to the way US and British companies behaved towards their employees when faced with a similar period of structurally induced stagnation between the early 1970s and the mid-1990s.[10] It appears therefore that management accepts the normative responsibility of preserving lifetime employment as a socially and culturally legitimate institution and takes measures to ensure the future financial and employment security of their regular employees, even if many of them may not end up actually working at their original employer.

If, in addition to considering the substantive manifestation of very long-term employment security and stability, we take into account the intentions of

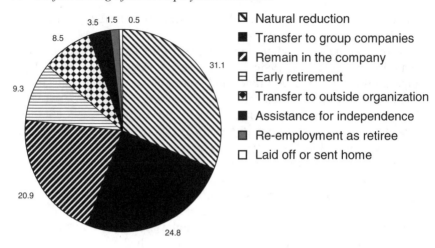

Figure 4.3 Employment adjustment of excess middle-aged white-collar workers by large Japanese corporations.

Source: NKSKK, 1995.

management then the future prospects for lifetime employment appear secure if perhaps slightly attenuated. Fully 56.4 per cent of employers said they intend to continue with the principle of lifetime employment (presumably unchanged), and 35.7 per cent intended to continue it with some modifications, adding up to more than 90 per cent of management wishing to preserve the system in some form or another (NKSKK, 1995). Three years later in the study by Chōgin Sōken Consarutingu (CSC, 1998),[11] only 3.3 per cent of employers thought that they should continue with the lifetime employment system unchanged, 25 per cent thought that there was not much need for change, and 61.9 per cent thought some gradual changes were needed, while 9.9 per cent thought they needed to change their system drastically. In the NRKK (2000) study of 690 companies,[12] 33.8 per cent intend to maintain the principle of lifetime employment, 44.3 per cent intend to continue it with some changes, 17.1 per cent believe some fundamental changes are necessary, and only 3.8 per cent say that they do not have lifetime employment at their company. Importantly, and implying that lifetime employment remains strong but is weakening, the study concluded by stating that, 'With regard to the custom of lifetime employment, it is difficult to think that there will be a drastic collapse in the near future' (NRKK, 2000: 33).

More recently, the SKSH (2000 and 2001a) studies also show that managerial commitment to lifetime employment is being maintained though, again, it may be weakening. Of 376 Tokyo Stock Exchange listed companies questioned in the 1999 survey (SKSH, 2000) 60.6 per cent wanted to maintain the system of lifetime employment while 25.2 per cent had no special preference and 10.7 per cent could not say either way. Of the 2000 sample (SKSH, 2001a), which consisted of 301 companies of which 166 were of more than 1,000 employees, 32.6 per cent wanted to maintain the system while 26.9 per cent did not and 40.2 per cent could not say either way. Comparing the two surveys one might conclude, first, that managerial commitment to lifetime employment is strongest among large corporations and, second, that a not insignificant minority of managers from all sizes of company are either not committed to lifetime employment one way or another or believe that it should be fundamentally reformed. This conclusion is backed up by other research by the Nihon Rōdō Kenkyū Kiko (NRKK, 1999) where, of more than 1,000 white-collar managers questioned, 19.8 per cent believed that lifetime employment should be maintained as a matter of principle, 59.5 per cent believed that some changes could not be avoided, and 18.1 per cent believed that fundamental reform could not be avoided.

The dependent attributes of the lifetime employment system

If we examine the employment system in large Japanese corporations from the perspective of seeing lifetime employment as a frame within which various dependent processes, systems, and attributes operate, the beginnings of a qualitative change to some of these can be observed. However, since the frame remains largely in place, these changes do not amount to a transformation of the system itself but an attenuation and a modification or, more accurately, a diversification and differentiation of employment structures and practices. While it is certainly the case that Japanese companies have continued to rely on the standard phased application of mechanisms for mitigating the effects of external economic difficulty (Araki, 2002: 22), substantive and qualitative changes have taken place, particularly in the areas of personnel management and development. However, it remains extremely difficult to make any firm judgements on the basis of current research as to how profound or permanent present developments are and what they signify.

First addressing the issue of the phased recruitment of entire cohorts of employees at or shortly after graduation, we have already seen above in the discussion of Nakata and Takehiro's work that the age of entry for males into many large Japanese companies continues to be in most employees' early twenties, confirming the assumption that companies continue to prefer to hire and retain regular employees fresh from university. Notwithstanding, it can also be seen from a number of other studies that hiring practices are undergoing some adjustments towards a more differentiated and more fluid system that makes greater use of external labour markets.

By way of example, companies are increasingly looking to hire mid-career recruits with specialized skills as well as dispatch and contracted workers who require little costly training and whose productive abilities can therefore be activated soon after they enter the organization. In a study of large corporations' recruitment strategies by the former Ministry of Labour (Rōdōshō,

2000a), it was found that 47.3 per cent of responding companies are introducing formal procedures for the mid-career recruitment of white-collar regular employees (62.5 per cent of services companies, 53.7 per cent of manufacturers), 45.3 per cent of companies had introduced the employment of dispatch workers, and 29.7 per cent of companies are continuing to diversify the hiring of new employees on fixed-term contracts.

Moving to the issue of long-term human resource development of white-collar employees, using Dore's (1973) schematic institutional dichotomy of a UK market and Japanese organization orientation as one of the bases of their analysis, Storey, Edwards, and Sisson found that Japan's career development systems were more uniform across industrial sectors and between companies than the UK, and were more robust, systematic, and long-term in their orientation. The authors stressed that the major difference between managers in the two countries was that Japanese managers did not constantly reaffirm the primacy of the market but had a more stable belief in the enduring long-term value of 'growing managers to meet the changing character of market conditions' (Storey, Edwards, and Sisson, 1997: 207).

Surprisingly, and somewhat contrary to expectations, they also found that British white-collar management track employees had a wider range of functional experience than their Japanese colleagues. This issue points to a widely held assumption that is increasingly coming to be challenged by recent empirical evidence as it accumulates. That is, Japanese white-collar employees are often believed to be, and believe themselves to be, generalists working towards achieving a management position through a career structure characterized by a received acceptance of the accumulation of broad functional experience within a single organization through regular movement and rotation among departments with different functional responsibilities. In contrast, the culture of career development in the UK and USA is strongly coloured by the assumption that white-collar business élites retain control over and ownership of their careers by actively and self-consciously building an upwardly rising spiral, or career chimney (Storey, Edwards, and Sisson, 1997), of increasing accumulation of skill, status, and salary through moving from one company to another within a specific functional specialization. This dichotomy appears no longer to be so sharp, if it ever was. Such were the conclusions, also, of a detailed comparative study conducted by the Japan Institute of Labour (1998).[13] In this study, although important differences between Japanese and other countries' human resource development practices were observed, such as greater continuity of employment in a single organization and fewer changes of employer in Japan, the main conclusions of the study can be summed up by stating that differences in career development practices, attitudes, and values among white-collar university graduate males in Western countries and Japan are not as sharp as before.

Nevertheless, Japanese corporations still practise broad-based and long-term career development and training for their regular employees and this is done in the hope and expectation that employees will remain with the company for most of their working lives. Imada and Hirata (1995), in their examination of the structure of career development and promotion for male university graduates at a heavy industrial manufacturer, found a typical three-tier pyramidal structure. Employees' careers commence with a seniority- and rotation-based system of socialization in the early years of their life at the company during which more than 90 per cent of employees experience and learn the company's core business before being promoted to positions where more content-rich specialized roles are encountered. This then proceeds to a speed-race system in employees' middle years when catching up with members of the same cohort who have been promoted more quickly is still assumed to be possible, and when skills are deepened and administrative and managerial skills begin to be acquired. Moreover, they found that if promotion to Section Chief by year 15 (about 40 per cent of employees) had not yet been achieved then there would be no further chances to catch up. Employees then advance to a tournament-style system in the company's upper echelons.

Within this type of system, which has been fairly standard across Japan's large firms for some considerable time now, it is becoming widely understood that companies are intent on long-term development of employee-managers possessing both generalist managerial and specialist functional skills and knowledge. Indeed, intuitively it would appear odd if Japanese companies did not try to do this, given the high levels of informal tacit[14] as well as formal specialist knowledge required in managerial positions today. Nakamura (1992), in a survey of 187 firms of more than 100 employees, found that many employees experienced specialist careers. Later, she found (Nakamura, 1995), in data from 334 respondents in a variety of large corporations, that companies try to develop employees into specialists after a few years of learning the basic principles of the company's activities in generalist customer-oriented departments such as the business development and sales divisions. Koike (1991) also found in his study of 60 large and medium-sized companies that later moves within the organization actually involved remaining within a specialization because although employees move from one department to another, more often than not they work within a single functional capacity. However, by moving between departments they also gain a broad knowledge of the company's activities.

If, however, we now examine these processes from the conceptually important and interrelated perspective of seniority-based pay and promotion, a diversification, relaxation, and rationalization of structures and systems seem to be appearing. Assembled together, the systems point to the introduction and strengthening of systems for promotion and payment according to ability and results, and the ongoing weakening of seniority- and age-based systems. Yatabe (2000) in his research of 31 companies of various sizes for the practitioners' journal *Chingin Jitsumu* found that 23 companies (74.2 per cent) had already discontinued age-related pay for management and 14 companies (45.2 per cent) had done so for employees, while all companies intended to discontinue it for management and 18 companies (58.1 per cent) for employees.

When asked why companies had originally introduced age-based pay, 16 responded that its purpose was to ensure a minimum salary and 13 companies said they had wanted to protect the living standards of employees. Asked why they were discontinuing it, 24 companies (77.4 per cent) said it was to strengthen results-based payment systems and 22 companies said it was in order to abolish seniority-based systems.

Looking at the larger study done by Chōgin Sōken Consarutingu (CSC, 1998), virtually all of the large corporations that responded believe either gradual changes (55.5 per cent) or drastic changes (38.7 per cent) are needed to the seniority wages system in their company. Only five out of 637 responding companies replied that no changes to seniority wages are required in either their own company or in general, and it is not clear from the data whether these five had already carried out measures to reform seniority-based wages and therefore felt that there was no more need to do so.

With regard to promotion, companies appear to be turning to more diversified systems and basing them increasingly on abilities and results rather than simply on seniority. According to a general survey of the labour situation in Japan by the Japan Institute of Labour (2001: 27) a greater number of companies are now adopting 'a more rapid advancement system' and there is a 'trend towards earlier promotions'. In their annual survey on employment management, the former Ministry of Labour's Policy Planning and Research Department (Rōmu Gyōsei Kenkyūjo, 1999) found that on average 85.2 per cent of companies based their decisions on promotion to Assistant Manager on ability and 80.1 per cent on results while 47.9 per cent used seniority as a guide. For promotion to Manager the figures were slightly higher for ability and results and slightly lower for seniority, indicating that seniority is progressively less important the higher the employee is promoted. The same research found that 51.5 per cent of companies with over 5,000 employees and 39.2 per cent of companies of between 1,000 and 4,900 employees had introduced dedicated career tracks for specialists.

These pay and promotion systems are being bolstered by the continuing introduction and development of systems of management by objectives (MBO). First introduced in the late 1960s, these are being steadily improved, broadened, and deepened and they signify a progressive rationalization of the often subjective and opaque process of evaluation for employee rotation, promotion, rewards, and assessment of abilities, achievements, and results. The ostensible consequences of the introduction and deepening of these systems are that employees are able to negotiate directly, more frequently, and in more formal circumstances with line and personnel managers over career development and near-term production and other targets in order to improve motivation and focus energies. In addition, through the formalization of feedback channels and procedures, employees are able to learn from management and personnel officers the results of evaluations and assessments of their performance. In research for *Chingin Jitsumu* (Nakajima, 2000), 46.4 per cent of companies stated they did so to improve motivation, 44.6 per cent in order to

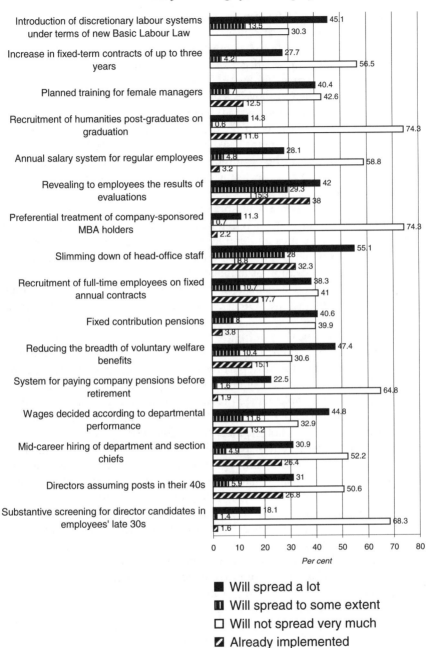

Figure 4.4 Actual implementation of and prospects for new personnel management systems.

Source: NRKK, 2000.

clarify evaluations, 42.9 per cent in order to unify organizational and individual objectives, and 35.7 per cent in order to activate the organization. Some companies, though still few in number and limited in scope, have also introduced what is sometimes called a *shanai kōbosei*, or an open internal system of advertising vacant positions, in order to facilitate the task of rotating employees and to give employees a greater sense of self-determination in the advancement of their career path (Iki, Hiroishi, and Mukai, 2000).

Continuing with the issue of the diversification of personnel management systems, taking data (Figure 4.4) from the Nihon Rōdō Kenkyū Kikō (NRKK, 2000) report, the beginnings of a pattern of tentative change and experimentation can be observed. Companies were asked whether they had introduced any of the measures described and whether they believed these measures would become widespread among Japanese companies. The message that the data conveys is that companies are aiming at modifying their organizational structures and employee management systems in the future and that these will have a presumed direct impact on corporate performance. The underlying motivation of management thus appears to be to boost productivity and make management more effective through the introduction of some modifications to the system of personnel administration while maintaining its basic structure.

However, what the data in Figure 4.4 also shows is the, as yet, quite small proportions of companies that have implemented even some of the more popular schemes. For the most part the data shows that management believes certain ideas and systems may become more popular in the future but that these are not being implemented in a widespread manner. This points to one of the central issues in the Japanese personnel management and lifetime employment systems. All of the most significant systems and attributes of the system are first and foremost predicated on the assumption that employees will stay at their companies until the mandatory retirement age. Second, and importantly, these systems and attributes are interdependent and have evolved together into the present set of intricate processes and systems over at least a half century of industrial development and are therefore very difficult to change. A fundamental reform or abolition of any one of them might destabilize the entire system so that it becomes almost unworkable. There is thus much talk of change both within and outside Japan and there is even some evidence of it, as has been demonstrated in these pages. However, there is no escaping the fact that lifetime employment and its corollary of seniority-based systems of pay and promotion continue to lie at the heart of the employment system in large Japanese corporations and reform, where it has occurred, has been implemented at the margins and has not yet penetrated into the core of the employment system.

The above discussions of reform to the systems of pay and promotion must be taken with a degree of caution. In the majority of Japanese corporations employees cannot be promoted until they have acquired the necessary skills and abilities to move on to the next grade, and salary increments are usually based on an employee having reached a certain grade or rank. For nearly all promotions there are stipulated minimum time periods to be spent acquiring the necessary formal and tacit knowledge as well as institutional memory needed to gain the recognized skills and abilities that fulfil each grade and rank's requirements. This knowledge and memory are acquired mainly through supervised experience in on-the-job training (OJT). It is thus difficult for managers to distinguish clearly between age and seniority on the one hand and skills and abilities on the other. In this respect, age and seniority are conveniently used as proxy indicators of skills and abilities and, thus, however management wishes to describe its policies and practices, pay and promotion on the basis of the former are, practically speaking, difficult to disentangle from pay and promotion on the basis of the latter. Moreover, under this regime any fundamental reform of the system of payment, promotion, or training would necessarily not only impact considerably on other dependent attributes but might also, as a result, compromise the integrity of the entire system.

Finally with regard to welfare benefits and pensions, companies are not only looking to reduce slightly the amount and comprehensiveness of benefits on offer but also attempting to tie these more closely to the needs of employees by constructing more flexible systems that involve employees choosing from a number of options. This system has been referred to as a *Cafeteria Puran* ('cafeteria plan') (Kirinoki, 2000). The options include portable pension plans for those who intend to change employer at some time in their career, flexible health and life insurance programmes, dedicated and individualized programmes of assistance for employees' families, and so on. These programmes are often organized in conjunction with company unions. For similar reasons some companies, Matsushita Electric being the most famous example, give employees the option of receiving their pensions while they work at the company instead of when they retire in their fifties, or later. In the Matsushita case, employees choose on entry whether to join the new system or to receive their pension on retirement and they are allowed to change once during the course of their employment.[15] These systems have been developed in recognition of, and perhaps to encourage, some employees' desires for a more flexible career structure.

To sum up, on the basis of the above figures and analysis, corporate management appears to be operating a policy of maintaining the basic structure of the established lifetime employment system and respecting its normative legitimacy while simultaneously attempting to make it more responsive to immediate market conditions. The substantive expression of this approach is a gradually falling proportion of employees being covered by the implicit guarantee of lifetime employment, a diversification of employment styles, and modifications to the internal dynamics. In the next section we will look at these issues in the light of evidence from four different companies' employment systems.

Field investigations

One could drown in the veritable deluge of statistics that is available in Japan regarding employment. These are produced with frequent regularity by all kinds of governmental, non-governmental, academic, and commercial organizations. Even with the enormous quantity of data that is available, of which the above is only a small fraction, it is still difficult to disentangle modern, rationalized, and individualized systems of employment and personnel management based on ability and results from more normatively and socially ascribed modes of organization based on seniority and presumed life-stage within a functional fictive-kin group. It is also difficult to judge precisely from such data the qualitative texture of employment conditions within Japanese corporations. This is particularly so within the framework of very long-term employment at a single organization that uses a highly structured and rule-bound system of on-the-job training as its principal mode of skill acquisition, where ability is judged according to the skills and experiences acquired, and where individual performance is difficult to assess accurately, as is the case with team-based white-collar work. It would be rash, therefore, to accept at face value the figures presented above and conclude that Japan's lifetime employment system is substantively though gradually evolving towards a more market-based system that places greater emphasis on individual ability and immediate results. It would be even more rash to conclude that the above figures indicate a move in the direction of a systemic convergence with the Anglo-American model of corporate management.

Lincoln and Nakata (1997) claim that Japanese companies are going to great lengths to cope with the prolonged stagnation and the globalization of economic competition by introducing substantive changes to the mechanics of the employment system. But they also concede that the changes that have thus far been introduced to great fanfare are, on closer inspection, perhaps more accurately described as signals to the workforce of the need for future change in the corporate structure and for diminished expectations on the part of employees in a more competitive environment. They suggest that companies' reluctance to broaden and deepen their restructuring efforts is a result, in part, of the normative legitimacy of the lifetime employment system as a national institution. Changes to it are therefore interpreted as a challenge to established post-war social and political norms as well as prevailing economic rationality. Is a transformation of the lifetime employment system taking place? What is its extent and significance?

In the following pages I will provide first an overview of the most significant modifications to the employment systems of the four companies investigated for this project and then go on to present some analysis derived from this data. These modifications closely resemble the general trends described above and, thus, to some extent bear out Lincoln and Nakata's conclusions. The chapter will then move on to describe some changes in the culture of employment in these four companies that management appears to be in the

Table 4.1 Overview of Companies A–D.

	Company A	Company B	Company C	Company D
	Established 1917.	Established 1917.	Established 1888.	Established 1951.
	4,862 employees as of May 2002.	4,919 employees as of May 2002.	10,977 employees as of May 2002.	17,559 employees as of May 2002.
	Manufacturer of optical products and precision machinery.	Manufacturer of automotive components, industrial machinery and sports goods.	Non-bank financial services.	Utility production and supply.
Sensitivity to external economic environment	Strong variability in sales of optical products due to consumer taste. Sales of precision machinery very volatile. Strong cyclical sensitivity.	Strong variability in sales domestically and internationally. Heavily reliant on customers' production schedules. Strong cyclical sensitivity. Over-capacity and competition in auto industry, having severe effect.	Stable sales. Some domestic cyclical sensitivity. Liberalization of price competition has had small effect on earnings. Strength of financial base largely unknown. Merger with another Japanese competitor in 2002 to consolidate market presence.	Extremely stable sales. Almost no cyclical sensitivity. Some secular sensitivity. Liberalization of domestic markets causing some reorganization.
Business group membership	Medium-sized peripheral member of large, powerful, and close business group.	Independent producer but maintains long-term (though attenuating) business links with main automotive assemblers.	Large core member of large, powerful, but loose business group.	Independent producer.
Regulatory environment	Little regulation domestically or overseas. Some regulation of optical and electronic products with possible defence uses.	Little regulation domestically or overseas.	Price competition until recently heavily regulated in Japan. Products and prices recently relaxed by Big Bang (April 1996 and July 1998).	Heavily regulated. prices set in negotiation with government ministry. Government pursuing liberalization fairly aggressively but gradually.

Sources: Company documents and interviews, newspaper reports, *Nikkei Net Interactive.*

process of trying to implement, and will draw some wider conclusions as to the significance of such change. In preparation for the following discussions I have provided in Table 4.1 a schematic representation of each company and its competitive position.

Change or transformation?

When looking simply at numbers of regular employees (Figure 4.5), while all of the companies investigated have responded to the slowdown in economic growth by reducing the number of regular employees on their books since the high point in 1994, none has done this through the use of mass lay-offs into the external labour force. Until 1994 Company C continued to increase numbers of regular employees the most rapidly of the four, whereupon reduction commenced which has reduced numbers to slightly above their 1989 level. Nevertheless, after the merger of its operations with a competitor in 2002, it has announced that there will be a reduction of more than 1,000 employees. All employee reductions have been achieved through the implementation of standard measures of reductions or freezes in new hires, early retirement measures, transfers to affiliates and subsidiaries, and diversification of employment styles.

Taking recruitment as an example of these measures, Company B recruited only five university graduates in both 2000 and 2001 compared to 102 and 113 in the peak recruitment years of 1990 and 1991. The company did not recruit any female clerical workers in 2000 and 2001 while it had recruited 106 and 101 in 1990 and 1991. Recruitment of high-school graduates for regular employment in manufacturing roles was down to 23 and zero in 2000 and 2001 from 115 and 156 in 1990 and 1991. Similarly, Company D recruited a total of 783 employees in 1990 as against 216 in 2000. The company reduced from 70 to zero the number of junior high-school graduates recruited, from 518 to 98 the number of high-school and junior-college graduates and from 163 to 83 the number of university graduates recruited in the same period. Interestingly, Company D increased its recruitment of mid-career recruits from seven in 1985 to 32 in 1990, 51 in 1995, and 35 in 2001.

In terms of the mix of employment types within each company, companies are pursuing a strategy of diversification and increasing their use of market mechanisms. For example, Company A, a consumer and industrial optical products manufacturer, effected a strategic reorientation to manufacturing precision engineering products; for the period of its restructuring it drastically reduced its intake of new graduate generalists and increased to 20 per cent of new hires its recruitment of mid-career specialists on fixed-term contracts from the external labour market. The company has also increased its reliance on female part-time, temporary, and dispatch workers for clerical roles. Meanwhile Company C, a non-bank financial services provider, in order to increase numerical flexibility among its large proportion of clerical workers as well as

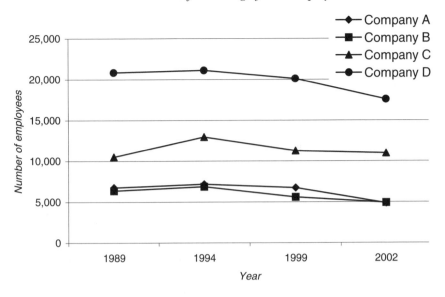

Figure 4.5 Number of regular employees, Companies A–D, 1989–2002.

Source: Nihon Keizai Shimbunsha, 1989–2002.

to reduce costs, has increased its use of dispatch, temporary and part-time employees while reducing its employment of permanent female clerical staff. The company has also begun using fixed-term contractees for specialist roles in computing and data processing but, unlike many financial services companies in Tokyo, has not yet resorted to regular and sustained use of the external labour market for market traders and analysts. Company D, on the other hand, as a near-monopoly regional utility provider has reduced its employment of regular staff by flattening the organizational structure and personnel hierarchy as well as increasing its outsourcing of basic functions such as bill delivery.

All four companies have continued to introduce a variety of mechanisms to reduce seniority-based systems and to try to activate employees' motivations and, presumably, their productivity. For example, Company A has abolished all distinctions between the *sōgōshoku* and *ippanshoku* career tracks that separated men and women into regular managerial and regular clerical employees in an attempt to increase intra-company competition between employees, to make more economically productive use of its female labour resources as well as to respond to a steady increase in demand for equality in the workplace among Japanese women. The company claims to have abolished all seniority-related pay and, in addition, performance-related pay rises as a proportion of the annual salary the higher up the company the employee proceeds. Forty per cent of pay is by results for non-managerial staff and 70 per cent for senior management, though the company would not divulge

the width of the spread within those bands that was actually paid to employees and managers.

Company B is a manufacturer of automotive components and heavy
equipment. It was badly affected by a downturn in demand for its products in
the early 1990s. The company has changed its training and evaluation system
from an on-the-job-based system to one based on management by objectives.
Alongside this the company introduced performance-related pay for employees and managers rising to 100 per cent of annual pay for directors. Nevertheless, the company admitted that, as of September 2001, no employee had
yet received a reduction in annual pay since the changeover in 1998. An interesting development in both Company B's and Company C's motivation
strategies, and one that is not unique to these two companies, has been the
introduction of a points-based retirement scheme whereby employees are
awarded points at the end of each year based on qualifications, rank and
grade achieved, and performance. The final pension is then calculated on a
ratio between the number of years served and the number of points gained
through the period of employment. Previous to this, both companies operated a retirement pay system based strictly on length of service. The system is
interesting because, while it seeks to unlock employee motivations as well as
to weaken the link between rewards and length of service, it is still based on
the premise that the employee will remain in a very long-term employment
relationship with the company because it is assumed that the payout will not
take place until the employee is well into his or her fifties.

One of the most significant of the reforms introduced by Company C has
been the creation in 1998 of a *shanai kōbosei*. However, on closer inspection,
it turns out that for the 11,000 or so regular employees who are qualified to
apply for the advertised jobs, there have been only 30 or so positions advertised each year since it was started and most of these are for international
roles that require transfer overseas. Thus, when interviewed, most employees
voiced some cynicism about the system. In its defence, management insists
that the system is still in its infancy and inconsistencies need to be ironed out
before it is broadened to include more positions. Nevertheless, this is a significant step because for the first time it introduces the market principle to
internal employment mechanisms. Even though the employment system in
large corporations has frequently been referred to as an internal market, it
has rarely operated under market principles as we in the West would normally
understand them. There had previously, for example, always been an assym-
metry of information between management and employees regarding
employment opportunities. Personnel departments had almost always negotiated with line managers and then simply assigned employees to departments
and tasks, often with less than a week's notice of the move (even if the position was in another country). Employees were often denied the opportunity
to bargain regarding their assignments. With the introduction of a *shanai
kōbosei* employees have for the first time been given information about vacant
positions for which they can choose to apply under a competitive regime, in a

similar fashion as they might in open labour markets. Although the number of positions advertised is still small and the number of companies offering such a system is also limited, it is nonetheless a significant development.

Moving now to analysing the data produced thus far, first, phased recruitment of predominantly male employees on or shortly after graduation from university, long-term employment at a single organization until the fixed retirement age, graduated training and promotion systems tied to length of service, and salary and reward structures based on assumed needs at the employee's stage in life remain central to the structures and functions of the employment system in large corporations. That is to say, the basic structures and ideologies of the lifetime employment system remain intact.

As stated above, although all four companies have, to varying degrees, reduced total employment, none has resorted to mass lay-offs in the manner that was characteristic of UK and US companies in their major restructurings of the 1980s. It must be remembered that unemployment in the UK in the early 1980s had reached more than 12 per cent of the total workforce with some regions experiencing levels of 20 per cent or more for sustained periods.[16] Although the official unemployment data under-reports and does not reflect the gravity of Japan's general economic and social malaise and does not reveal to us the real effects of present conditions on individual workers and their families, particularly those who work in small and medium-sized enterprises, there is little doubt that the present wave of employment restructuring, while severe for those who are on its receiving end, is by no means as severe as that which occurred in the UK. This can be attributed to, among other things, the seriousness with which large corporations have stuck, however unwillingly, to the lifetime employment principle.

What is beyond the reach of this research, unfortunately, is the extent to which large corporations are able to externalize their difficulties onto subsidiaries and subcontractors, where dismissals and bankruptcies appear to be an all too common solution. Nevertheless, the example of Company B is perhaps indicative of how a company's position within this hierarchical network of relations constrains or even determines the options available to management. Out of the four companies researched, Company B has had the most difficulty in this regard. Although employment of regular workers has been steadily reduced since the mid-1990s, the company has achieved this through dramatically reducing and at times freezing recruitment, transferring employees to subsidiaries and subcontractors, transfers to new business departments, natural turnover, and early retirement. The principal cause of this reduction has been the company's position as an automotive components supplier to mainly much larger and more powerful clients. These large automotive assemblers have put extreme pressure on the company to reduce prices for its products. In order to protect long-term implicit contracts, the company has been forced drastically to reduce labour costs while still trying to maintain the principle of lifetime employment. Although the other three companies have taken measures to reduce employee numbers and streamline operations none has been under quite the same kind of hierarchically imposed external pressures and therefore they have retained greater flexibility.

Second, restructuring of the dependent attributes of the employment system is substantive and represents an ongoing and gradualist shift from stressing seniority and ability to a progressively greater emphasis on ability and results. The stage at which seniority becomes less important is earlier in employees' careers and results-based calculations are being factored into the pay and promotion of all regular employees and, in particular, management.

All four companies have placed greater emphasis on individual ability and performance at the expense of age and seniority in pay and promotion. Company A now no longer has either an age- or a length-of-service-based component in its basic salary, preferring to pay according to the employee's rank and the line manager's evaluation. The company appears to have the widest pay differentials based on academic qualifications of the four companies and it does not any longer discriminate in pay or promotion against mid-career recruits. Nevertheless, it is difficult to see how, as is the publicly stated intention of management at all four companies, seniority can be substantively eliminated if promotion continues to be constrained by minimum service periods and employment continues to be dominated by long-term acquisition of company-specific skills through on-the-job training and experience, particularly for employee and junior management ranks. In addition, although mid-career hiring from the external labour market has increased and become formalized, as a system (especially at Company A) it is, as yet, a temporary phenomenon driven by exceptional needs in exceptional circumstances and will take time to embed itself into the organization as an integral feature of corporate recruitment.

Third, personnel management, pay, promotion, welfare, and retirement pension systems are becoming progressively more geared towards the abilities, performance, and needs of the individual employee as these progressively become more differentiated with the opening out of Japanese society in general. All four companies have proceeded to implement and deepen such individualized personnel management systems though, interestingly, Company C appears to be quite progressive in this area, for example in its introduction of the *shanai kōbosei*, an annual salary review system (*nenpōsei*) for assistant managers and above, and a performance points-based retirement and severance payment system.

Company C is a financial institution in a sector which has until recently been heavily regulated by the government. In 1996 and 1998 reforms were introduced to liberalize[17] price competition in Company C's sector and reduce barriers between different sectors of the financial services industry. These 'Big Bang' reforms have sparked a period of restructuring across the industry which shows every sign of intensifying further as and when institutions restore themselves to financial health and foreign financial institutions gear up, expand, and entrench their Japanese operations. Moreover, it is an open secret in the financial services industry that many employees are not so much interested in the content of their work as in the monetary rewards that come with it. Significant also is the fact that, more than in any other industry, Japanese financial institutions must compete with foreign institutions on their own turf. Foreign, but particularly American, institutions compete very fiercely and sometimes successfully for the best Japanese graduates[18] and their efforts have also led to the recent appearance of what passes for a fluid external labour market for skilled and qualified mid-career university graduate recruits.[19] Thus, it is perhaps to be expected that rewards should be incentivized in such a manner by Company C.

To be sure, all four companies have introduced various individualized personnel management and reward systems but the extent of these systems is still questionable. Significantly, in interview some employees admitted to feeling that these reforms as yet amount to *tatemae*, or window-dressing, for the purposes of persuading employees that the company is pushing through rigorous reform, rather than being anything permanent and substantive.

Fourth, with reference to the wider but crucial issues of low or stagnant growth combined with the intensification of global and domestic competition, due to the twin impacts of economic globalization and domestic liberalization measures, increasing competition is having a measurable impact on companies' business activities and internal management systems, causing them to pay greater attention to market efficiency. As discussed above, although this is reflected in all aspects of the employment system becoming progressively geared towards individual ability and performance it would still be wrong to assert that the employment system is now based on individualism as a positive ideology. Team-based systems, evaluations, and rewards are still dominant, though it might be difficult on the basis of results from just these four companies to make any firm judgements as to how this is played out in a practical sense across Japanese industry. However, some preliminary and general conclusions can be made about the issues of globalization and liberalization which, if tested using a representative sample, might yield some interesting results.

It appears that the four companies can be divided into two pairs of two companies: those who do business in already substantially unregulated international markets and are exposed to the effects of intensifying global competition (Companies A and B), and those who have until recently been somewhat protected from the full force of competition by government regulations and have recently been exposed to intensifying competition due to domestic liberalization measures (Companies C and Company D). Of course, the two phenomena are indissolubly linked, however, they are also separate issues and can be seen as such in their effects on corporate systems.

Both Company A and Company B have felt the need to initiate more numerically significant employee redeployment and restructuring programmes than either Company C or Company D, for example. The cause of this is that both companies appear to be more determined and have proceeded further, with varying degrees of success, in their attempts to explore new product development opportunities and to expand into new markets. Both Company C and Company D occupy significant positions in mature established domestic markets and are unlikely significantly to increase their sales. Although both companies are making efforts to expand into new areas, these remain in their very early stages. Company C has begun to advertise for mid-career recruits to bolster these initiatives though Company D has taken the other route of transferring some employees over to newly created subsidiaries, hence the appearance of a rapid decline in regular employees in Table 4.1 above. Moreover, both Company C and Company D, but particularly D, appear to maintain a stronger intention to maintain lifetime employment as a normative principle.

As yet, economic globalization appears to be a more powerful force for substantive restructuring than do domestic liberalization measures. This may be because liberalization measures have been implemented only recently and gradually and so their full effects have yet to be played out, particularly in the case of Company D where partial deregulation of its business came into effect only in March 2000 and competitors will need a considerable time to invest in and establish the required fixed capital to be an effective challenge to the regional monopolies. Moreover, there is a degree of debate in the academic and popular literature as to the actual extent of government deregulation measures and, consequently, their effect or lack thereof.

If, however, we consider domestic liberalization to be the first of a two-stage process of institutional and structural modernization with globalization as its second stage, then it is surely only a matter of time before both Company C and Company D too become exposed more fully to comparatively atomized global markets and, accordingly, the competitive pressures and disciplines they impose upon participants. Their response to this cannot be predicted but, if the current climate is anything to go by, then the options open to management in ensuring company survival and prosperity would seem to have become very restricted indeed.

All four companies appear to be introducing more flexible systems of organizational management in response to the rapidly changing and unstable external economic environment. Companies A, B, and D have all introduced a *gurūpu seido*, or group system, to replace the more traditional *ka*, or section system, that Company C still operates. The group system places a leader at the head of a group who, in informal negotiation with other group leaders and employees within the department, then chooses group members at any time according to the department's requirements. Movement of employees between groups within each department is more fluid than under the more rigid system of sections which is controlled by the personnel department and, regardless of business conditions, takes place in April at the beginning of the financial year. In this way companies feel that they can respond rapidly and decisively to external developments as they occur by giving managers more discretion and responsibility. In principle, group responsibilities have thus become more project-based, with employees being gathered together for the purposes of carrying through specific tasks. As and when these tasks are completed or added to, the group may change its composition. Again, one must be careful not to take these developments too literally since they are, in effect, modifications rather than transformations of existing team-based working arrangements, but managers do appear to be satisfied that flexibility and rapidity of response have been improved as a result. Moreover, they appear to be more similar to the fluid and changeable internal arrangements of Anglo-American corporations than the apparent bureaucratic rigidity of the previous system.

The drive towards institutional and structural as well as numerical flexibility can, in addition, be observed in all four corporations in their increasing use of temporary, part-time, and dispatch workers while at the same time reducing total employment. As Beck (2000) observes, this is a development occurring across not only the whole Japanese labour force but the whole of the developed world and represents a shift towards a new labour force paradigm where insecurity and instability are becoming structurally endemic to all layers of society as a result of the globalization of production and trade following the liberalization of markets.

In summary, therefore, companies are in the midst of a programme of restructuring which, because of the gradualist nature of reform procedures, may take some years to complete[20] The measures already taken do indeed indicate a gradual shift away from the closed and organization-oriented system described in the previous chapter towards a more outward-looking and market-oriented position. However companies say that, as yet, they wish to achieve this without having to abandon the lifetime employment principle. According to this analysis, therefore, the reforms undertaken do not yet represent a fundamental transformation of the employment system. Such a development would require not only a transformation of the substantive manifestations of lifetime employment but a fundamental change in the ideology of corporate management.

If we are to take Britain and the United States as our model and assume that Japanese companies will eventually complete a restructuring programme of similar significance to the one achieved in those two countries between the late 1970s and the early to mid-1990s, then we can say that Japanese corporations are, in a systemic sense, in the midst of a restructuring programme that will, in time, amount to a substantive transformation of the entire corporate system and will signify a convergence towards a global standard that is a hybrid version of the Anglo-American system. However, this scenario is by no means inevitable, even if some Japanese managers believe it to be, since the system itself rests on, or is embedded in, a set of normative social and ethical assumptions and beliefs. For a transformation of the employment system to occur, a sea-change would also be required in this arena of Japanese political and social life. It would require the emergence of individualistic ideologies of liberal self-determination in the form of a mass culture organized around a future-oriented reflexive project of the self. Until we examine the world-view that underlies the system of employment we will not be able to understand more clearly and deeply what kind of system it is becoming, not only in terms of its texture but, in addition, in a material and systemic sense. To this end it is first necessary to examine the ideologies and cultures of employment from the perspective of management.

The managerial ideology of lifetime employment

From the perspective of management, large Japanese corporations remain committed to the principle of lifetime employment, at least publicly, in a normative sense. However, its cultural and ideological basis may be undergoing some modifications which, when we observe its substantive manifestations might appear to be comparatively inconsequential, but have the potential for both heralding and being representative of a profound transformation, not only of employment, but also of Japanese society as a whole. This is because the ideology of Japanese management towards the entire post-war corporate system appears to be undergoing a change towards viewing it as an anachronism incompatible with a changing external environment and, thus, requiring substantially more deep-seated reform than that which has been attempted hitherto. Further, Japanese managers believe that these reforms will, if implemented in their entirety, represent a convergence towards a global corporate standard.

Managers attest to their continuing commitment to lifetime employment. However they also reveal, perhaps unwittingly, a feeling and a realization that the system's normative power may not be suited to the new circumstances they find themselves within and that its mechanics may be something of an incongruity in an era characterized more by fluidity, change, and globalization than by rigidity, constancy, and internationalism.[21] Nevertheless, there remains a deep feeling among most managers that the lifetime employment system has been and still has the potential to be enormously beneficial in terms of corporate effectiveness, particularly if one takes the view, as managers undoubtedly do, that to be effective in an environment characterized by long-term employment the corporation must maintain an atmosphere of social interdependency and consensus. Thus, a cultural shift towards an acceptance of, if not desire for, change to even this most sacrosanct of Japanese post-war institutions is beginning to take place. But also present, reading between the lines of conversations and interviews, is a feeling of fatalistic regret, or even mourning, for the probable passing of an institution that has come to represent some of the certainties, securities, and comforts of the past. Japanese managers accept the perceived inevitability of convergence on global patterns of management but do not at all appear to relish the prospect or wish to accelerate its arrival.

The following statement reveals a matter-of-fact recognition of this state of affairs as this manager recognizes that the cultural underpinnings of the lifetime employment system are under threat as the system moves closer towards global, or Anglo-American standards, in a systemic sense. In the last sentence of this excerpt he reveals that he sympathizes with the difficulties that employees may have but, taken with what comes before, he quite subtly implies that the days of lifetime employment security may indeed be coming to an end.

> But you know that Japanese society is different from the UK. We still think that we should guarantee employment for the employee's whole life if we could. We don't give up that. Generally, we have come to think about costs and we think we should pay more to high-quality employees but we still don't think about firing people.
>
> The difference between British and Japanese companies is . . . the weight paid to stakeholders . . . In America it is the shareholder and management manage in their interests. In Japan it is still the employees who are large stakeholders. The important point is that the Japanese system is coming closer to the US or British system in this respect.
>
> . . . In Japan we have traditional ideas and traditional values and so it is still hard to fire someone. It is changing but very slowly. Mainly it's moving closer and closer to the UK and US, but in Japan it is still very hard to find a new job if you lose your job.
>
> (General Manager, Company D)

The next manager recognizes the pressures for greater fluidity that are arising out of participation in globalizing markets but he laments the probable loss of the human quality of long-term relationships of trust that can develop within the Japanese system.

> I was the president of the Singapore subsidiary of [this company] and, maybe you know, Singapore has a very liberal employment system and the fluidity of the labour market is very intense. But, against that, you can still hire good people. If I ask which is best then I would say that Singapore has become too liberal. Employees can enter and leave companies too easily. But, in Japan, it is a little solid. There is no flexibility. If you say that Japan's situation is bad then you might say that Singapore is good. But, if we both worked at the same company . . . then our feeling of trust would grow and become strong easily if we worked for a long time . . . ten or so years together . . . and we both knew that we both had the intention of staying here for life. But in Singapore if you have to work next to someone who might leave after three months then . . . In that meaning, the feeling of security and trust is not strong.
>
> (General Manager, Company C)

More than simply speaking directly, Japanese communication strategies rely on the listener understanding and responding to implied meanings. This is especially true when one is trying to maintain proper harmonious and polite long-term social relations while talking about difficult and controversial subjects. From listening to Japanese managers, I have little doubt that there is a profound feeling among many of them that the synergistic constellation of more or less favourable circumstances that existed for more than 30 years after the establishment and entrenchment of the post-war system, which in large measure facilitated Japan's reconstruction and transformation into one of the world's richest and most technologically advanced nations, has all but come to an end. In fact, it would not be an exaggeration to state that the opposite state of affairs is gradually coming to take shape, at least in the minds of Japan's managerial élites. That is to say, a series of external structural developments and changes appear to be conspiring against the Japanese corporation so that standard approaches to weathering economic difficulty, while continuing to be of use, are no longer perceived as being sufficient and, thus, in addition to internal structural reform of the principal functional attributes and institutions of the Japanese corporation, change to its cultural and ideological foundations is also rapidly becoming a necessity rather than just a consideration.

These developments include: long-term prospects for low or stagnant domestic economic growth; intensifying global economic competition; continuing long-term domestic de-industrialization; a gradual collapse of the 1955 political system on the domestic front and a rapidly globalizing international political arena; complex demographic difficulties that include low birth rates and an ageing population; a gradual but steady relaxation of protective government regulations including the 'Big Bang' financial reforms; the achievement of a materially affluent society; fundamental changes to domestic and international consumption patterns; an increasing proportion of smaller and more diversified cohorts of young people graduating from university; changes in the attitudes and value patterns of young people in Japan and elsewhere; rapid and sustained advances in communications and information technology; and so on. There follow statements by managers from each of the four companies researched about some of the difficulties with which they are faced.

> The question of liberalization is a serious one for [our type of] company. We need to think about what kind of [utility] company we wish to be in the future as circumstances are changing . . . One more thing is the falling birthrate, which is reducing the population . . . Another thing is that industries that consume a lot of [our product] are shrinking in favour of a service-oriented society and economy.
>
> (General Manager, Company D)

> First, more and more people are investing in [our products] for a more peaceful life. From now on [the company] will not just be offering [our standard products] but other financial products. That's the Big Bang. With that competition will increase enormously, but if we don't overcome that then [the company] will disappear. In order to do that, the foundation will be [our present business] . . . If we work hard we can earn

more profits and open up new areas of business. If we don't do that and stay with [our standard products] then we won't succeed with the Big Bang . . . If we don't say to ourselves, not just in our core area of business but realistically, 'How can we provide a service?' especially in terms of providing measures for the ageing society, then we won't succeed.

Another problem is that our generation and the younger generation are different. For me work is the company. [The company] is my work. For younger people, they want work that suits them. If they don't find work at [this company] that suits them then . . . When I entered [the company] I wanted to work here for more or less the rest of my life, so I looked for work that suited me inside [the company]. It was that kind of way of thinking. I doubt, after the collapse of the bubble, that young people think in that way. Since the collapse of the bubble there are a lot of people who have joined the company and within three months have left and joined a different company . . . People now look for work that is suited to them and are strict about that.

(General Manager, Company C)

The situation is changing dramatically. We have a low-growth period and there is much more severe international competition between companies. So if we compare with before, with that and the ageing of society, then internal costs have increased greatly and we have to do something.

(Manager, Company A)

A: Until now there has been the Spring Wage Offensive (*Shuntō*) in Japan. At that time the main industries make their decisions early and so this has an effect on suppliers and their negotiations. If [a major automotive assembler] raises its wages by say 3 per cent then we cannot raise ours any higher. There are many reasons. One thing that is often said is that, if suppliers raise their wages higher then the contractor will ask for parts costs to be lowered. Because of international competition every year is getting more difficult and they ask us to lower costs and so we cannot pay our employees more than they do. They don't say to us that we cannot raise our wages in this way but from our point of view we cannot and they know this.

. . . Nowadays we need creative people and people who are independent and who don't have to rely on others and those who can set their own goals and challenge themselves. It's not that we don't need the cooperative atmosphere of before, we consider that now to be a given, but we need those types of people in addition to that and it is difficult to recruit them in this atmosphere.

Q: So, how does the company motivate such people and keep them if you can't pay them any more?

A: That is a big issue. One thing is that we clearly understand that the company's and the individual's needs are mutually compatible. We ask people what their purpose is for being in the company and so on and try to explain to them how that fits in with the company's plans as well as trying to put them in places that they want to be in. If people's aims don't coincide with the company's then we tell them that we want them to be like so and so. We try to make a direct mutual connection between the individual and the company. This system has gradually become more effective. Of course we look most closely at performance and that is coming more and more to affect pay and other things. We also clearly tell them how we think about their performance so that they can understand why someone else in their year group became a manager ahead of them. This is an important difference from when I joined.

(General Manager, Company B)

From reading the above four interview excerpts a number of different issues come to the fore. One is that each company, depending on its industry and position within it, faces different difficulties and structural developments that require different solutions and this, inevitably, is contributing to a diversification of personnel management and employment systems. Another is that these statements barely conceal a feeling that the rigidities of the corporate system, and within that lifetime employment, are something of an inconvenience in their efforts to reform and restructure themselves. However, what is also significant is the degree to which management in all four companies appears to feel that it is being buffeted by external forces that they are unable to weather using so-called traditional means. And finally, the last statement reveals, possibly accidentally, a more subtle but no less important development. Companies, in addition to modernizing internal systems and structures to deal with the exigencies of a new era, are in the initial stages of a liminal strategy to modernize (meaning both to bring up to date and make reflexive, or individualize) the consciousness of their employees.

Re-fabricating the Japanese salaryman

Starting with a subjective overview of changes to the employment system over the past 30 years or so, Table 4.2 is an English translation of a chart constructed by a Personnel Manager from Company A. Although the data is not strictly representative of all four companies, it is an interesting document because it summarizes much of the post-war external environment surrounding the company and the company's managerial response to it. It is also interesting because it substantiates and puts into context much of the data and discussions presented above.

Moreover, Table 4.2 shows that although changes to the employment system have taken place gradually over a period of some 30 to 40 years, if one looks at the three periods in aggregation some quite substantive changes have indeed taken place both in the external environment and in the principles and practices of employment management in the company. These changes are clearly in the direction of establishing a more market-based and individualized employment system and have, at least on the basis of the above data, been proceeding in a gradualist fashion for quite some considerable time. Thus lifetime employment, in an institutional and organizational sense at least, must be seen as a permanently evolving, responsive, and dynamic system rather than as a static phenomenon that has remained virtually unchanged throughout most of the post-war period. In addition to this, what is now coming to be the case in Company A as well as in other companies is a managerial policy of implementing changes to the underlying culture and ideology of lifetime employment.

In April 1998 Company A printed and distributed to all its employees a four-page foldout document entitled *Jinji Bizhon 21* ('Personnel vision 21'). Explicitly recognizing the incompatibility of the employment system with external conditions, the company describes a 'greatly changing economic and management climate' that demands the conscious and deliberate construction of 'a new type of company and employee that correspond with the social and labour environment'. The document describes this new era as being characterized by accelerating international competition, severe competition in technology, greater pressure to achieve customer satisfaction, environmental problems, the falling birthrate and ageing of society, an increasing desire by women for equal participation in the labour force, changes in people's work consciousness, and the diversification of enterprise activities.

The company predicts, somewhat optimistically, that the twenty-first-century economic system will be 'free . . . fair' and 'global' and to meet this challenge it is pursuing a bottom-up strategy of reinventing the internal mechanics and philosophies of the organization through a 'plan, do, see' and a 'scrap and build' approach. That is to say, the basic foundations of all the institutions and structures upon which management and employees relied in order to navigate their way through the world of work will be examined for their compatibility with the new era and if any are found wanting they will be replaced and re-examined in a never-ending process of reflexive reconstruction and reform.

Moreover, management wishes to construct a new relationship between company and employee that is based not on a dissolution of the self into the corporate body in order to forge a long-term village-like community of mutual dependence among a closed hierarchy of organization-oriented salarymen but on the 'realization of an independent spirited professional body that is a partnership between the company and the individual for the joint ownership of values and results'. This body is based on a realization of each person's responsibility to 'actively raise his own value' and for each individual to 'feel a sense of that which makes life worth living'. However, this 'strengthened organizational character' is to be arranged around 'a small group of talented people' while also recognizing 'the diversification of employment structures'

Table 4.2 Personnel system changes at Company A (1960s–1990s).

	External environment	Management style	Employment system	Education and training
1960s ↓	High-speed economic growth.	Seniority-based treatment.	Job grade system.	Cycle of HR training is utilization to rewards (long-term HR development). On-job-training with off-job-training. Rotation-based flexibility.
mid-1970s ↓	Low growth. Ageing of the labour force. Lack of administrative posts. Expansion of higher education. White-collarization.	Ability-based treatment (in reality seniority style).	Ability- and qualifications-based system.	Individualized rank-based study and training.
1990s ↓	Low growth. An ageing society. Increase in labour costs. Diversification of values (individualization). Diversification of employment structures and flexibilization of labour markets. Flattening of organizational hierarchies.	Ability- and results-based treatment.	Intensification of ability and qualifications based system with results added.	Specialist education. Compatibility with internationalization.

such as 'the use of dispatch and contract workers and foreign employees and increasing temporary transfers'.

By any standards this is an impressive document in the sense that it maps out a comprehensive ideological foundation for the future relationship between the employee and the corporation. Clearly, it is the product of some serious and lengthy research and discussion. Importantly, Company A is not unique in pursuing this strategy of constructing a new corporate ideology that begins the process of cutting the umbilical cord of emotional interdependence between employee and company that has existed in Japan for so

	Pay, promotion and rewards	*Recruitment and labour force management*
1960s ↓	Rank-based wages.	Lifetime employment and inflexible labour markets.
	Length-of-service and age-based promotion and wages (ability not reflected).	Corporate loyalty.
	Educational background-oriented administration.	Phased recruitment.
	Long-term promotion and salary system.	Enterprise unions.
	Length-of-service-oriented retirement pension system.	
mid-1970s ↓	Ability-based pay	Increase in mid-career recruits.
	Separation of promotion and rewards.	
	Increasing importance of experience and ability leading to length-of-service-based pay and promotion.	
1990s ↓	Ability-based salary with results reflected.	Diversification of employment styles.
	Clarification of ability and qualifications leading to intensification of promotion orientation.	Further increase in mid-career hiring.
	MBO system leading to clear understanding of results.	Increase in use of dispatch workers and foreign employees.
	Introduction of content-based pay elements.	Increase in transfers.
	Revisions to service-based promotion and salary	Early retirement systems.
	Intensification of ability- and results-based systems.	

long. Also in 1998 the Human Resources Development Centre at Company D produced a new guide for all employees to develop themselves entitled *My Try Next: Jiko Henkaku no Tame no Kyōiku Shien* ('My Try Next: educational support for self-reform'). This document too places responsibility for a conscious strategy of self-development and self-transformation squarely on the shoulders of the individual employee through the construction of a step-by-step guide for the realization of individually generated and company supported employee autonomy, creativity, and growth. The document's cover is peppered with the Chinese characters for 'Competition, Autonomy, Mission,

Reform, Creation, Change, and Speciality'. The same company has even distributed to all its employees credit-card-sized mission statements on the new management and personnel policy. In encouraging employees to carry this at all times in their wallets the company is surely doing all it can to develop in employees a new and modern consciousness that focuses on developing employee individuality and autonomy as well as an orientation towards a future that is assumed to be dominated by global competition and individualistic and reflexive transformation.

Believing that the globalization of Western capitalism, like so much from the West that arrives uninvited in Japan, has a level of inevitability about it that is eroding the ideology of difference within modern capitalist development that the Japanese corporation has until now successfully maintained, management undoubtedly feel that they must at least collude with its apparently unchallengeable power, embrace it, work with it, and then remould it to suit their own particular circumstances and needs. Sensing the incompatibility of the systems and ideologies of employment within their companies with a globalizing modernity that stresses flexibility, fluidity, and rapidity as well as change, reflexivity, growth, autonomy, and individuality, managers are striving hard to catch up with and adapt to circumstances that appear always to be just ahead of their grasp.

Consequently, managers are not only in the midst of reforming and remodelling the mechanisms and structures of their corporations but they are also embarking upon a liminal strategy to refashion the basic consciousness of their employees in an effort to fabricate[22] within them the mentality of global capitalist modernity. While ostensibly, though paternalistically, conceding to employees the right to determine themselves and to realize an authentic self, management also unwittingly sends out the message that the employee is, paradoxically, compelled to be free to determine himself so long as that self is commensurate with corporate needs. To be sure, as Hazama (1997 [1964]) and others have often pointed out, the post-war culture and ideology of lifetime employment were and are themselves a fabricated imposition, however, contemporary developments appear to be the deliberate development of a Japanese version of Casey's (1995) 'designer culture'. For Japanese managers, admittedly themselves capitulating to the perceived strength and irresistibility of what they view as the globalization of Western capitalism, are embarking on an intentionally fabricated alteration of the employees' personalities and values. This new managerial culture compels the employee either to pursue a self-generated reflexive project of the self that conforms to the human resource needs of the corporation or face being restructured out to the periphery of the corporation and, thus, career failure.

Put another way, Japan's corporate managers appear to be in the, as yet, early stages of developing and implementing their own corporate dystopia. Like Casey's American corporation, this is not so much a proactive strategy but more a late and defensive response to the perceived exigencies of an economic globalization that pitches management between the isolationist rigidities and incongruities of the post-war Japanese corporation and the dis-consonant artificiality of a complete convergence with the Anglo-American system. Second, it is a belated acknowledgement of the inevitable mass psy-chological consequences of a rapid material expansion that is generating the kinds of social dysfunctionalities and predicaments that demand for their solution deep-seated changes in the Japanese self and, consequently, Japanese society as a whole. It is, in its essence, a struggle by management to fabricate a new modernity out of the decaying structures, customs, and cultures of the post-war order in an attempt to fend off, or at least hold at bay, through an orderly retreat, the apparently unrelenting advance of the seismic sea-wave that is the globalization of capitalist modernity.

It is perhaps disingenuous to stress to employees the principles of 'a part-nership between the company and the individual' or 'joint ownership of a sense of values' and 'joint ownership of results', as Company A does in its *Jinji Bizhon 21* document, when at the very same moment management, first, is determining the values upon which the company will henceforth be based and, second, is espousing a new system of corporate governance that places greater importance on the role and importance (read power) of shareholders. In addition, these statements reveal another and more significant message which is somewhat at odds with what management wishes to convey. At one time the company and the employees could not be separated for they were one and the same, at least in the consciousness of company members. There would have been no meaning in the word partnership because they were not separate entities with a potential for conflict. Therefore, the idea of partner-ship that this message sends to the employee, subliminally, is the *separateness* of the employee from the corporate community and, of course, the real owners of the corporation's sense of values.

One can imagine the effects on the consciousness of employees of such a cunning, seductive, and yet unintentional about-face after they have spent nearly 20 years in an education system that itself inculcates an ideology of sacrifice for the common good and the merging of self with community for the purpose of securing long-term security, stability, and continuity for all, and then joined the embodiment of Japan's twentieth-century solution to the contradiction between the globalization of capitalist modernity and the maintenance of tradition and community. For despite the refreshing libera-tion from national corporatism that management espouses, employees have little option but to comply. Moreover, even if one does comply there is no guarantee of success since, first, management decides who will join them on the upper echelons of the corporate ladder and the space is becoming pro-gressively more limited; second, the very survival of the corporation is now no longer certain; and third, success itself, in a reflexively individualizing modernity, is emptied of meaning if it comes laden with the compulsive requirement to comply to other people's criteria for living.

To be sure, Japan, too, has been and is a colonizer and an exporter of ideol-ogies and systems with which other countries, and the companies within them, feel they have no option but to compete through a radical intensification of the work process and an imposition of a fabricated modern consciousness. And this process, of course, in turn reflects back upon the Japanese corporation and so on and so on in a never-ending mutually defensive intensification of global competition and, thus, the work process.

Accordingly, managers and, by default, employees too have become willing and active though somewhat unwitting and defensive conspirators in the apparently inherent and self-regulating tendency of capitalist modernity to penetrate into and control and manipulate ever wider areas of the world, ever more areas of human activity, and ever deeper realms of the human consciousness.

5 Working under changing employment relations

Since the collapse of the Bubble Economy in the early 1990s the idea of the complete abandonment of the lifetime employment system has been mooted from various perspectives on an increasing number of occasions. Indeed, if one were to take some popular books at face value, one might be forgiven for thinking that the system exists now in name only as a convenient fiction and has, in actuality, already collapsed. One of these, entitled *Sararīman Hōkai* ('Fall of the salaryman'), goes so far as to claim that the 'age of lifetime employment has ended' (Utsumi, 2000). Another, referring to the oft repeated and rather dreary Japanese colloquial expression that attempts to enforce conformity to normative standards, 'The nail that sticks up will be hammered down,' is titled *Denai Kugi wa Suterareru* ('The nail that doesn't stick up may be thrown away') (Terao, 1998).

How are salarymen coping with this apparently new era that threatens radically to alter the conditions under which they work? Are they developing an individual, autonomous, and authentic modern consciousness with respect to their careers and the institutions of their employment? If so, how can this consciousness be described and what are its characteristics? Moreover, can it be said that it is change at this level that is driving, or at least facilitating and heralding, a transformation in the institutional and organizational environment?

Needs, desires, and values

Whether deliberately or not, a large proportion of research into work consciousness has been greatly affected by the writings of the American psychologist Abraham Maslow. His most important book, *Motivation and Personality*, introduces the concept of a 'hierarchy of needs' to describe the structure of human motivation. This is a five-tiered hierarchy that proceeds from physiological needs through safety, belongingness, and love needs to the need for esteem and, finally, self-actualization. In this schema, once one need has become 'chronically gratified' (Maslow, 1987 [1954]: 18), the individual transfers most of his or her energies towards achieving the next level.

Many scholars have tried, at times rather unfairly, to discredit Maslow's work, principally because his research conclusions were based on a narrow range of subjects[1] and the structure of human motivation is more complex and fluid than this rather simple and mechanical structure might allow. Although Maslow understood that humans are integrated beings and motivations are therefore complex psychological and physiological states, at a basic level, he claimed, human motivation might be understood through this hierarchy. Nevertheless, his work not only continues to influence research into human motivation and life and work values but it has come to be incorporated into, and has helped to shape, public discourse about these subjects throughout the world, perhaps even affecting the structure of motivation itself through enhancing and influencing public understanding of the phenomenon.[2]

Two of the most significant conceptual issues to have come out of Maslow's work are the division of his hierarchy into a simplified system of physiological needs and psychological desires, and the relationship of these two states to the subject of values. It is important to distinguish needs, desires, and values since, first, unlike desires, needs describe physiological insufficiencies which, if denied would threaten an individual's existence, and second, desires describe a psychological preference for achieving a state that is ethically neutral (Pryor, 1979). Values, on the other hand, while they are indissoluble from needs and desires, have an ethical dimension that is largely absent from the phenomena that Maslow and his successors have tried to describe. Since ethics are determined by belief and custom as well as by actual conditions, values will tend to possess a greater complexity and a greater variation between cultures than either needs or desires.

Further, although theoretically needs and desires are predominantly etic phenomena (McGaughey, Iverson, and De Cieri, 1997) and thus might show variation according to criteria such as economic or geographical context, the particular outcomes of needs and desires will depend on the particular cultural circumstances that each person encounters and will therefore also be coloured by emic variations.[3] Accordingly, different groups of people will *value* certain modes of expressing their needs and desires over others and these modes will be different across cultural and ethical boundaries according to each group's customs and systems of belief.

Values, and their combination with needs and desires, become even more complex when we connect them with the question of how people negotiate their life-paths through the institutional systems of capitalist modernity. For when cyclical patterns of ascription as externally imposed guides for behaviour have to a large extent disappeared, the substantive manifestations of human motivations will necessarily be coloured much more by the problem of ends and means. That is to say, in capitalist modernity end states, as they represent the concrete outcomes in social life of needs, desires, and values, must be achieved by individuals in negotiation with others, within prevailing institutional constraints, and by using the means that they deem necessary, possible, and ethical.

To be sure, when looked at in this light, Maslow's hierarchy is somewhat simplistic when applied to human motivation and its relationship with social behaviour on an individual level but, as both Inglehart (1990 and 1997) and Watanabe (1997) successfully argue on the basis of an enormous quantity and variety of longitudinal research data, it may be applied as a general schema to the structure of needs and desires at the level of mass society. The principal weakness, however, of Inglehart's and others' adoption of Maslow's work, is that they too often fail to include the extra dimension of values and they neglect to describe critically and concretely what self-actualization is as a state of mind, how it feels and functions, and therefore how it underpins the new society that they describe. If indeed the end state of self-actualization is becoming the new psychological mechanism of social regulation in capitalist modernity, as Giddens, Inglehart, and others in one way or another appear to claim, then it is important that we understand more completely than hitherto what it is. Maslow himself (1987 [1954]) used the term 'peak experiences' without focusing too hard on the details of how it functions in social life while Inglehart for the most part avoids the problem. Giddens describes an ongoing 'reflexive project of the self' but, again, does not adequately describe its functional characteristics.

This is an important issue to pin down when we attempt to analyse and understand social development because not only does it impact on the types of institutions and structures that people construct in order to filter their consciousness into concrete reality but it also guides us towards an understanding of what individuals value as their most preferred end state. More specifically, if a Maslovian-type hierarchy can be observed on a societal level, and as most Japanese people's physiological needs are now chronically gratified, then they will surely, on the whole, concentrate on satisfying their psychological desires. Further, if in a general sense people's desires for security, belongingness, and prestige become chronically gratified through an implicit guarantee of very long-term employment and promotion within a large and well-respected community-like corporation, then surely they will begin to make greater efforts towards achieving authentic individual self-actualization. And if work has become one of the principal loci in modern society for the substantive manifestation of an individual's authentic consciousness then the modern corporation, as it is the most widespread, complex, and developed organizational form in capitalist modernity, will perhaps be the principal site upon which people may wish to realize such a state.

Flow

Although he does not make this claim for himself, probably the most comprehensive examination to date of how the system of needs, desires, and values might function at a deep level, or what self-actualization might be and what it might feel like to experience, is the work of Mihaly Csikszentmihaly (1988 and 1997) and the group of scholars who are gathering around him to research the concept of what he calls 'optimal experience' or 'flow'. He describes it as a consciousness that derives from what he terms the 'emergent teleonomy of the self'. That is to say, the reflexive free will that humans possess and which links together but is distinct from either genetic or cultural teleonomy[4] enables them to discover experiences that lead to a psychologically negentropic[5] and developmental state that is profoundly fulfilling but requires increasing levels of sophistication and challenge (Csikszentmihaly, 1988). I will leave it to Csikszentmihaly himself to describe how flow functions and what its significance is for self and society.

> In our everyday activities, either by chance or by design, we come in contact with experiences that we have never been exposed to before . . . Some of them . . . will be negentropic – that is they will increase the order of the self because they will be congruent with already established goals. Therefore they will produce a sense of exhilaration, energy, and fulfilment that is more enjoyable than what people feel in the normal course of life. When this occurs, a person will tend to replicate this state of being in preference to others. The activity that produced the experience will be sought out again and again. To the extent that this is done, the self will be built on the model of emergent goals.
>
> The evolution of consciousness – and hence, the evolution of culture and ultimately the evolution of the human species – hinges on our capacity to invest psychic energy in goals that are not modeled exclusively on the teleonomy of genes or cultures. When we step beyond motivations based on pleasure, power, and participation, we open up consciousness to experience new opportunities for being that lead to emergent structures of the self. This is autotelic motivation, because its goal is primarily the experience itself, rather than any future reward or advantage it may bring.
>
> . . . The universal precondition for flow is that a person should perceive that there is something for him or her to do, and that he or she is capable of doing it. In other words, optimal experience requires a balance between the challenges perceived in a given situation and the skills a person brings to it . . . any possibility for action to which a skill corresponds can produce an autotelic experience.
>
> It is this feature that makes flow such a dynamic force in evolution. For every activity might engender it, but at the same time no activity can sustain it for long unless both the challenges and the skills become more complex.
>
> (Csikszentmihaly, 1988: 28–30)

Although this is an exceptionally powerful idea with profound implications for every area of human activity, what Csikszentmihaly does not adequately describe is, first, the preconditions necessary for people to encounter and experience flow in their lives and, second, though he hints at it, how people might behave if they are prevented from experiencing flow by external institutional structures and mores. Taking a somewhat more libertarian line Se (1999) attacks the first problem by urging us to liberalize and marketize our institutions in order that people might be allowed to pursue 'experiments in living' so that they may discover by education and trial and error what activities enable them to gain such enjoyment and fulfilment. His argument is persuasive but it fails to pay enough attention to the need for individuals to build self-actualization onto and around an already existing foundation of security and stability.

Csikszentmihaly (1988) alludes to the second question by suggesting that another way to build the emergent self is in relation to instructions endorsed by the social system and to become part of it, thus merging one's being with that of the greater whole. Interestingly for these discussions, he uses the faithful employee as one of his examples of a manifestation of this solution. In the process the self loses its autonomy, but in exchange gains identification with a larger and more powerful entity. Thus, the teleonomy of self might be organized around goals that involve participation. Nevertheless, this solution requires abnegation of other goals in order to experience the sense of belonging and merging. Csikszentmihaly recognizes the excessive rigidity and resulting instability of this solution since the apparently selfless members of such a community will, where there is incompatibility between the system and its external circumstances, contribute to destroying the system itself because individuals' desire to replicate a sense of belonging begins to take precedence over the requirements of the system to adjust to any new or emerging circumstances. Further, Csikszentmihaly (1988: 27–8) argues, 'if these were the only sources of motivation, human behaviour would remain the same over time. Yet consciousness evolves' and 'attention has become focused on more and more differentiated stimuli' and this will gradually cause the system itself to implode as its members begin to choose their own individual routes into experiencing flow or, in the context of this research, self-actualization.

Nevertheless, as Csikszentmihaly might agree, although the two are closely related and intertwined end states, flow does not equate to self-actualization. More accurately, flow might be described as the feeling an individual experiences as he or she achieves his or her emergent goals. These goals might themselves equate roughly to a Maslovian hierarchy of needs and desires. Putting the above discussions together we might then describe self-actualization as a coming together. It is a feeling of deep enjoyment and fulfilment (flow) that comes with the achievement of having all one's goals, as they emerge, become chronically gratified and of having new goals emerge and become gratified in their place in a sustainable and upward trajectory of experience and achievement. It is a feeling of being challenged in one's work and private interests but being able to rise to those challenges, overcome them, and develop oneself and deepen one's relationships as a result. Moreover, it is also a feeling, and this is important, of simultaneously not being threatened by basic insufficiencies and insecurities. How this manifests itself in social life will differ from one society to another according to the values that it and its individual members hold dear. We might speculate that the Japanese may, therefore, place greater importance on deepening their emotional interdependency at the expense of what they might see as a more self-absorbed and perhaps self-indulgent emphasis on individual self-development in Anglo-Saxon societies.

Accordingly, we cannot also avoid the conclusion that Csikszentmihaly makes with regard to the selfless route into experiencing flow. The Japanese corporation, having for so long provided a context for the achievement of a socialized version for Japanese society of selfless flow and self-actualization, may now be structurally and institutionally incompatible with a new set of external circumstances and, thus, the context for the achievement of self-actualization as well as the process of its substantive realization may now be on the cusp of a transformation.

Work values in Japan

There is a widespread feeling in Japan that a fundamental change has occurred in the system of values that has helped to propel it to its place among the rich countries of the world. This feeling is not confined to academics and media commentators but is also common among ordinary adults and young people.

Fujioka (1989), says that time is the missing ingredient because Japan lacks the refinement of a culture that, like a good wine, has mellowed. Adopting a more academic approach, some scholars have painted a rather depressing picture of mass social-psychological decay. It has been argued that the various pathologies described are a consequence of the rapidity of Japan's achievement of affluence, an incompatibility between Japan's traditional value system and the demands of global capitalism, and the lack of a clearly defined direction now that the explicit national goal of material parity with the West has been achieved (Hirooka, 1986; Mouer, 1989; Ohira, 1990; Allison, 1994; Kato, 1994; McCormack, 1997b; and Tao, 1998).

Clearly something is afoot. For how can it be that in the space of ten years Japan has gone from being the society that the West should study and try to emulate to being the one that the West should understand for the purpose of avoiding making the same mistakes?

Focusing more narrowly on the salaryman's work consciousness, his experience of work, and his relationship with the institutions of his employment, and echoing similar research done in the United States some 20 years earlier (Jurgensen, 1978 and Yankelovich, 1978), some have suggested that young people in Japan are developing a new set of work values and that this phenomenon is intimately linked to the achievement of an affluent society (Nitto, 1993; Schlosstein, 1993; Herbig and Borstorff, 1995; Yamakoshi, 1996; Imada, 1997). Their thesis claims that the structures of employment have not changed dramatically since the establishment of the post-war system and, therefore, have become inconsistent with the emerging consciousness of Japan's young people which is being formed within a radically different material environment where the problem of scarcity exists only for those on the margins of society.

As a result, the emergent goals associated with this new consciousness appear to be: less attention to achieving material stability and security and, because these can now be taken for granted, a steadily increasing desire for individual self-determination in controlling one's career trajectory as well as one's life biography in general; a greater desire to experience individual self-development and self-fulfilment through deep involvement in the content of one's work and at the expense of long-term absorption and participation in organizational socialization; and an increasing desire by younger employees to enjoy participating in and developing family and other relationships as well as leisure pursuits external to the corporation. More precisely, the consequences for the Japanese lifetime employment system and the corporation as a whole are likely to be profound since they strike at the long-term organization orientation that lies at the heart of its successful operation.

To have one's cake and eat it?

Are wealth, security and stability, prestige and self-esteem, good social relations, self-actualization, and the experience of flow in the achievement of these goals mutually contradictory objectives to expect to gain from working in a large bureaucratic capitalist and modern organization? Intuitively it would seem to be difficult for people to attain all of these objectives simultaneously from a single workplace or even, for that matter, if one includes other life spheres such as leisure, religious, educational, and community activities as well as personal relationships. Nevertheless, it is testament to the centrality of work in capitalist modernity that this is precisely what Japanese employees appear to wish to achieve.

The Raifu Dezain Kenkyūjo[6] (Kato, 1999) gathered data from 2,210 people between the ages of 18 and 69 on a series of lifestyle topics including work. This research shows how work appears now to occupy a crucial role in the satisfaction of a diverse range of needs, desires, and values among Japanese people. Figure 5.1 shows males' desired workplace characteristics and their perception of the substantive implementation in their workplace of these characteristics. For these respondents the most desirable workplace characteristics (in order) are where one can: develop one's abilities, get a good salary, have responsibilities, have a secure job, have interesting work, have trustworthy superiors, and have like-minded colleagues. Substituting this data for a Maslovian hierarchy would be too simplistic and, moreover, there is the additional problem that the respondents were of different ages and backgrounds, thus clouding the issue of whether a new set of work values is developing among the young. Nevertheless, it is clear that these respondents wish to satisfy a broad range of needs and desires from their work and that security and stability of employment, while remaining important, is, even in the present circumstances, not the most highly valued among them.

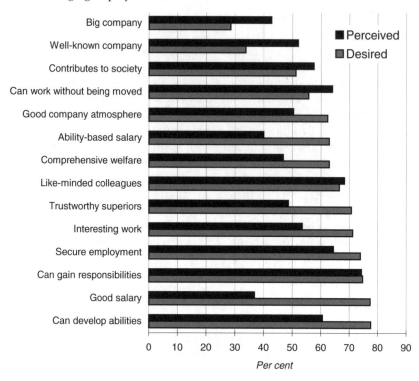

Figure 5.1 Male workers' perceived and desired workplace characteristics.
Source: Kato, 1999: 179–80.

The second important point is that some respondents felt that there was a mismatch between their objectives and what they feel their workplace is actually delivering for them. Of the 14 attributes listed, in only five cases did respondents feel that the company is providing more than they desired and four of these were the least desired attributes. The greatest differences between respondents' desires and perceived company performance were over material rewards, with some respondents feeling that they were not being paid enough, that the method of calculation was not sufficiently based upon their abilities, and that the company welfare packages were inadequate.

There were also negative differences between respondents' desired work content and what they felt they were being offered, confirming the suspicion that Japanese employees seek, but to a certain extent appear to be frustrated in their efforts to gain, more interesting as well as more challenging work. Whether this represents a desire for self-actualization and flow is difficult to answer; however, at least some kind of relationship cannot be discounted. Nevertheless, it can also be said that a substantial number of respondents' needs, desires, and values are being delivered by the workplace.

The idea that many Japanese would like to gain both greater security and more material rewards from their work as well as experience more spiritual or psychological satisfaction is also born out by a number of government studies. It can also be shown that employment security and stability, for the majority of the people questioned, are at least as important as any psychological rewards accruing from their work. Statistics produced by the Prime Minister's Office (Sōrifu, 2000: 161)[7] showed 52.9 per cent of more than 7,000 respondents saying that their ideal work would provide income security and stability, 34.9 per cent replying that their ideal job would have an enjoyable working environment, and 34.2 per cent responding that it would give them an opportunity to make good use of their specialist knowledge and abilities. Since the previous study in 1997, the first figure has increased by 3.7 and the second and third have been reduced by approximately 1 per cent each. In addition, the number of people responding that their ideal job would be one without fear of being made unemployed had increased from 14.7 to 17.3 per cent and the number of people stating that they wanted the opportunity to earn high income had fallen from 9.2 to 7.6 per cent of the sample. Clearly, fear of unemployment and the resulting feelings of insecurity appear to be increasing, adding to the feeling that life may not be what people wish it to be[8] or what they believe it could be. However, the figures also reconfirm that a substantial proportion of Japanese do indeed appear to feel secure enough also to expect psychological enrichment from their work.

Nevertheless, the changes in these figures may also point to the continuing but perhaps temporary effects of the present period of stagnation. What is also interesting is that, when asked which of either more money or more free time they would choose, the proportion opting for more income has fallen from a high of 53.3 per cent of respondents in the 1994 study to 48.7 per cent in 2000. The number opting for more free time rose to 34.2 per cent from 29.4 per cent during the same interval (Sōrifu, 2000: 164), possibly suggesting that material rewards per se are becoming less important in relation to the opportunities to enjoy, or actualize, them that extra free time might bring.

Importantly, in the same survey, respondents were asked what they thought was the most important purpose for people to work (Figure 5.2). Rather than being asked to list their work preferences or desires, they were being asked here to list what they valued from among a range of choices offered. The results were a slight contradiction to the previous data because income came out as the second most important value, slightly lower than working to discover one's *ikigai*, or something that makes life worth living. The third most important value was working to develop one's talents and abilities and the fourth was doing one's duty as a member of society. However, as has already been discussed, values possess an ethical dimension that desires might not and thus it should be no surprise in this case if the responses seem, at first glance, to be contradictory. What is also interesting about this data is that more women than men believe that discovering one's *ikigai* is the most important reason for working, perhaps suggesting that for some men discovering one's

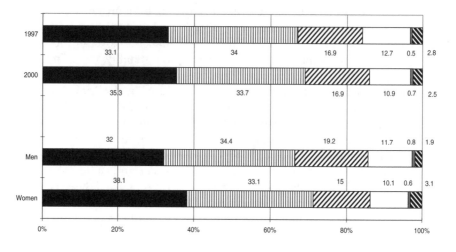

- **■** Work to find something that makes life worth living
- **Ⅲ** 'Work to earn money
- **◪** Work to develop one's talents and abilities
- **□** Work to fulfil one's duties as a member of society
- **▣** Don't know
- **◩** No answer

Figure 5.2 What do you think is the most important reason for people to work?

Source: Sōrifu, 2000: 159.

ikigai must take second place to the more pressing value, or serious duty, of supporting oneself and one's family.

When we link these figures to major lifestyle indicators a pattern does appear to emerge. Figures from the Ministry of Public Management's *Monthly Statistics of Japan* (Sōmushō, 2002: 24) show that in the period 1995 to 2002 average monthly cash earnings for regular employees actually fell by nearly 25 per cent from ¥408,900 in July 1995 to ¥309,100 in May 2002 while average monthly hours worked have remained steady (159.1 hours in July 1995 to 156.9 hours in June 2002) (Sōmushō, 2002: 27). In the same period average monthly income for workers' households fell from ¥570,817 in July 1995 to ¥441,284 in May 2002 while average household expenditure has stayed more or less the same (¥438,307 in July 1995 to ¥413,945 in May 2002) thus decreasing household monthly savings by more than 75 per cent from an average of ¥86,935 per month in July 1995 to ¥20,563 in April 2002 (Sōmushō, 2002: 144). Given these indicators, and if one also takes into account that bank interest rates on savings have been near zero for some years now, one could forgive Japanese people for feeling somewhat less well-off and less secure than previously. What is perhaps more surprising, therefore, is that the data presented above on employees' work preferences and values have not moved towards more material concerns as much as one might have expected under such severe macro-economic conditions.

Career choice

Consequently, it would seem that, in general, Japanese people strongly value and desire employment security and material comfort but these are not as dominant objectives as perhaps they once were. One of the best ways of finding out if this is indeed the case, and of understanding what other work attributes and characteristics are becoming more highly desired and valued, is to look at data regarding job search and job-changing activity since, if a person forgoes the opportunity of lifetime employment at a single organization and the steadily rising and secure salary that comes with it, then desires and values other than employment security and income stability must necessarily be coming in to play.

In recent figures produced by the employment research company Rikurūto Risāchi[9] and reproduced in the 2000 White Paper on Labour (Rōdōshō, 2000b),[10] when asked whether they looked for and soon found work as a regular employee, 64.6 per cent of respondents graduating out of education in 1999 replied that they could not and instead, even if only temporarily, became *furīta*.[11] Of those, 22.1 per cent said they became *furīta* because they could not find regular employment, 15.6 per cent said that conditions at positions open to them were not to their liking, and 41.2 per cent said that they did not wish to be a regular employee. Clearly, although some young people are involuntarily unemployed, a considerable number would rather be in insecure and unstable work than in a job that may be secure but is not to their liking.

In research on people's reasons for choosing their first company (Rōdōshō, 2000b),[12] there appears to have been a marked shift away from security and prestige towards self-actualization issues. The number of men aged 20 to 24 who chose their company for its size and name value fell in the period between 1985 and 1997 from 11.1 to 6.3 per cent and the number who chose their company for its future prospects and survivability fell from 25.3 to 4.1 per cent. Moreover, the number who chose their company on the basis of the work content rose from 26.7 to 32.2 per cent. Interestingly, the 1997 figures include the additional answer of choosing the company on the basis of making good use of one's talents and abilities. Men scored 18.5 and women 12.9 per cent on this issue. By adding these figures to the ones for work content, we can see self-actualization reasons scoring 40.7 per cent for men and 52.8 per cent for women.

On the issue of long-term employment at a single organization, there is a trend towards more self-determination and flexibility, though the desire for security and continuity remains strong. Figure 5.3 shows longitudinal data on the question of how long newly hired employees wish to remain at their

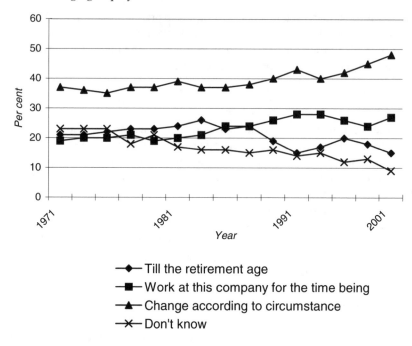

Figure 5.3 Until when do you intend to work for this company?

Source: SKSH, 2001b: 82.

company. While a dramatic change in sentiment is not evident, at least until the 1990s, a steady increase towards changing employer according to one's circumstances and keeping one's options open is taking place. A determination to work at the company until retirement is falling gradually and more slowly.

Further, when examining the question of wishing to change employer across all age groups a clearer picture begins to emerge. Figure 5.4 shows data from the former Management and Coordination Agency's *Basic Survey on the Employment Structure* on job-changing consciousness by age. Although all age groups show a secular rise in wanting to change jobs, predictably, younger people showed the greatest rate of increase. Despite there being a fall for some age groups between 1987and 1992, the curve resumed its upward trend for all age groups by 1997. Interestingly, for the youngest group the proportion of people wishing to change employer at some time in their career rose over the 26-year period by an outstanding 307 per cent. Admittedly the curve began from an extremely low initial level of only 7.1 per cent in 1971, attesting to the normative strength of lifetime employment and the extent of the desire for employment security and income stability in that era. However a change in consciousness is indeed evident.

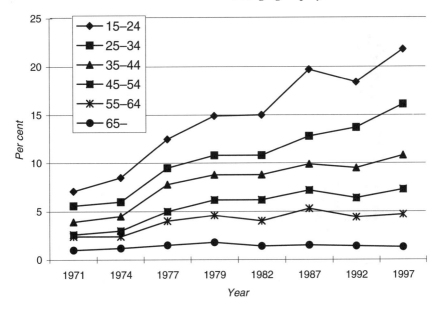

Figure 5.4 Rate of those wishing to change employer by age group.

Source: Sōmuchō, 1971–97.

Moreover, in more recent figures collected by the Ministry of Public Management (Sōmushō, 2002: 21) the number of persons wishing to change jobs has continued to increase. The number of full-time employees wishing to change jobs rose from 5.19 million people in 1995 to a peak of 6.92 million in August 2001 before falling back slightly by 2002.

Looking now more closely at actual job-changing activity and taking figures for young people in the early stages of their career, the number of young people changing employer is rising. The 2000 White Paper on Labour (Rōdōshō, 2000b) presents data from the entire labour force on job changing in the first three years after graduation from school or university. Fully 33.6 per cent of those graduating from university in 1995 had changed employer at least once in three years since graduation. This compares to 23.7 per cent of those who had graduated in 1992.

However, focusing now more closely on male university graduates working for large corporations, Figure 5.5, from a survey by the Japan Institute of Labour (NRKK, 1999), shows the number of organizations that responding university graduate males have worked for since graduation. It compares two groups and traces their career paths; those who graduated in the 1983–4 period and those who did so between 1989 and 1991.[13] Confirming the institutional continuity of lifetime employment, after 15 or so years since graduation, 69.9 per cent of the first group are still at their original employer while,

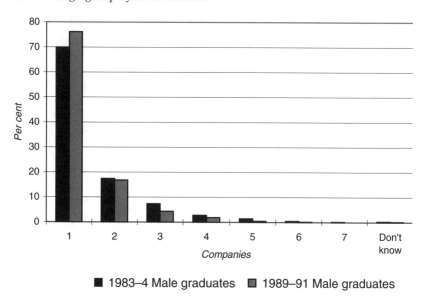

Figure 5.5 Number of companies worked at since graduation.

Source: NRKK, 1999.

of the second group, 76.1 per cent are still with their original employer. This confirms data produced by the Nihongata Koyō Shisutemu Kenkyū Kai (NKSKK, 1995), which shows 81 per cent of university graduate male white-collar employees still at their original employer.[14]

When the respondents to the NRKK study who had changed employer were asked the reasons for leaving their original employer, the results show less preoccupation with financial concerns among the younger group and, importantly, both groups placing much greater emphasis on work content (Figure 5.6), perhaps indicating a greater desire for self-actualization rather than concentrating more narrowly on employment security and stability. Interesting, also, is the proportion of job changers responding 'other', though it is impossible to speculate why these people changed employer other than to say that the options available in the questionnaire did not conform to their particular circumstances.

Further, another study by the same organization (Japan Institute of Labour, 1998) compared Japanese data on job changing among white-collar managerial employees with that of the United States and Germany, the most representative examples of the two dominant Western economic models. The proportion of Japanese managerial employees who had experienced a change of employer stood at 18.2 per cent while the figure for Germany was 70.3 per cent and for the USA 81.8 per cent. When the age for entering the new company was taken into consideration, 48.1 per cent of Japanese who had

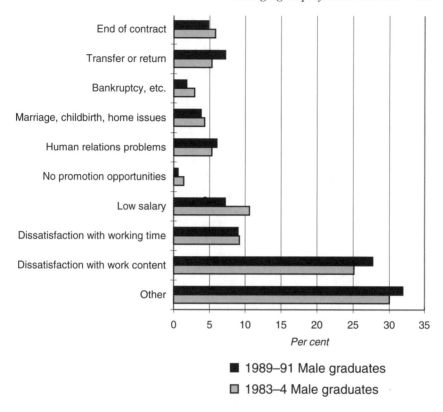

Figure 5.6 Reason for resigning from original employer.

Source: NRKK, 1999.

changed employer did so before they were 30 and 71.7 per cent had done so before they were 40. For Germany, the figures were 33.3 per cent and 77.6 per cent, and in the United States, 34.3 per cent and 76.5 per cent. Thus, far fewer Japanese white-collar managerial employees experience a change of employer than in other developed countries and, second, while in all three countries nearly all employer changes had taken place before the age of 40, a significantly higher proportion of Japanese had done so before the age of 30. This confirms that changing employer among white-collar managerial employees in Japan is rising among the young and may also indicate a perception of the continuing strength of structural barriers to career change, especially in later life.

Taking data again from the Nihongata Koyō Shisutemu Kenkyū Kai (NKSKK, 1995) research project and examining the salaryman's attitudes towards the institutions of his employment, a picture of satisfaction punctuated by some fears and frustrations emerges.

On the subject of satisfaction with one's work, levels appeared to be consistently high, with average levels of satisfaction registering 75.4 per cent of the 4,063 respondents (27.5 per cent satisfied and 47.9 per cent mostly satisfied) and 23.9 per cent dissatisfied (4.3 per cent dissatisfied and 19.6 per cent mostly dissatisfied). Satisfaction levels did rise slightly with age and by size of company though this cannot conclusively be interpreted as a generational difference since dissatisfied people will presumably have a greater tendency to leave the corporation, particularly when young. However, on the subject of salary, satisfaction levels were much lower, with more dissatisfied people than satisfied. 42.5 per cent were satisfied (9.6 per cent satisfied and 32.9 per cent mostly satisfied) and 56.7 per cent were dissatisfied (17.1 per cent dissatisfied and 39.6 per cent mostly dissatisfied). Moreover, the younger the employee the higher his dissatisfaction with financial rewards; 65.6 per cent of 24- to 29-year-olds and 66.8 per cent of 30- to 34-year-olds were dissatisfied. Arranged by hoped-for career path, 70.3 per cent of those who wanted to become independent of the company were dissatisfied with their financial rewards. Asked about their satisfaction with the company in general, 61.1 per cent said they were and 37.9 per cent not.

Importantly, there appears to be a rough correlation between satisfaction with work or with wages and with the company in general, with 84.4 per cent of those dissatisfied with their work also expressing dissatisfaction with the company and 72.2 per cent of those dissatisfied with their wages also dissatisfied with the company. Looking at the opposite scenario, 71.5 per cent of those satisfied by their work and 81.6 per cent of those satisfied with their salaries are also satisfied with the company. There seems to be, therefore, a relationship between both material and psychological satisfaction, and, further, between these two and satisfaction with the general work context and the organization as an entity. What the precise nature of these relationships is the data cannot tell us but it does suggest that salarymen place a very high importance upon both their financial situation, or livelihood, and gaining fulfilment from the content of their work and that these issues not only are, in a very real sense, inseparable from each other but also have a very great impact upon an employee's overall perception of his employing organization.

Moving from the issue of satisfaction with present conditions to that of desired career path and job-changing consciousness among salarymen, although a majority of respondents in this study wished to remain at the same company till retirement, their reasons for doing so are predominantly negative, in the sense that existent conditions and structures appear to be holding them back rather than being positive reasons for them to stay (Figures 5.7 and 5.8). While more than half of all respondents over the age of 35 wish to remain at their company, probably until retirement, when their reasons for not wanting to change employer are considered, except for the over 55s, more than half of them do so not because they are happy with their present conditions, but because they feel either that leaving would cause their situation to get worse or that moving would be too difficult.

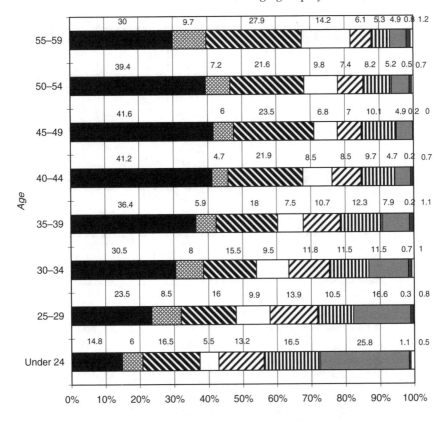

Figure 5.7 Desired career path.

Source: NKSKK, 1995.

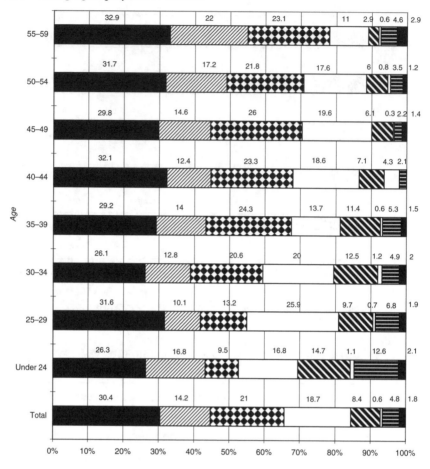

I am satisfied with my present job

I am satisfied with my present working conditions

I would lose salary and pension benefits

I don't have any useful qualifications or specialist abilities

Even if I changed job nothing would change

The company I wish to move to does not recruit mid-career

Other

N/A

Figure *5.8* Reasons for not wanting to change job.

Source: NKSKK, 1995.

What is also interesting about this data is the relative lack of commitment by younger employees to long-term employment and their lack of satisfaction with their jobs and, in particular, their working conditions. Further, younger employees seem to be expressing a somewhat negative approach to remaining with their employer. Such an apparent belief in the strength and rigidity of employment structures keeping young people, who one would normally expect to be the least risk averse, from realizing their personal objectives does not bode well for the future of the corporate community as a viable institution in a cultural sense. Given these conditions, what might be the consequence to the lifetime employment system of a sustained recovery in Japan's economic growth trajectory and increasing fluidity in labour markets? Of course, this type of question is merely speculative, but it does alert us to the possibilities inherent in the relationship between motivation, culture, structure, and social action and can help us feel our way towards understanding how social systems are developing. However, if young people remain company- rather than job- or skills-oriented then, even if they only possess negative reasons for remaining, it is unlikely that a viable and dynamic labour market, such as those that exist in Western countries, will emerge, since these markets function on the basis of skills and attributes being traded between employers and employees in a similar, though not identical, manner to commodities. Thus, it is important that we investigate and analyse in a qualitative sense how younger employees are coming to view their careers, jobs, and employers.

Field investigations

In the light of the theoretical system that is gradually coming to take shape, it remains necessary to find out some of the principal qualities of the salary-man's needs, desires, and values and whether he feels he is able to achieve their substantive realization within the employment system as it is presently unfolding. Moreover, in this period of intensifying global economic competition and domestic institutional reform, how is the Japanese salaryman adapting to and coping with the demands of the emerging personnel and management paradigm? Conversely, how is he directing and negotiating his life and career within the demands of a continuously developing employment environment?

Career start

Despite the broadening of the higher education system to include nearly half of each cohort of young people, and the encouragement of young people by educators and parents to choose their own career according to their own desires, values, and abilities, being a regular employee at a large corporation is still the preferred career among the graduates of Japan's élite universities. Of the 1998 graduating class from Doshisha University in Kyoto, reputed to be the most prestigious private university in the Kansai region, 64.4 per cent of graduates (66.1 per cent of male humanities and social science graduates and

Table 5.1 Principal recruiters of Tokyo University graduates (1997 and 2000).

Employer (1997)	No. of graduates	Employer (2000)	No. of graduates
NTT (Telecomms)	34	Hitachi (Electrical/electronics)	44
Tokyo-Mitsubishi Bank (Finance)	25	Sony (Electrical/electronics)	32
NHK (Broadcasting)	24	IBM Japan (Electrical/electronics)	28
IBJ (Finance)	19	Science Research Institute (Research)	24
Sumitomo Bank (Finance)	18	Toshiba (Electrical/electronics)	22
Sumitomo Trading (Commerce)	17	Nihon Denki (Electrical/electronics)	19
Sony (Electrical/electronics)	16	Mitsubishi Heavy Industries (Transportation machinery)	16
Tokai Bank (Finance)	16	Accenture (Management consulting)	15
Tokyo Marine (Finance)	16	Mitsubishi Electric (Electrical/electronics)	15
Mitsubishi Corp. (Commerce)	15	NTT Data (Telecomms)	13
NTT Data (Telecomms)	15	Mitsui Chemicals (Chemicals)	13

Source: *Tokyo Daigaku Shimbun*, 2 June 1998: 1; 12 June 2001: 1.

74.2 per cent of engineering graduates) became regular employees of corporations with more than 1,000 employees (Dōshisha Daigaku, 1999). In addition, of the 1997 and 2000 graduating classes from Tokyo University, certainly the most prestigious if not the best public university in Japan and the favoured recruiting ground for the national bureaucracy, large corporations were the principal career choices for those with both undergraduate and postgraduate degrees (Table 5.1).

By way of comparison, in 1997 Tokyo University sent just 22 graduates and post-graduates to each of the Ministry of International Trade and Industry and the Ministry of Agriculture, Forestry, and Fisheries, while the Ministry of Finance recruited only 12 graduates.[15] In 2000 these figures had risen to more or less previous levels with 32 graduates going to the Ministry of Transport, 31 to the Ministry of Finance, and 24 to the Ministry of Economy and Industry.

While the majority of company employees interviewed for this research said that neither their parents nor their teachers had coerced them into choosing a particular route other than giving either a gentle steer towards something respectable and stable or simple encouragement and support for whatever career they felt their children would be happy with, most employees felt that there were limitations, restrictions, and obligations that weighed upon their ability to do so. These included the individuals' own aptitudes and abilities, the structural limitations of the recruitment system, and individuals' needs, desires, and values where sometimes these were in conflict. However, respondents rarely expressed any strong feelings of disappointment or frustration at being prevented from achieving their objectives in a pure sense, instead they more or less accepted their situations with equanimity, and even willingly and enthusiastically took on the challenge of negotiating a successful compromise between fulfilling the demands of their circumstances and obligations and the objectives that they had set out to realize for themselves as individuals.

From the interview extracts below we can understand a little about the varied and complex situations that individuals find themselves in when having to make their career choices and how they reconcile their accumulated experiences and present circumstances with their own developing desires and values. Importantly, although employees did sometimes express great interest in the content of their work and its subject matter, the extracts below point towards the continuing strength of a company rather than specialist career orientation among white-collar salarymen. On the whole, what these men still appear to want and have been conditioned to expect to do is, primarily, join an organization and then use their talents and develop their interests over the long term within that context. Also interesting, however, are the differences between interviewees' systems of desires and values, how these have come to take shape, and how these are reconciled with external issues such as choice of organizational type and career direction.

The following employee of Company D was well aware of both his own desires and those of his parents and managed to find a good compromise between the two. Company D is a near monopoly regional utility provider with almost no operations outside the region that it serves. Joining it has meant that he has been able to satisfy his desire to join an organization, develop his particular interests and abilities, and fulfil his familial duty of looking after and supporting his parents in their later years by remaining in his local area.

Interestingly, it became apparent through the course of my fieldwork that Company D was a preferred employer among some young men who are the eldest sons of their families, or *chōnan*, and who take the traditional duties of that position seriously. Although the company did not profess to any policy of preferring to recruit eldest sons and has no statistics on their number, a substantial proportion of the men I met were *chōnan* and informed me that they chose this company because it provides stable and long-term employment with little or no prospect of being transferred to a distant location. Importantly in this regard, although the company is not a public entity it has the feel of being one both to employees and to local people, and it is well respected as an establishment institution, thus being attractive as an employer to those people wishing to be regarded as reliable and respected members of their local communities.

Q: What were your aims at high school and at university?

A: At that time I had no concrete ambitions, though I wanted to join a company. Coming from a rural area, with no trains or businesses I wanted to become a salaryman . . . I thought to myself that I didn't have the confidence or ability or money to start my own business . . . It was only at university that I began to think more clearly.

A normal company didn't really suit me either . . . I thought that administration and planning probably suited me more so . . . In Japan, when looking for a job, one doesn't really think about the content but more the type of company, and [this company] doesn't have a large sales force.

Q: During your high school and university days, what kind of hopes did your parents and teachers have for you?

A: When I was at high school they had no specific hopes. When I went to university in Kobe they wanted me to return [here] and become a local government official. But I didn't want to do that because I felt that it doesn't offer much chance for self-development. But, I am the eldest son so for my parents' sake I thought I should search for a job with [this company] in this area . . . I didn't feel a really strong obligation to return, but coincidentally I felt that [this] was a suitable company and my parents were happy too.

(Senior Staff, Company D, age 32)

The next employee contrasts with the previous one in the reasons for his choice of company. In common with most respondents he candidly admits to not having any particular ambitions or desires and to joining his company because he wanted a high salary in order to be able to afford an affluent lifestyle. In this way many graduates of Japan's more reputable universities appear to drift en masse every spring into employment in large corporations as if it is a rite of passage for the sons and daughters of the urban middle classes. He also points to the assumption held by many that the content and style of white-collar work in large corporations can be quite similar and therefore, in his reasoning, there is little to choose between them except as to whether one can enjoy as well as afford to enjoy the social aspects of working with like-minded colleagues.

> Honestly speaking, without really thinking about anything I entered the company. The only thing I thought about was that there are a lot of seniors (*sempai*) from my university kendo club here. Among those seniors there are many very good people and I wanted to work in a company where there are a lot of good seniors from (my) university.
>
> . . . also, completely different companies all have a personnel division that does the same personnel work and the general affairs division does the same general affairs work. The only difference is the product being sold and the style. So I wasn't particular.
>
> More than the work I wanted a high salary. When I chose the company I had the impression that once you join a company you start early in the morning and finish late in the evening. So, of course, a high salary would be great . . . While working I want to work hard and while playing I like to have the money to afford what I want to do.
>
> (Employee, Company C, age 23)

The following two employees chose their companies according to the type of product that the company manufactures. Both men could not realize their principal ambitions so chose something that they felt would be a satisfying alternative. Interestingly, many respondents from the two manufacturers claim to have chosen their company because they have an interest, and for some almost an obsession, in the products it manufactures. Yet, as is the case with the two men above, few of the respondents at the two service-oriented companies made this claim except to say that they wanted to join a company that provides a public service.

> I like cars and I wanted to work at a car manufacturer and contribute to making cars that people like. I applied to a few but I couldn't make it. I heard that this company was recruiting and it looked interesting.
>
> (Employee, Company B, age 25)

> *A:* I didn't have any particular ambitions. I mostly wanted to enter university and I thought that I could choose what I wanted to do while I was there.
>
> . . . I did what I wanted but still I didn't have the talent to do what I really wanted, which was to be a comedian.
>
> *Q:* Why did you choose [this company]?
>
> *A:* At high school I liked photography and I knew a lot about cameras.

> So when I was looking for a job this company was interesting . . . It has a
> strong brand image so I thought it would be a good company.
>
> (Employee, Company A, age 30)

If we compare the above extracts with employees' recollections of their
reasons for choosing their companies in chapter three, a couple of important
but quite subtle contrasts emerge. Above we can see evidence of a received
acceptance of conditions and relationships being a constraint on and a challenge to people's decisions and behaviours. We can also see a desire on the
part of some to take on and conform to certain externally ascribed duties and
expectations. However, what is different from before is the element of a
slightly more refined and inner-directed reflexivity. While the younger respondents often willingly adjusted to existent conditions and their own circumstances, they also demonstrate a somewhat deeper level of reflection regarding
their own situation, the possibilities open to them, and the relationship
between their desires and values, the decisions they make, and their responsibility for the courses of action which they embark upon. More evident than
with the older respondents is the element of a considered choice from a
number of varied possibilities with quite different outcomes. This choice is
considered in the sense that, although most employees as students may have
simply enjoyed what is often called the moratorium between the serious business of high school and company life, when the time came nearly all of them
made their decisions on the basis of it being the most preferable option given
what they perceived about their own particular circumstances and their desires,
values, and expectations.

There is, in addition, a difference between the generations in that few
younger employees made mention of seeking employment as a salaryman in
order to escape from difficult material circumstances. Some employees did say
that their parents had suffered in their youth and that they had responded to
their parents' advice and fears in their choice of a career characterized by security and stability, but none expressed that they themselves had had to endure
such circumstances and had sought long-term secure employment at a single
organization for that reason.

One other issue to come out of the interview data is that employees expressed mixed messages concerning the contrast between choosing a company
and choosing an occupation. Most employees seemed to choose their company
because the company's business as a whole and its social role coincide with
their system of values and what they want to do in terms of work content.
Many showed that the choice of a company or an occupation is a double-sided
problem and is as much a predicament to be solved as it is a liberating opportunity. Many engineers and technicians were able to express, within a still
largely company-oriented pattern of thinking, an orientation towards a particular occupation but those who graduated from university with a generalist
degree such as law or economics and who expected to go into white-collar
administrative work at a corporation were, like their elders, oriented towards

being a member of a company organization first, and working in a particular field was subordinate to that end if not completely absent.

Lifetime employment at a single organization

Turning now to the related issue of permanent employment at a single organization, we must ask the questions; what expectations do young people today have towards the implicit lifetime employment contract? What role does lifetime employment play within the system of desires and values of men working in today's large corporations?

This next employee, like nearly all respondents, expresses his expectation on joining of the company providing lifetime employment yet he feels that this expectation is no longer tenable in the long term. He believes the company is strong in the medium term but, unlike earlier generations, and probably as a result of some recent high-profile corporate bankruptcies, is not confident that the company will survive long into the future. The result is that he is anxious for his future security and feels that, rather than passively relying on the company to provide this, he should actively secure his future by developing tradeable skills as a hedge against possible company collapse. Nevertheless, he is not taking any action on this matter yet and this implies that his fears for his security may not be tremendously strong. In addition, he also hints at a feeling of self-realization about his life and work that might be similar to Csikszentmihaly's description of flow.

Q: When you joined did you want to stay until the retirement age?

A: Yes. Especially since there is no feeling of this company being weak or about to collapse.

Q: What about the work content?

A: Well, it's not a game but when I think of something and it is realized I feel the sense of happiness similar to that of winning a game. It's not just this work either, but lots of things.

Q: Do you have any fears that the company will go under?

A: Basically I do. I think it will be around for the next five years . . . but ten years or 20 years in the future? I don't know if the company will be here with me in it when I am 60 . . . 30 years from now. I have no idea and so I think it's a little dangerous.

Q: When you entered the company did you worry about that?

A: No.

Q: So, 30 years from now you feel the company may go bust. Are you doing anything about it?

A: I think I must do something but I'm not doing anything. I could do the real-estate dealer qualifications or something but I couldn't say, become a lawyer or a doctor or anything like that.

(Employee, Company A, age 30)

The next employee more clearly states his intention to take advantage of the security that lifetime employment offers but also subordinates that interest to his desire to find satisfying work to the point of forgoing security for satisfaction. Of course, this preference has not been tested in his employment as yet but it is something that he believes enough to state out loud.

Q: When you joined did you want to stay until the retirement age?

A: Well, looking from the outside I didn't really know what kind of work was involved. Before knowing that I couldn't really make that kind of a decision, but basically I thought I'd be here until the end.

Q: Was that one of your hopes for joining the company?

A: Yes, sort of. But first was whether the work gave me a sense of satisfaction. Until now the company has given me that sense of satisfaction, I think. More than a feeling a security, well I definitely have a sense of security, but if I had work that wasn't satisfying I couldn't continue it.

(Assistant Manager, Company D, age 32)

In contrast, the next employee declares that he wishes to live and work in what he perceives as a dynamic and 'fast moving' environment and thus professes to be not at all attracted to lifetime employment at a single organization. Again, perhaps he is trying to express a preference for flow over the security of a stable but somewhat static and possibly uninspiring job that comes with lifetime employment.

A: For myself, I don't have the feeling that I will stay at this company for the rest of my life and so, if I change my job then I will need strength and ability and I will have to develop it objectively for the future so that if a chance comes along then . . .

In this company what will happen probably is that I will be posted to various offices and then return to the head office and then be promoted. It is quite a narrow career and if I look at the present system then I might want to change at some time in the future.

Q: To what?

A: Well, something to do with computers or media. Not just a hardware or software maker but one that does both. Computer makers . . . are very flexible and fast moving companies and I think they are really impressive . . . I'd like to go to a company where I can have more control over my future.

(Employee, Company B, age 24)

Following on from the previous respondent, this next employee goes further to state that the culture of lifetime employment among employees themselves is changing towards a more fluid way of thinking. It is significant that respected and trusted individuals such as university professors are influencing their students in such a manner and these statements are then being confirmed through real experience. Moreover, this man expresses grave doubts about whether he could be happy in the type of working environment that he believes exists under lifetime employment. He worries about his private life and the effect on his personal relationships, yet goes on to state his desire to be a good company member by not selfishly disrupting others' work if he were to leave. Here we see an emerging conflict between desires and values being played out in the employee's mind as he grapples between what he prefers for himself as an individual and how he values his image of himself, or his self-identity, as a decent, diligent, and unselfish member of his company.

A: I feel that our generation doesn't think all the way to their retirement age. At university too a professor said that this age is not one where people will join a company and stay till their retirement. When I entered the company I felt that quite strongly about the place.

Also, when I look at my seniors and their wives and children I look at the image of my own future. The wives say that their husbands are always at work. I wonder if I could be happy taking that road . . . I don't feel the company will make me leave but . . .

Q: So, do you think seriously about your future a lot?

A: Yes. Recently . . . at first I had the image that it would be natural to work here till the retirement age and then retire but I felt very enclosed and recently I have seriously thought that when it got tough would I really work through it? But I have a strong desire to do a proper job and not to be a bother to others . . . when I think about that I don't think of leaving.

(Employee, Company C, age 25)

The next employee has clearly been influenced by spending a part of his life in the United States. Not only does he not see himself working in the same company for the rest of his working life, he also wants to work overseas and appears to prefer what he considers to be more freedom in his working life.

His opinions of his generation's preferences however conflict with the previous respondent indicating, perhaps, his desire to present himself as different from other Japanese and as an individual. On the other hand, the previous respondent, while presenting himself as different, also expresses a desire to fit in with his colleagues.

Q: When you joined did you want to stay until the retirement age?

A: No. If I have a chance I'd like to work somewhere else. I have a strong desire to leave Japan and work overseas for some time.

Q: What would you like to do?

A: I haven't any definite ideas and media-related work would be difficult so I think I'd like to give hotels a try. I don't want to work for this company all my life.

Q: Are you thinking seriously about this?

A: Yes. I am thinking seriously about it. My university friends are different . . . they want lifetime employment at one company. That way of thinking is strong. The friends I have from elementary school in America are different, they are more like me.

Q: So your experience in America was very influential?

A: Yes, very much, I think . . . It gave me the freedom to do what I want.
(Employee, Company D, age 26)

Finally on this subject, this employee shows how it is possible to have an enjoyable career within the context of lifetime employment and for him this is achieved through movement between positions. Further, he also shows how marriage and a growing family often influence employees' preferences in favour of taking advantage of the security and stability that lifetime employment offers.

Q: When you joined did you want to stay until the retirement age?

A: Yes, when I entered I had no intention of leaving. Before I entered the company I didn't really know what I would be doing. When I was placed in the regional sales office, I had no idea before that I would be posted there. But, contrary to my expectations, after I started, I found it was great fun. I was able to speak to various customers . . . Of course, change is fun and interesting isn't it?

Q: You were married recently, weren't you? Your way of thinking, has it changed?

A: It has changed a little. When I was single, speaking honestly, I thought it would be OK to leave the company if I wanted. Of course, after marriage those thoughts changed. But still there's just the two of us so, if I were to leave it wouldn't be a disaster. However, if we have children I'd really have to think hard about it wouldn't I?

(Employee, Company D, age 26)

It seems, therefore, that most employees originally joined their companies in the expectation that they would work there until the fixed retirement age. However, in the short period of time since the late 1980s the expectation of being able to work at the same company for the whole of one's working life has undergone a revision. Nearly all respondents suggested that they either may not in future be able to take advantage of lifetime employment or for one reason or another might not wish to do so. However, the gap between what people say they wish to do and what they actually do is often substantial. All of the employees in the above group had joined their employer immediately upon graduation from university and, although some expressed a desire to move, all were still at their first employer. As the last respondent shows, people may change their opinions, feelings, desires, and values through the course of their lives and, in addition, their circumstances may change so that desires become redundant or more difficult to achieve than previously.

It is also well known in Japan that employees may express a desire for change early on in their careers but will gradually accommodate themselves to their employers in the course of the period leading up to their first management position after approximately 15 years in employment. This accommodation is no doubt due to a number of factors of which personal circumstances, rising incomes, greater responsibility, and more interesting work tasks are probably the most important. Nevertheless, although we must caution against understanding present developments as a mirror of Anglo-American modern individualism, there is a steadily though gradually growing desire among employees for more fluid careers that may involve working for a number of different employers. This might be interpreted as a move in the direction of Western-style multi-company specialized career chimneys.

On the whole employees expressed a basic satisfaction with the structure and attributes of the lifetime employment system in that it provides them with security and a feeling of belonging, opportunities for personal growth and development, and even for some opportunities for a genuine feeling of self-actualization and deep enjoyment in work. The above extracts confirm that the issues of security and self-actualization may sometimes be in conflict but are not mutually contradictory and might even be mutually sustaining. Moreover, where they are in conflict employees seemed to express the possibility that they would be prepared to forgo the former for the latter and where they are not in conflict, or where the employee does not value self-actualization too highly, lifetime employment at a single organization is an attractive career choice. The attractiveness of lifetime employment must also be considered from the perspective that employees do not ever remain long in one position, and are thus required to do work that is progressively more complex and more challenging.

The following extracts attest to the variety of ways in which the lifetime employment system provides the institutional context for the long-term realization of employees' desires and values sometimes even, as is the case with the following employee, against his expectations and desires.

Q: Has your career up to now been ideal?

A: Ideal . . . well . . . I don't know. For example, . . . soon after I entered . . . I said that I really didn't want to go into land administration as I imagined it would all be dirty and complicated administrative work. Then . . . I was sent to [a regional] office . . . It's an extremely small, remote, rural place. I had written that I really didn't want to be sent there or do [that work]. So when I received my written appointment it said [that work] at [that] office. I was shocked. It was what I most didn't want to do. But I didn't know anything about it so . . . once I went there to see for myself, it was completely different. [It] has been the most interesting experience I have had. I'm that kind of person. In Japan there's the expression *kuwazugirai* meaning disliking a certain food before having tried it and then trying it and liking it. So, I had that kind of experience.

. . . Looking back, I think every workplace I have been to has been very interesting.

(Director, Company D, age 56)

The following employee found that his posting to study in the UK for a year enabled him and his wife to rediscover an appreciation for their leisure time, an opportunity he feels he may not have had if he had not joined his company.

Q: Has your career up to now been ideal?

A: Mmm . . . well . . . If you can say ideal then it is ideal. Working in legal affairs was work that I like and being fortunate to be sent to [a British] university to study, and now in sales, it is the work that I requested when I entered the company, so I am thankful that it has been ideal.

Q: What kind of influence did your time [in Britain] have?

A: Very much. It made me recognize once more the importance of quality of life. Japanese company men normally place their company and work ahead of their families but, being sent to Britain for a year while young, it taught us both how to have fun in our lives. Of course on my return I had to do overtime, but definitely, it changed my way of thinking. It's really idiotic to only work and not have fun.

(Employee, Company D, age 34)

And this employee expresses his satisfaction in the company having facilitated his starting and maintaining a fulfilling family life.

For me, as I said before, my personal life is important. It is very uncommon among Japanese businessmen, but for me my family comes first. When I graduated I accidentally found [this company] and then I found my wife. My wife worked [here] too. So, I found my wife and then had children and earned a salary to pay for my wife and children. I had various good chances and promotions too. And so I am happy at the company. Even if there are various problems at the company it is basically a good and fair company and so, therefore, so far I am happy.

(General Manager, Company C, age 48)

This employee responds that the lifetime employment system in his company gives him the opportunity both to do work that he loves and to fulfil his goal of developing himself within the corporate context.

Q: So when you joined the company you expected to stay with the company until you retired and you were happy about that?

A: Yes. That was common sense for most students at that time.
    . . . I have many friends from my university days. We have a party every six months, and every time eight or ten people come and have dinner and drink, no one yet has changed his job. I don't know if they are happy or unhappy, but for me it's great and I love to do the work at [this company]. I don't have any plans to change company.

Q: Do you feel that the future of the company is in a sense your own future too?

A: Yes.

Q: So you want to work for the company to help the company progress and as a result you will also progress with it. That is generally your feeling?

A: Yes, that's my goal.

(Group Leader, Company B, age 45)

Although this next employee expresses dissatisfaction about what he calls 'the way of working in Japan', his experience working for the company overseas and subsequent opportunity to work in the company union have enabled him to achieve some measure of success in his goal of achieving change in the company. As a result he is 'happy' in his work at the company and the union.

Q: Did you want to go overseas, then?

A: Yes that too. I didn't want to live there forever but I wanted to learn about it. I thought at that time and now that there is no option but to change the way of working in Japan and so I thought I would like to work at least once overseas and learn about it first hand. After that I would be able to help change the way of working in Japan and in the company. Three or five years would be OK . . . I just wanted to do it once. So when I found that I could do it here I was extremely happy.

Q: Are you helping to change the way of working in Japan now?

A: Well . . . I hope so. I am working at the union now and I can have some influence, I think. That makes me happy.

(Employee, Company B Labour Union, age 30)

And this employee expresses satisfaction that he is able to work towards his objectives in terms of both the content of his work and the rewards, both material and psychological, that come with it.

Q: So, what makes you satisfied?

A: I have two things. One is to do what I want to do. In my case that is to do what I am interested in . . . management or business administration. I want to increase my knowledge to have a high ability in that . . . if I can. One more thing is . . . in Japan . . . the corporation has a high performance level by international standards but . . . employees' salaries are not high compared to Europe and North America. So, I would like to increase my salary. So I want to do what I want to do and increase my salary. Put those together and that is my definition of satisfaction.

Q: Within those two things, are you satisfied?

A: Well, yes, I think. I am working hard at what I want to do and I believe I am performing well and doing a good job. I am enjoying it too. If you work hard and perform well then because you are motivated and so on, the enjoyment and the money follow. So yes, I am satisfied.

(Employee, Company A, age 28)

It is by no means the case, therefore, that lifetime employment in a single organization is not suited to the needs, desires, and values of at least some employees. It is also true that the system has the flexibility and dynamism to enable some employees to satisfy desires and values that go well beyond the need to secure their material circumstances. The system of long-term training gives these employees the opportunity to enhance their skills and abilities, discover new things about themselves, experience a variety of different activities and tasks, and fulfil a diverse range of values both within and outside the work context.

However, as the next set of interview extracts shows, there is also a feeling among many employees that the institutionalized structure and attributes of lifetime employment, although they are undergoing some modification and adjustment towards a more economically rational and fluid system, are a hindrance or a barrier to some in their efforts to achieve a realization of their desires and values.

The following employee wishes that he were able to have more control over the direction of his career and choice in the opportunities offered to him as well as greater material rewards from his work. He also expresses the feeling that the 1950s system is now old-fashioned and in need of change, hinting that it is the system of seniority pay and promotion that is constraining him from achieving what he wants from his work.

Q: Are you satisfied with the lifetime employment system?

A: Well, basically I am half satisfied. The other half says it is old-fashioned. I would like the 1950s system to disappear. Well . . . if you compare with foreign companies there is still seniority promotion and so on but . . . compared to before it is collapsing little by little. I would like it to collapse still further.

Q: Why?

A: There are various values now. For example, as I said before, if you want to do a certain job it is still difficult to progress and so on. I would like more choice in guiding my own career. Also, the salary, compared to before is not rising like it did during the bubble. I would like it to rise more now. The annual salary system would be a good thing . . . I would like the working environment to be improved too. But I think the most important thing now is the seniority promotion system.

(Deputy Manager, Company A, age 47)

The next employee says that lifetime employment has a tendency to prevent him from getting the most out of his family life. Moreover, he opines that the system may be a hindrance to corporate development and even has some negative social effects in preventing employment mobility at a time of economic difficulty and increasing fluidity in external labour markets. He believes that lifetime employment may even be on the point of disappearing as a result and hopes that the whole system might change in the near future.

Q: Are you satisfied with the lifetime employment system?

A: Well . . . lifetime employment is still to be expected at Japanese companies but if you look at the global standard then it is just Japan, I think, that has lifetime employment. I don't think those conditions will continue. I don't know about our company either. In fact, for me I don't think lifetime employment is a wonderful thing. That is to say, the company doesn't have a tendency to change. Of course, I have to work for a living and I am married and at this time my family has become more important to me than the company. So I want to spend more time with my family and the way of always working that the lifetime employment system encourages is not suited to that kind of lifestyle.

Socially too the lifetime employment system has various harmful effects, I think. Now the economy is weak and some of my relatives are searching for work . . . they can't get work in the areas that they would like to. One of the causes of that is Japanese companies' placing importance on lifetime employment and the excess of older workers in companies. That's not the whole reason but it is one reason. So from now the number of people looking for work will increase but companies are keeping their older workers and older practices . . . companies are not looking forward to the future . . . Of course the problem requires the country to provide adequate welfare for older people so that they can feel confident about leaving work. So, I'd like to see a radical reform of the whole system.

(Employee, Company A, age 30)

This next employee supports changing the salary system to one that rewards an employee's contribution rather than his length of service, perhaps hinting that he feels he has not been properly compensated while others may have been given more for less. This feeling is common among younger employees who are perhaps impatient to progress within what is perceived by some to be a slow and cumbersome system of promotion.

Q: Are you satisfied with the lifetime employment system?

A: . . . Do you understand the seniority system? In that, those who have been at the company a long time are highly evaluated, speaking in extreme cases, even if they can't do the work at all. So long as they are here, they are ranked, or evaluated highly. Even if they do nothing. That's, to begin with, a bit strange and so an ability-based system is better, where even if you are young, if you can do the work then you are evaluated highly. Until now, even if you do good work, better than those who have been here ten years, and you've been here five, then they are evaluated higher than you. That was the system. Now, they intend to change it. You should be evaluated properly and just because you have been here a long time you may not be evaluated highly.

(Employee, Company C, age 28)

This employee, a senior manager at the company, feels that he has not been able to develop the specialist skills that he wanted to acquire and that the company's system of frequent rotation of employees between posts is at fault in his case. In his opinion this has not only harmed his career and caused him personal disappointment but it has also not been of great benefit to the company either.

A: Speaking for myself, with my personality and style of work, if I had been made to do one type of work it might have benefited me and the company but, . . . on the contrary, unfortunately, my career in the company has not been that kind of a journey. In fact, I was never posted to a position that I could definitely do, only indirectly so. For example now I am in [this department] and it's my first time here.

Q: So you worked a long time in work that you didn't have much interest in?

A: More than that, there was work that I wanted to continue with but I was always being moved around.

(General Manager, Company D, age 48)

This employee has the opposite problem of perhaps not being moved enough, at least not enough to be able to develop the specialist skills that he wants to acquire.

Basically, the work I have done is not the work that I had hoped and asked for. I asked to be moved but I haven't been.

Also, I am not learning any special skills. There are no special skills needed for this type of work. So, as far as that is concerned I feel that my career is not really developing.

(Employee, Company D, age 30)

The above extracts return us nicely to the notion of self-actualization and Csikszentmihaly's idea of flow. While the statements reveal to us the very real joys, satisfactions, frustrations, and disappointments that employees encounter, and endure during the course of their working lives, they do not tell us in enough depth whether they are experiencing deep fulfilment and enjoyment in the content and contexts of their work. The following extracts explore these issues in more depth.

For the following employee, fulfilment in his work comes from enjoying and being absorbed in his work and private life and, importantly, his feelings of success in his life hinge on being able to experience such enjoyment. He believes that working at the company is enabling him to achieve such a feeling.

> *A:* For me it is my sense of fulfilment, I think. In my work and private life it is my sense of satisfaction. If that disappears then I will feel I have failed in my life.

> *Q:* Concretely what do you mean?

> *A:* Enjoying my work and private life. Giving something to society and giving to my family.

> *Q:* Do you feel satisfied now?

> *A:* Yes. Maybe you would call me a company man because I stay here till late at night but I enjoy it. The work is very interesting and I can become absorbed in it.
>
> (Manager, Company D, age 41)

Like the above employee, for this man feelings of fulfilment come from both his work and non-work life and he also has a clear and well-articulated idea of how he can achieve satisfaction by realizing his thoughts through his work tasks. In addition, he clearly feels that material security and comfort are vital to this endeavour. But, nevertheless, he does not feel fully satisfied in either his work or with his lifestyle.

> If I had to choose then I would have a reasonable lifestyle and be able to realize my thoughts through my work. To some extent I can do that. I can say it is half and half. My salary is quite good and my work is quite interesting . . . I have a lot of responsibility and so on . . . but neither are one hundred per cent.
>
> (General Manager, Company D, age 50)

In common with many engineers and technologists who are promoted into management or asked to perform white-collar work the following statement attests to a feeling of not being challenged by the work tasks and, thus, feeling a sense of boredom and lack of adventure which leads to frustration. Interestingly, this man's statement shows how security can be a foundation for satisfaction but that once it is achieved, other desires become the focus of one's attention which, curiously, may be contrary to the need to feel secure.

> *A:* I thought a feeling of security was important, and of course it is comfortable here. But it is also boring and so a more adventurous feeling,

if possible, would be a good thing for me. I wanted a feeling of security but, I also wanted to do certain things that I am not able to achieve.

Q: Like what?

A: I wanted to achieve something in my work. I wanted to enjoy it too but it has been boring recently . . . I used to work in engineering and that was very stimulating but I have been doing the same office work for some time now and I cannot develop my abilities in this job.

(Manager, Company D, age 47)

Work can also be frustrating to the point of driving employees to express themselves in quite extreme terms, as in the following interview extract. This employee feels that, contrary to his expectations, white-collar work is now no different from working in a repetitive job on a production line, with all the feelings of boredom and lack of self-esteem that that kind of work might entail. He is very critical of managerial work and sees it more as an exercise in enhancing employee security rather than developing the company's business activities. In this way, like the previous employee but in a more extreme manner, he is expressing a desire for risk and adventure.

We white-collar workers are now the blue-collar workers. We must work to a manual and we cannot differ from the bureaucratic rules . . . we are not allowed to use our abilities. In Japan the manager's most important task is to hedge risk and not to take it. This means lots of meetings and shared responsibility which becomes another form of employment security.

. . . Our job has lost much of its meaning now . . . we cannot take decisions and enjoy the adventure of working in a dynamic company.

(Manager, Company C, age 38)

This next employee explains clearly and simply a common refrain among salarymen and that is the value of conformity to social norms, of not appearing too distinctive and working closely and cooperatively with one's colleagues in order to progress. For employees intent on promotion there is a difficult balancing act to be negotiated. To be promoted more quickly than one's peers it is important to be noticed but, conversely, in order to get on one must not disrupt the working atmosphere and personal relations within work groups by being too noticeable or by progressing too quickly. Many times employees spoke about this atmosphere being quite different from their impression of the typical American company that, in their opinion, rewards distinctiveness and individuality above conformity and teamwork. Moreover, for this employee, such a mode of work, while being an artifice at one level of consciousness, also provides a feeling of fulfilment for the employee.

A: We don't have an idea of the 'American Dream' in Japan. It is much better for us to live like everyone else and not to be so unusual. If you are unusual you will not be able to be a part of the group and that means your life in the company will be uncomfortable. More than enjoying your work it is important to cooperate with others and work together for the company. If you can do that and enjoy it then you can get self-actualization working for a Japanese company, I think.

Q: Can [you] do it?

A: Yes. I think so. Maybe you should ask my colleagues about whether I can. I feel satisfaction that we can produce good products together.

(Manager, Company D, age 40)

Caught between two modernities

The interview extracts presented above are intended to demonstrate in employees' own words that their situation in Japan's corporations is a complex and subtle one which relies on a nuanced combination of each individual's experiences and circumstances as well as his personal system of needs, desires, and values and that these aspects of their lives are inextricably enmeshed together. In this way David Plath's (1983 and 1989) sensitive discussions and analyses of the employment and life-consciousness of Japanese people are interesting because, rare among researchers of Japanese society, he uses life-course analysis to ask the important question of whether self-realization is a situational response to external conditions and the public discourse of social life or whether it is an internally generated autonomous unfolding of the self.

Quantitative survey data alone cannot inform us about this issue. For the results of such research efforts often tell us more about the standpoint and objectives of the researcher rather than those of the researched. More importantly, in an effort to discover how individuals feel, think, and behave, these approaches, regardless of the substantive nature of people's previous experiences and present circumstances, can lead to a shutting out of the richly textured contexts and understandings that constitute people's lives as they are lived. Consequently, and all too often, they fail to alert us to the multiple and layered understandings that people possess regarding the complex nexus between self, family, institution, and society that unavoidably must inform the route that an individual follows from needs, desires, and values through to decisions and, thence, actions.

Plath theorized that Japanese society has very recently encountered a series of radical shocks to received common understandings of the life-cycle, the most important of these being mass and extreme longevity and the introduction and development of modern capitalism. In other words, people are having to learn to cope with and adjust to the demands of a very long life in a society that has hitherto relied on custom, social relationships, and inter-subjective understandings for expressing and substantiating its values. They are now having to reconcile this in concert with a high-technology economy and the rhythms of production and consumption that are contained therein.

As Plath perceptively notes, the life-course approach places an emphasis on the self as the agent of its own development and is, by its very nature, there-fore a critique of the conventional view of a subsumed and context dependent Japaneseness. Borrowing from Julius Roth's (1963) groundbreaking research, in Plath's description timing is essential to self-realization in the Japanese context. The interaction of, and balance between, interdependent people's timetables are essential to the realization of the self-conscious and self-directed individual's life, career goals, and values. He concludes with a sensitive and perceptive contrast between a particle model of human develop-ment dominant in the West, that places the lone individual at the centre of an atomized universe composed of competing and colliding individuals, and the Japanese view where the locus of personal development and realization is not solely in autonomous and self-interested individuals but in the circle of human relationships, ideologies, and material circumstances within which each individual is actively and willingly, yet also unavoidably, enmeshed. Importantly, also, as a consequence of his method of research and analysis, Plath criticizes structuralist interpretations of Japanese social life as being inadequate to describe the way an individual is not so much compromising his own self-actualization by accepting and acting upon the claims of others but may well indeed be increasing the range and quality of the self and its realiza-tion through combining the realization of his own objectives and values with a socialized moderation and enhancement of his individual singularity.

As the responses presented above demonstrate, many Japanese employees undoubtedly possess a deep appreciation of their roles and obligations within the complex web of relationships that constitute their lives. Moreover, they are also acutely concerned about fulfilling these roles and relationships, not so much out of a reluctant sense of duty, but because these aspects of their lives are valued for their potential to enhance social life in an integrated and synergistic manner. That is to say, for many the total outcome for the individ-ual and the rest of society that accrues from the fulfilment of social obligations transcends the personal consequences that might result from the limitations and restrictions placed in their way by external exigency. Many of the employees above, both young and old, understand this idea implicitly and completely and thus *individual* self-actualization, in the sense of flow, or 'optimal experience', has hitherto not been the most important part of the Japanese value system. For these employees self-actualization includes, perhaps even is dominated by, interpersonal relations within a collective sin-gularity[16] because Japanese people cultivate these and value them in an ethical or moral sense. In this sense, self-actualization is impossible without the relational dimension.[17] While the individual experience of flow outside the relational context is undoubtedly something that many employees seek (and they may be disappointed if they do not achieve it), it is but one part of their system of needs and desires. It is not valued in the moral sense in the same way that it is valued within the relational context. Thus lifetime membership of the corporate community, although it may not result in the most individually fulfilling life, and may be somewhat of a disappointment if that is the case, is valued primarily for the relational synergies and opportunities that are unleashed by such a system.

Nevertheless the demands of modern capitalism are complex, powerful, internally contradictory, and thus inherently unstable. Hyper-development, modern consumer culture, the discourse of individual self-actualization that now pervades our consciousness, and the globalization of liberal democratic market capitalism are challenging the integrity of the Japanese self and its compatibility with the post-war system of bureaucratic organization. More than simply demanding the establishment of a flexible global standard for employment and management systems, economic globalization, and the achievement of affluence are challenging the Japanese system of needs, desires, and values and causing it to undergo a shift towards something that more closely resembles the Western-style achievement of individual self-actualization that at times contradicts and supersedes the relational dimension.

What is becoming clear is that a new consciousness is emerging in Japan and it represents a rupture with the past. It is the slow and gradual appearance of an autonomous and perhaps even atomistic liminal reflexive consciousness that seeks to construct a new institutional structure that creates the circumstances necessary for the living out of an individual reflexive project of the self. Thus, the days of institutionalized lifetime employment at a single organization as the only normative employment paradigm for Japanese men appear to be numbered, for this reason as well as others. Management itself is partly responsible for this unfolding as it seeks to fabricate a new modern consciousness of individual responsibility and motivation among employees as well as institute a more flexible and, consequently, more insecure employment structure.

The interview extracts above do not present us with a particularly inspiring or uplifting picture of personal achievement or happiness. Japanese company men for the most part are, at present, having great difficulty trying to live out their lives as dutiful salarymen and family members as well as meeting the demands of the new modernity. Most continue to suffer the consequences of living on the edge of rigidity and stability on the one hand and flexibility and insecurity on the other. No doubt many salarymen dutifully proferred a modest front to me, the researcher, as is demanded by Japanese behavioural aesthetics, but more than that, although most were possessed of a keen and intelligent reflexive individualistic rationalism and understood the emerging and developing context of their working lives, they also remain committed to the normative demands of the corporation as a context for the realization of their relational selves. Consequently they appear to exist in a social-psychological no man's land between the somewhat ponderous, pedestrian, and closed transitional modernity of the post-war corporation and a dynamic open-ended global hybrid modernity that is beginning to take shape around and within them.

6 Conclusion

Japanese capitalism and modernity in a global era

In recent years research into socio-economic development, globalization, and convergence has become more sophisticated as it has taken greater account of the possibility of differing levels and directions of analysis within the same study. And yet, curiously, there is now probably more disagreement on the issue than ever.

As an example of this research Darbyshire and Katz, in their examination of employment systems in the automotive and telecommunications industries of seven different countries including Japan, found four cross-national patterns of employment. Yet, within this pattern of apparent convergence, they found that there is increasing diversity of employment systems within countries and that this is due to a differential implementation of policies at both the plant and even individual levels which is itself due in part to declining union influence over the setting of employment standards (Darbyshire and Katz, 2000: 263–83).

A year earlier Whitley considered the conditions necessary for capitalisms to change their characteristics and perhaps converge and listed them as the growing internationalization of firms and markets, changes in national political and economic arrangements, and geopolitical shifts (Whitley, 1999: 183). Approaching the problem from the perspective of the international political economy of business he looked at, among other things, the Japanese employment system and theorized that:

> For leading Japanese *kaisha*, for example, to change the labour management practices significantly they would have to develop new ways of recruiting, rewarding, training, promoting, and organizing their core employees . . . While this is possible, it is extremely improbable without major changes in state policies, family structures, and the education and training system, as well as in inter-firm relationships and, probably, firms' boundaries.

> (ibid.: 186)

Whitley starts his book with his conclusion by predicting that, 'Convergence to a single most effective type of market economy is no more likely in the twenty-first century than it was in the highly internationalized economy of the late nineteenth century' (ibid.: 3). While this type of prediction is difficult to refute, principally because there is no way of telling either way how the institutional arrangements of world capitalism will present themselves 100 years from now (if indeed capitalism will exist at all), in keeping with Whitley's long-wave prediction, there is little doubt in my mind that the institutions of Japan's, Britain's, and the United States's social and political economies are, generally speaking, more similar today than they were in 1853 when Commodore Perry sailed his Black Ships into what is now called Tokyo Bay. Therefore one must conclude that in the intervening period there has been a degree of convergence. This convergence can be seen in all manner of structures, processes, and ways of life from the structure of politics and government, through the institutional arrangements of the economy and systems of social stratification, down to the structure of the family and even the micro-behaviours that constitute individual people's daily lives.

However, it is also undoubtedly true that from time to time cross- and counter-currents have emerged that have challenged and even rolled back this process or created entirely new social arrangements. For example, in the arena of business and production organization, it can be said that the Japanese have developed some genuinely innovative systems with the result that there has been some Japanization of British and American systems in recent years.

Nevertheless, the general, but not exclusive, direction of convergence has been in the direction of the West. This is due in no small part to a self-conscious and successful adoption and adaptation by the Japanese themselves of selected Western institutions, technologies, and systems of thought. These include, for example, representative political institutions, a largely meritocratic educational system based on the principles of secular and reflexive rationalism, and, in business, the early application of Scientific Management in pursuit of mass production in manufacturing (Tsutsui, 1998). Furthermore, we can extend a similar argument to virtually any region of the world. The causes of this worldwide long-wave convergence have been the expansion of European and then American forms of capitalist modernity via the processes of imperialism and its latter-day cousin economic globalization.

This is not to say that Japan and the West are identical. Such a claim would be absurd. This is not to say, either, that the process will continue indefinitely into the future until they do become identical. There will probably soon be a time when the process ceases and perhaps even begins to move in the opposite direction. This may happen, for example, when and if the contemporary form of the nation state is replaced by a different form of political and legal economy that allows for a greater amount of self-determination at the provincial and even community level rather than at the supra-national level as is occurring at present. Or it may happen when and if China and India mount a serious challenge to US hegemony.

Moreover, what is also important to an understanding of social life, in addition to attempting to understand what is actually happening in people's lives, is an understanding of what people think is happening in their lives and how they feel about it. Consequently, in this sense, there is little doubt that the Japanese people think and feel that their cultures, institutions, and organizations are becoming more like those of the West more than do Western people think that their cultures, institutions, and organizations are becoming more like those of Japan. Thus, at this level, there is at least a perception of convergence by Japan upon the West. Much of this perception might be put down to confusion over its causes, whether they be industrialization and the achievement of affluence or any Westernization that is a result of economic or cultural globalization. But we cannot condemn such thoughts and feelings among the people of Japan and the West to pure confusion and ignorance and claim clarity of thought for ourselves as scholars. And there is no doubt in my mind therefore, having lived and worked in Japan for more than eight years and having gone through the process of researching and writing this book, that a large measure of this convergence is not simply public misperception or a consequence of the achievement of affluence, but that some kind of Westernization is really happening and has been happening for quite some time now. Japanese capitalist modernity is indeed converging on Western forms of social and economic life. The causes of this are extremely complex and, as previously discussed, lie as much in the path to development that the Japanese chose for themselves as they do in the expansion of Western capitalism and modernity into Japan.

If we accept that social life at its most foundational level is embedded in systems of belief and how people perceive themselves and their circumstances, then perhaps the most powerful determinant of the likelihood of, for example, systems of business organization to converge on or diverge from one another is culture. As much as business systems are rooted in the institutional arrangements of the political economy, individual actors working within them will bring to and develop therefrom different understandings of those systems depending on their background and the cultural and social milieu in which they live. In turn this will in part determine actors' propensity to promote, comply and collude with, capitulate to, or resist change and, thereby, influence the possibility of convergence. However, culture itself is a dynamic process that is inseparable from, and deeply affected by, other arenas of social life (Inghilleri, 1999). It is a state that is achieved by actors through the daily construction and reconstruction of common understandings and customs, via a process of inter-subjective negotiation. Moreover, culture itself will be influenced in some way by the institutional structures and processes that business organizations bring to bear on their members and stakeholders. Thus, if the values that managers and employees bring to the circumstances of the work, for whatever reason, develop in new directions, so might the institutional bases of the work organization. And, in turn, if the institutional bases of the work organization change then so might the foundations of culture.

In keeping with these discussions, Rowley and Benson analysed the human resource management systems of four Asian countries, including Japan, at the three levels of system architecture (guiding principles and basic assumptions), policy alternatives (appropriate fit between policies and architecture), and practice process (implementation and techniques) (Rowley and Benson, 2002: 98). What is significant about this research is that it rests on the premise that, to be successful, the practical implementation of policy must in some way be embedded and accepted within the deep structure of basic assumptions and beliefs. In other words, culture matters. More significantly, their research shows little evidence of any change in Japan at the level of system architecture but some change in Thailand and South Korea as a result of the shocks experienced during and after the 1997–8 Asian financial crisis. Consequently, in their discussion, Rowley and Benson conclude that there is little prospect for convergence by Japan due to gradual or evolutionary change, though some prospect for convergence if there is a revolutionary change that causes a reconsideration by employees and management of the deep structure of the human resources management system.

Kuruvilla and Erickson also present an analysis of changes in Asian industrial relations systems and suggest that these changes are similar to those undergone by Western countries. They conclude that there are two types of change to Asian systems and these are in response both to an increase in external competitive pressures and to changes in the priorities of management away from focusing on stability and peace towards increasing numerical and functional flexibility. They identify systems that have smoothly adapted to change and those that have fundamentally transformed themselves. Investigating Japan, they found the 1990s showed an 'acceleration of changes already under way, as well as changes in other practices that constitute the core of the system' (Kuruvilla and Erickson, 2002: 182). Of the changes already under way they identify a change in managerial strategy as being among the most significant (ibid.: 213). The cause of these changes has been in large part the recession of the 1990s. Nevertheless, they imply that although this acceleration of changes may be the beginnings of a radical and discontinuous transformation in the future this has not yet happened. Interestingly they conclude by stating that competitive pressures are 'pushing IR [industrial relations] arrangements in Asia in the same direction as it has in the West, which suggests the possibility of convergence' (ibid.: 222).

Review and conclusions

In this book I have examined Japanese capitalist modernity along two dimensions of analysis. The first proceeds from theoretical argumentation through methodological depth to empirical data collection. The second runs from analysis at the level of the individual through the organizational setting to the contexts of national systems of institutional arrangements and the historical development of the wider socio-economy. There are, to my knowledge, no recent studies of the Japanese lifetime employment system that observe the cultural underpinnings and structural components of the system from the point of view of both management and employee and set these empirical observations in the context of discussions regarding the development of Japan's capitalism and modernity.

It is my belief that it is only through this type of analysis that the academic discipline of area studies, in this case Japanese studies, comes into its own as an important contributor to social science and, ultimately, our understanding of the world in which we live. Disciplinary studies such as sociology or economics, while they undoubtedly produce works of great explanatory power, occasionally fail adequately to come to grips with, and therefore explain, the nuanced and culturally-based understandings that actors bring to their circumstances, especially when those understandings and circumstances are located in societies that are outside the mainstream of Western civilization. Conversely, area studies on occasion has the tendency to work under the premise that beliefs and behaviours are necessarily particular to a group of people when it might be more appropriate to view them as being derived from living under a set of socio-economic or political conditions, in this case capitalist modernity, that cross over the boundaries of culture. Undoubtedly, social life is a combination of both particular and universal, or human, causes and consequences and this understanding has led me to conduct this study in order that the assumptions of both sociology and Japanese studies might be equally represented.

I began this book by presenting a rationale for researching capitalist modernity in Japan through an empirical investigation of the lifetime employment system in large corporations. Although this is rather a narrow study from which to be extrapolating conclusions as to Japan's development, as the chapter argues, the lifetime employment system lies at the centre of the crossroads between Japanese contemporary culture and its capitalism and modernity and between the individual, the organization, and society.

I then developed this theme by examining some of the principal academic literature on capitalist modernity and socio-economic convergence. It is worth saying here that there is an enormous body of literature on these topics and, therefore, in examining it I have used literature that is predominantly sociological and Western in origin, or at least takes a Western perspective to the issues that this book deals with. This is not so much to cast Japan in an inappropriately Western framework, nor is it an attempt to ignore other perspectives on modernity but, through studying Japan in these terms, I hope to be able to make the universalist leanings of some Western sociology more sympathetic to and inclusive of the Japanese and thereby non-Western experience. These discussions bring together both theoretical and empirical research on social life under Western capitalist modernity and how it is related to a particular way of living in and looking at the world; what Giddens (1990) refers to as a 'reflexive project of the self'. However, I also stress that life under capitalist modernity in Japan may possess different qualities precisely because Japan and Japanese social life have developed under different historical circumstances and out of a different cultural milieu. In addition, I feel it is important to note that this book is but a snap-shot of a rather narrow and particular aspect of Japanese socio-economic life and, while I try to extrapolate my conclusions beyond the confines of the lifetime employment system in large Japanese corporations, I do not wish to make a claim to a definitive description and analysis of Japanese social life in the early twenty-first century.

The middle three chapters of this book concentrate more closely on the lifetime employment system itself. Chapter three presents the idea that the post-war Japanese corporation occupied an intermediate or transitional stage in the development of capitalist modernity in Japan in that the fabricated cultures of managerial familism and then welfare paternalism served to entrench and reinforce a semi-ascriptive way of life for the salaryman within the structure of lifetime employment. Salarymen themselves appear to have been more or less content to live somewhat passively and uncritically within these circumstances because they afforded the material security and stability of permanent employment that they needed and desired. The recollections by managers of working in their companies at that time are necessarily going to be retrospective rationalizations of their thoughts and behaviours, however they do correspond well with the academic research from the same period.

The next chapter presents data on the structure of the contemporary lifetime employment system and then goes on to examine it from the perspective of management. In it I put forward the thesis that, although the frame of lifetime employment remains largely in place, there are modifications occurring in a gradual fashion to its dependent attributes. Moreover, it appears that management is embarking on a process of attempting to re-fabricate the culture of lifetime employment towards a more fluid and market-based system that is, at least in the eyes of management, more congruent with an external environment characterized by globalization and liberalization.

Chapter five then examines lifetime employment from the perspective of the contemporary Japanese salaryman. Like the previous chapter it first discusses secondary quantitative data and then goes on to present primary research findings. I argue that there is pressure for reform coming from inside the corporation as salarymen themselves are also questioning the cultural and structural bases of the employment system. However, as the chapter also shows, it is by no means a foregone conclusion that they wish Japanese forms of employment to converge on Western models. Many salarymen maintain a deep affection for the lifetime employment system, the security and stability that it brings, the relationships it generates, and the possibilities for self-development and self-actualization within the corporate career pattern that it affords. Moreover, while recognizing the present global ascendancy of the American economic system, they retain a certain pride in the Japanese exceptionalism that it signals to themselves and others both inside and outside Japan. Nevertheless, the contemporary Japanese salaryman has grown up under different circumstances to the early post-war generations. They have grown up within a materially affluent and secure society and have come to take these things somewhat for granted. Contemporary society offers young people a much greater variety of opportunities and places fewer normative expectations upon them so that they are required to make choices about their lives and reflexively construct their future biographies in a manner that was neither possible nor expected in earlier decades. Consequently, while there is pressure for change coming from within Japanese society and within the Japanese corporation, taken together the motivations underlying such pressure are not so clear and unambiguous as to suggest a desire for an easy convergence on Western-style employment systems, labour markets, and patterns of social and cultural thoughts and behaviours.

In all three of the middle chapters I presented extensive extracts from my research interviews with Japanese salarymen and corporate managers. This was done in order to present their thoughts and feelings as much as is reasonably possible in their own words and so that readers might be able to judge for themselves more clearly the validity of my analysis and conclusions. While it is impossible really to know how much these men presented me with their real thoughts and feelings or a rationalized interpretation of what they thought I wanted to hear, I feel that what they communicated to me was, in general, not only a good representation of their circumstances but a good indication of a gradually individualizing and increasingly reflexive approach to their work and their lives. This in itself is indicative of a move towards Western forms of social life.

Whitley is entirely correct when he states that there are many obstacles to a complete realignment of the institutional arrangements of Japanese capitalism along Western lines (Whitley, 1999: 186). There are tremendously powerful inertial effects present within the educational and legal systems to name but two of these obstacles. However, these are only obstacles to the extent that the Japanese people wish them to be. Indeed, reform to both the educational (Hood, 2001) and legal (Araki, 2002) systems is taking place, though of an incremental and gradual rather than revolutionary nature. The fact that reform has only proceeded in this manner indicates to me that there is support for it but it is weak and ambiguous. For example, there is resistance to reform along Western, or global, standards partly because the Japanese people adhere to beliefs and customs that they value in and of themselves. In general, they feel an emotional attachment to institutions and practices such as the lifetime employment system partly because these are Japanese and contribute to Japanese people's sense of identity and partly because they contribute to a way of life that most Japanese people continue to prefer to live by. Of course Japanese people feel that their society produces many injustices and inequities, however that does not mean that they wish to adopt Western solutions to their problems. In fact, and in general, the reverse is true. I have a strong sense that most Japanese feel that by adopting Western solutions they would lose much of what they value in social life and incur substantially more pain and difficulty than they regard as strictly necessary. Thus they seek Japanese solutions to, among other things, the present extended period of economic stagnation.

However, there is undoubtedly pressure from both within and outside the corporation to adapt to the forces of globalization and for some this means reluctantly adopting, or at least modifying, some global standards of corporate organization. As this research shows, this is not so much a positive or optimistic but mostly a reluctant adoption and adaptation. In a manner similar to the Meiji period reformers who adopted Western-style technical modernization as a policy designed to strengthen Japan in order to resist spiritual Westernization, today's Japanese managers on the whole wish primarily to preserve the organization for the benefit of all its stakeholders in order to maintain the strength and durability of the Japanese competitive challenge. However, their feeling is that this is becoming progressively more difficult to achieve as the post-war system and the consensus on which it was built come under the twin pressures of economic globalization and the consequences of the achievement of material affluence.

Just like managers, salarymen are also caught between a system to which they feel a great deal of emotional attachment and a sometimes impatient desire to make experiments in their lives in order to achieve what they believe may result in a greater degree of personal happiness and self-fulfilment. However, as this research shows, many feel that to actually go through with these dreams and desires itself has wider consequences that pose a threat to the integrity of the Japanese system; and so they banish what they consider to be selfish thoughts from their minds and commit themselves to lifetime employment and the organization. Others, however, genuinely feel let down by a system that threatens to unravel a lifetime of expectations and yet feel powerless to defend what appears to them to be a lost cause. Still others embrace the emerging consciousness and work to gain personal benefit from it.

In the opinion of many Japanese managers and salarymen, there has already been a good deal of convergence on Western forms of corporate organization, though this may not be so apparent if one studies only visible or empirically measurable systemic developments. While there have undoubtedly been some structural modifications resulting in the increasing importance of external employment mechanisms and an increased marketization of systems, as this research shows, most of this change has occurred only at the margins of the system. However, by studying the cultural foundations of the system and the values and attitudes that Japanese participants bring to lifetime employment, it is possible to detect some significant changes that have already taken place in the value orientations of both management and employees and other developments that have the potential to herald more substantive structural change at the core of the system. Because these changes are in many respects unwelcome developments it is impossible to know how they may play themselves out in the future, though I suspect there will be increasing resistance by the Japanese to convergence on Western forms of capitalist modernity for some time to come and that the Japanese will maintain a sense of justifiable pride in a system that, partly because of its exceptionalism, retains many competitive advantages.

Moreover, what some may regard as merely tinkering at the margins and as minor changes of emphasis, may appear to Japanese participants who have worked within the system on a daily basis for many years as substantive enough to signify a dramatic transformation. Our propensity to opt for either modification or transformation as words to describe the development of a social phenomenon may depend more on our own temporal, emotional, and aesthetic frames of reference than they do on the actual data that we unearth. For is it not the case that, when examining change, perception is nearly all, especially when one group prioritizes a different set of criteria from which to understand a set of phenomena? Those Western social scientists who work under the short-term, rationalist, and goal-oriented assumptions and premises of political economy and business studies and who therefore adopt positivist research programmes that examine formal structures may detect little or no shift in the institutional arrangements of Japanese capitalism over the past decade or so. However, those Japanese people who work and live within an organizational culture that emphasizes a long-term process-oriented attention to aesthetic form as well as relational and emotional depth may perceive current developments as being a wrenching and potentially disastrous transformation when compared to the aesthetic and emotional composition of the 1950s and 1960s Japanese firm.

And under these circumstances does it really matter so much where the truth actually lies? For does not perception decide for us how we understand what we see? Are not Western social scientists and their non-Western research subjects therefore at times talking past, instead of with, one another? Thus, rather than impose our truth onto others who have no wish to see things as we do, is it not more important to try to understand how others perceive their truth in their own words and in terms of their own values and assumptions? In this way not only will we grope towards a more authentic representation of social life worldwide but we may also learn to live with each other with greater tolerance, understanding, and appreciation.

Notes

Preface

1 Out of respect for the self-identity of informants, throughout names have been printed in the order in which they have been presented to me. That is to say, if individuals have introduced themselves to me with their given names before their family names I will mention them in the text in that order. This principle also goes for written material. Thus, Francis Fukuyama is presented in the English fashion and Tominaga Ken'ichi in the Japanese.

1 Introduction: researching Japanese capitalism and modernity

1 The terms the 'West' and 'Western' are highly problematic, as are 'Asia' and 'Asian'. By the 'West' or 'Western' I mean, in a general sense, Western Europe and North America. However, although Western countries and cultures such as Spain and Ireland without doubt possess unique characters of their own which give colour to what might very loosely be called Western culture, the principal countries involved in the outward expansion of industrial capitalism and capitalist modernity have been the United States and Britain. Thus, when I talk about the West and Western in this context I mean what might be called the Anglo-American system, or model, of political and social economy.

2 A formal definition for work is difficult, and by its very nature may differ from person to person. Unpaid domestic labour may be called work, as can unpaid academic study at school and university, creative and performance art, entrepreneurial enterprise, or virtually any activities, including criminal acts, that have an instrumental purpose. That is to say, work activities can be valued in themselves or for their psychological benefits, but for an activity to be considered 'work' there must always be, in addition to any other purposes, an extrinsic or instrumental aim or motivation for its performance (Brown, 1999: 919–21).

3 While many researchers (for example Florida and Kenney, 1991) assume that employees in small and medium-sized enterprises are necessarily exempt from inclusion, Araki (2002: 19) claims that as much as 87 per cent of the workforce are 'permanent workers with indefinite period contracts'.

4 Both these two *manga* series have, as their main protagonists, young and handsome salarymen who battle ceaselessly and selflessly for the benefit of their companies against the pernicious influences of self-centred adversaries from both within and outside the organization. Both characters regularly encounter systemic frustrations in the course of their battles but, after enormous struggle, are able to overcome the seemingly insuperable obstacles they encounter. Of course, both characters are also devastatingly attractive to women. See Motomiya, *Sararīman Kintarō* (n.d.), and Hirokane, *Kachō Shima Kōsaku* and *Buchō Shima Kōsaku* (n.d.).

5   These details are taken from a video recording of a 1997 Fuji Television special documentary news item about the history of the salaryman. I was shown the video in a Japanese language class at the Japan Foundation Language Center, Kansai, in the summer of 1998. However, after much effort I have been unable to gain a bibliographical reference. I also tried, unsuccessfully, to gain a reference directly from Fuji Television.

Kinmonth (1981) places the origins of the term at around the same time but sees the salaryman's origins in the low-level government employees colloquially termed at the time *koshiben* because they carried lunch-boxes tied around their waists, and the newer *gekkyū-tori* of private industry, so termed because they received a monthly salary.

6   Fully recognizing the fundamental importance of women in the workplace, this aspect of Japanese modernity does not lie within the parameters of my research. While understanding the limitations this places on the generalizability and validity of my findings, in keeping with Gilligan's (1996 [1982]) and others' work on the differences between men's and women's world-view as well as women's and men's experience of modernity (Sayer, 1991), I prefer to leave an analysis and description of women's role in Japan's development to other more qualified researchers.

7   Please refer to Table 4.1 (page 87) for a schematic representation of each company and its competitive position.

8   In the interests of preserving the anonymity of respondents I have decided not to reveal the names of any of the four companies whose data is used in this research project.

9   These periods were chosen because they represent the height of the post-war period of rapid economic growth (late 1960s), the period of instability of the mid-1970s, and the period with which my research is primarily concerned (late 1990s to early 2000s).

10 *Nikkeiren* has now merged with *Keidanren* to form *Nihon Keidanren.*

2 Japanese capitalism and modernity in theoretical perspective

1   For example, modernity has been for much of its history a masculine condition and a masculine consciousness. Moreover, different industrial classes have different experiences of modernity, especially when we incorporate the capitalist process within it. Thus we must be mindful of differences of understanding and experience both between societies and between sections of a society when we make judgements across time and space as to the generalizability and applicability of theories of capitalist modernity as a social condition.

2   David Williams (1996) goes further to claim that the Japanese challenge to Western social scientific epistemology is so powerful that it represents, in Kuhnian terms, 'revolutionary science' as opposed to the 'normal science' of social scientific studies of Western countries.

3   After the American functionalist sociologist Talcott Parsons. In, among other works, *Toward a General Theory of Social Action* (1951) he argues that in order to maintain social order people must perform four functions. They are adaptation (economy), goal-attainment (polity), integration and pattern-maintenance (society), and tension-management (culture).

4   R. H. Tawney's distinguished work, *Religion and the Rise of Capitalism* (1975 [1922]), describes in eloquent detail the economic developments in England and elsewhere in Europe that prepared the ideological ground for the transformations of the Renaissance and Reformation. The introduction of market principles into trade, the development of sophisticated financial instruments, the increasing acceptance of the merchant's profit as well as that of the money-lender, the taming of large areas of previously waste agricultural land, and so on. Basically, Tawney's

thesis is not a direct repudiation of Weber's work but he opts for a more nuanced understanding of the way developments in the late Middle Ages prepared the way for the Renaissance and Reformation.

5 See Maslow (1987 [1954]).

3 Lifetime employment in post-war Japan

1 Kinmonth (1981) points out that long-term continuous employment was a characteristic of large Japanese enterprises and governmental institutions as early as the Meiji period, however, by the Taisho and early Showa years there was a surplus of graduates from private universities trained in what he translates from a 1928 *Asahi Shimbun* article as the 'flunky learning' of subjects such as law or economics. Although larger enterprises were moving in the direction of long-term employment of élite white-collar graduates during this period, as Kinmonth concedes, there was endemic insecurity for white-collar graduates of private universities as well as a tendency among major employers such as Mitsui and Mitsubishi to take advantage of this by enforcing compliance and conformity to corporate values through the ever-present threat of being laid off.

2 See, for example, Lincoln and Kalleberg (1991).

3 President, Company C, in-house magazine, May 1967: 2.

4 This feeling was confirmed on reading the 1968 entrance ceremony speech of the Company A (optical and electronic products) President's speech. Again, he stressed the nature of working as a thoughtful, creative, productive, and cooperative person because all aspects of the company's activities rely on interdependent cooperation between employees as well as with other companies and the development of long-term relationships between employees.

5 See Imada and Hirata (1995) for a more in-depth analysis and description of this structure.

6 Those who left the corporation early very often did so not for reasons of moving to a similar position at another company for higher rewards, as is often the case in the United States and United Kingdom, but in order to start their own business, take over a family business, or look after ageing parents. Even under the high growth regime of the 1960s this movement of personnel out of the corporation served to facilitate the pyramidal structure of promotion by naturally shrinking the size of the cohort without management resorting to reduction measures.

7 With nearly all corporations operating a similar system of acquiring a broad range of skills through learning by doing, an effective and fluid external labour market, one that is based upon the trading of specific labour capabilities for a mutually understood market price, became practically impossible for white-collar university graduate males. A secondary labour market of this type has operated in Japan for virtually the whole of the post-war period but this has for the most part been confined to blue-collar work in small and medium-sized enterprises. Consequently, the economic sociology of Japan has repeatedly stressed a basic dualism between primary and secondary markets and systems.

8 In the course of my field-work and in discussions with Japanese from all walks of life this was explained to me on many occasions.

9 On a visit to a Japanese electronics company in South Wales in 1997, the Japanese company president explained to me that he found great difficulty in trying to persuade British white-collar employees to adapt to Japanese job-rotation systems. In fact, he had given up trying. He claimed that British employees look for a job that is defined by its content, for example marketing, accounts, personnel, and so on, and they try to develop professional expertise in that field in order to increase their attractiveness in terms of a fluid external labour market. He explained that, by contrast, he found Japanese white-collar employees much easier to manage because

they identified first and foremost with the company and, as such, did not object to being moved to positions away from their area of expertise. Indeed, he said, because the Japanese employees expected to remain at the company until retirement they felt they had no need to develop professional skills that can be traded on the external labour market.

10 Sugimura (1997) certainly believes that the Japanese salaryman gained personal fulfilment principally from diligently working within a productive community but that this aspect of working within the corporation is waning with increasing individualism.

11 This idea was first described to me by a salaryman who himself had studied sociology at post-graduate level and had recently resigned from his company.

12 Moreover, the very survival of the term 'salaryman' leads one to surmise that Japanese men in white-collar work do not see themselves, and are not regarded by others, as professional specialists. Otherwise would they not be called accountants, investment bankers, insurance actuaries, and so on, as they are in the West?

13 'Sararīman dokuhon: anata no yokubō wa nani gata ka', *Shūkan Asahi*, 26 May 1974: 16–23.

14 'Sararīman jidai', *Nihon Keizai Shimbun*, 19 March 1967: 11.

15 Japan Management Association.

16 'Sararīman jidai', *Nihon Keizai Shimbun*, 12 March 1967: 11.

17 'Nōryoku jidai no tenkin sakusen', *Asahi Shimbun*, 30 March 1967: 7.

18 '"Nenkōjoretsu" ga kawaranai ga jakunensō hodo kakusa shukushō', *Nihon Keizai Shimbun*, 7 April 1974: 3.

19 These ideas were stimulated by a presentation given by the historian and anthropologist of nationalism Benedict Anderson at Kyoto Seika University on 13 June 2000 entitled 'Memory and forgetting: nationalism in Indonesia and Taiwan'.

4 Re-fabricating lifetime employment relations

1 See Dore (1986) for a description and survey of these forms of employment.

2 Company data was from the following automobile assemblers: Hino, Honda, Isuzu, Mitsubishi, Mazda, Nissan, Subaru, Suzuki, Yamaha, Daihatsu, Toyota, and Nissan Diesel.

3 Company data was from the following department stores: Hanshin, Matsuzakaya, Hankyu, Daimaru, Izutsuya, Isetan, Sogo, Takashimaya, Mitsukoshi, Matsuya, and Tokyu.

4 Company data was from the following supermarkets: Daiei, Inageya, Ito Yokado, Jujiya, Izumiya, Mycal, Nagasakiya, Yuni, Seiyu, and Jusco.

5 At the time of writing my original PhD manuscript, Sogo, a major department store operator had filed for bankruptcy protection under new US-style measures that came into effect in April 2000. Nagasakiya, a supermarket chain, in 1999 had also been in such difficulty that it has now been taken over by the US investment company Cerberus. Moreover, the Saison Group, which owns Seiyu amongst others, was in serious financial difficulty as a result of its over-investment in real estate during the bubble period. (This information was compiled from various newspaper and television sources.)

6 Given that more than 90 per cent of Japanese attend secondary education to age 17/18 and then more than 40 per cent attend an institution of further or higher learning it would be difficult to achieve much lower levels of average entry age if there was anything approaching a functioning external labour market for mid-career recruits in these industries.

7 In English the Nihongata Koyō Shisutemu Kenkyū Kai is the Japanese-style Employment System Research Group, Chōgin Sōken Consarutingu is Long-Term Credit Bank Research Consulting, Nihon Rōdō Kenkyū Kikō is the Japan Institute

of Labour, and Shakai Keizai Seisansei Honbu is the Japan Productivity Center for Socio-economic Development.

8 The Japanese government is moving towards raising the age for pension eligibility to 65 in an effort to reduce the expected future revenue pressures of an ageing society. Passed in 1994, the Older Persons Employment Security Law now prohibits management from setting a mandatory retirement age under 60 (Araki, 2002: 28–9). However, with early retirement packages being offered to (and forced on) employees, the real age of retirement from large corporations continues to be in an employee's fifties. Large numbers of press reports attest to the fact that many are forced or at least are strongly encouraged to retire 'voluntarily' and are thereupon transferred either to affiliated companies or into the external labour market where they must compete for employment.

9 See Araki (2002) for an excellent summary of the current legal situation that surrounds employment in Japan. Although statutes do not regulate employers' freedom to dismiss there is a large amount of legal precedent that constrains employers' ability to dismiss employees with indefinite periods in their employment contracts (ibid.: 18–32). Moreover Araki calculates that approximately 87 per cent of the labour force are protected from arbitrary discharge in this manner (ibid.: 20). Nevertheless, Araki also states that case law may be on the point of change and that employers may be given more freedom to dismiss arbitrarily in future (ibid.: 26–7).

10 It is important to note here that government intervention in labour markets through employment subsidies for loss-making firms and support for the construction and other industries that soak up workers temporarily is much more heavily used in Japan than in the UK or USA, with the consequence that the full potential effects on employment of economic stagnation are not felt in the same way as they may be elsewhere.

11 This study consisted of questionnaires returned by the management of 645 companies, the majority of whom are listed on the Tokyo Stock Exchange. The focus of the questionnaire was on the future of the Japanese corporate system in the twenty-first century.

12 In comparison to the other two studies this one is interesting in respect of the various ownership structures and the size of companies represented. Three hundred and sixty-seven companies are listed on the Tokyo Stock Exchange with the rest being either subsidiaries or independently owned companies. Moreover, the study includes a substantial number of companies of fewer than 1,000 employees.

13 Publications in English from the Nihon Rōdō Kenkyū Kiko are cited under the English name Japan Institute of Labour. Those published in Japanese are cited under the acronym NRKK.

14 See Nonaka and Takeuchi (1995) for an excellent description of how this is achieved and how it then confers advantages for the Japanese firm.

15 This information was provided during an interview with a personnel manager from Matsushita Electric Industrial in April 2000. Of those recruited in April 1998, 44 per cent opted for the early payment plan, to the great surprise of the company which expected perhaps 10 per cent to opt for this system. As of January 2000, 5 per cent had changed to the standard system, leaving 39 per cent still on the early payment system. According to an *Asahi Shimbun* article ('Matsushita Denki "Saki-barai kyūyō seido"', *Asahi Shimbun*, 10 January 1998, p. 12), engineers especially favoured this system, preferring performance-related pay over security of employment.

16 Significantly, also, it was precisely the wave of restructuring in Britain and the United States in the 1980s in which the ideology of 'a job for life' was crushed from without by the ideologically driven economistic reform measures of the Thatcher and Reagan eras and collapsed from within as a result of the changing

work values and working behaviours of younger people (see for example Yankelovich, 1978 and Bernstein, 1997).

17 See Malcolm (2001) for a more detailed description of these reforms and their effects. In addition, deregulation is often used in English to describe these reforms, but this is an inaccurate translation of the terms *kisei kanwa* and *jiyuuka* as well as being an inaccurate reading of the situation. *Kisei kanwa* means a relaxation of regulations and *jiyuuka* means liberalization. Both these terms are more appropriate descriptions of actual conditions, the latter being more natural in English.

18 Since May 1999 Doshisha University in Kyoto, the most prestigious private university in the Kansai region, has held an employment fair for its students where participation is exclusive to foreign companies. The event is dominated by American financial institutions and, according to the university careers service, is very well attended by students.

19 See Beck and Beck (1994) for more details on this point. Moreover, this phenomenon was confirmed in informal interviews at both a Japanese and a foreign securities trading company that took place in August 2001.

20 This view was expressed to me in interview with the General Manager of the Research Department of the Centre for the Industrial Renovation of Kansai, July 2000.

21 By internationalism I mean the respect for, as well as an acceptance or even insistence upon, the interconnectedness of difference between separate national systems and characteristics. This is in contrast to globalism which assumes the penetrability and even irrelevance of nationality and national borders. Internationalism can perhaps be assumed to be a characteristic of the mid- to late twentieth century and globalism of the late twentieth and early twenty-first centuries.

22 In this sense *fabricate* is used to convey the idea that the new employee consciousness is a deliberate falsity for the purposes of the corporation's competitive success. Furthermore, the idea of brittleness or transitoriness is also intended in the use of this word, meaning that the new consciousness lacks the strength and permanence of a truly modern consciousness because it is being manufactured from without rather than developed and cultivated from within.

5 Working under changing employment relations

1 Maslow's subjects were predominantly white American males and this has led to the criticism that his work is biased in a number of important respects.

2 By way of example, the term self-actualization (*jikojitsugen* being the Japanese translation) was in part derived from Maslow's work. Hamada's (1998) book, titled *Shigoto to Jikojitsugen no Ii Kankei no Tsukurikata* ('Creating a positive relationship between work and self-actualization'), is an attempt to clarify the way to self-actualization through work and the employee's relationship with the company. The book is loosely based on Maslow's work and directed at salarymen who might feel confused by the new world of work in Japan and elsewhere. It advises them to respond by ditching the past and looking forward to a new future of individuality, creativity, and a sense of responsibility for oneself.

3 Although all people experience hunger if they do not eat and they seek to satisfy that hunger by eating food, precisely what someone eats and how the food is prepared and consumed will be different between cultures and individuals and this will be influenced greatly by what people value as ethically correct behaviour. Moreover, people in all cultures make friends and fall in love with each other though they may express that friendship or love in different ways according to the ethical and cultural values that exist between different groups of people.

4 Both genetic and cultural teleonomy are evolutionary and developmental processes that are, to a large extent, beyond the capacity of individuals to direct. In modern

society, where relatively liberal social regimes are combined with the security and stability of material wealth, the teleonomy of the self becomes relatively more important because of the possibilities opened up for the exercise of choice and of experiments in living.

5 Csikszentmihaly uses the terms negentropy and negentropic to mean the opposite of entropy and entropic. That is to say, where entropy means a tendency towards decay, simplicity, and uniformity, negentropy suggests a tendency towards growth, complexity, and diversity. Inghilleri (1999) describes entropy as a permanent state for all inanimate objects and negentropy a natural and essential state inherent in all living things.

6 Literally translated into English as the Life Design Research Institute, this research body was set up and sponsored by Daiichi Seimei Hoken (Daiichi Life Insurance Company).

7 The research was conducted in December 1999 and published in 2000. Out of 10,000 people over 20, 7,022 agreed to face-to-face interviews and out of these 3,223 were men and 3,799 women. This question asked respondents to say what kind of work they thought was ideal. Respondents were allowed two choices out of a possible nine. The other studies in this series that are mentioned here were conducted in May 1994 and May 1997.

8 Oswald (1997) claims, quite convincingly, that lack of fear of unemployment is a much greater influence on people's feelings of well-being than material prosperity.

9 Recruit Research Company.

10 This research was reproduced in the CD-ROM that comes with recent Labour White Papers. The number of respondents and the size of the sample were not given. In addition, it is not clear whether respondents were senior high-school or university graduates or both.

11 *Furīta* is a shortened version and combination of the English word 'free' and the German word '*Arbeiter*' and is used to describe those people who either cannot or choose not to gain regular and secure employment on graduation from high school or university. Instead they usually take a series of low-paid but convenient part-time and temporary jobs in predominantly service-oriented work such as in retail and eating and drinking establishments.

12 Reproduced in the Labour White Paper CD-ROM, this research covered 20- to 24-year-olds. Produced by Rōdōshō (Ministry of Labour), the title of the survey is *Jyakunen Shūgyō Jittai Chōsa* (1985 and 1997).

13 The 1983–4 group was comprised of 648 men (34 per cent at companies of more than 1,000 employees and 31.4 per cent at companies of 999 or fewer) and 383 women. The 1989–91 group was made up of 641 men and 661 women. The respondents came from companies of various sizes, unlike the 4,063 respondents of the Nihongata Koyō Shisutemu Kenkyū Kai (NKSKK, 1995) who all come from companies of more than 1,000 employees.

14 Although the percentage changing employer is higher in the more recent study, as it covers a wider range of companies in terms of their scale, a precise comparison between the two studies in this respect would be problematic.

15 The *Tokyo University Newspaper* article from which the first half of this data is compiled stressed that banks and securities companies, as well as central government ministries, had experienced a reduction in popularity in recent years due to the series of scandals that had engulfed the finance industry and the bureaucracy (*Tokyo Daigaku Shimbun*, 2 June 1998).

16 See Sato's (1988) essay on the feelings of *Bosozoku*, or motorcycle gang members. In this article Sato clearly expresses the idea that Japanese gang members experience flow through the activities of the gang as a single entity.

17 See Sugimura (1997).

Bibliography

Newspapers, magazines, etc.

Asahi Shimbun
Nihon Keizai Shinbun
Nikkei Net Interactive
Shūkan Asahi
Tokyo Daigaku Shimbun

Books and articles

Abegglen, J. C. (1958) *The Japanese Factory: Aspects of its Social Organization*, Glencoe, IL: The Free Press.

Abegglen, J. C. (1973) *Management and Worker: The Japanese Solution*, Tokyo: Sophia University and Kodansha International.

Abegglen, J. C. and Stalk, G., Jr (1985) *Kaisha: The Japanese Corporation*, New York: Basic Books.

Abo, T. (ed.) (1994) *Hybrid Factory: The Japanese Production System in the United States*, New York: Oxford University Press.

Allison, A. (1994) *Nightwork: Sexuality, Pleasure and Corporate Masculinity in a Tokyo Hostess Club*, Chicago: Chicago University Press.

Araki, T. (2002) *Labor and Employment Law in Japan*, Tokyo: Japan Institute of Labour.

Ashkenazi, M. (1996) 'Some influences of Shinto on Japanese business practices', in Kreiner, J. (ed.) *The Impact of Traditional Thought on Present Day Japan*, Monographien 11, Tokyo: Deutschen Institut für Japanstudien.

Bauman, Z. (1995) 'Searching for a centre that holds', in Featherstone, M., Lash, S., and Robertson, R. (eds) *Global Modernities*, London: Sage.

Bauman, Z. (1998) *Globalization: The Human Consequences*, Cambridge: Polity Press.

Beck, J. C. and Beck, M. N. (1994) *The Change of a Lifetime: Employment Patterns Among Japan's Managerial Elite*, Honolulu: University of Hawaii Press.

Beck, U. (2000) *The Brave New World of Work*, Cambridge: Polity Press.

Bell, D. (1996 [1976]) *The Cultural Contradictions of Capitalism*, New York: Basic Books.

Benson, J. (1998) 'Labour management during recessions: Japanese manufacturing enterprises in the 1990s', *Industrial Relations Journal*, vol. 29, no. 3: 207–19.

Bernstein, P. (1997) *American Work Values: Their Origin and Development*, Albany, NY: SUNY Press.

Brown, R. K. (1999) 'Work and leisure', in Kuper, A. and Kuper, J. (eds) *The Social Science Encyclopaedia*, London: Routledge: 919–21.

Casey, C. (1995) *Work, Self and Society After Industrialism*, London: Routledge.

Chalmers, N. J. (1989) *Industrial Relations in Japan: The Peripheral Workforce*, London: Routledge.

Chandler, A. D., Jr (1980) 'The United States: seedbed of managerial capitalism', in Chandler, A. D., Jr and Deams, H. (eds) *Managerial Hierarchies: Comparative Perspectives on the Rise of Modern Industrial Enterprises*, Cambridge, MA: Harvard University Press.

Cheng, M. M. and Kalleberg, A. L. (1997) 'How permanent was permanent employment? Patterns of organizational mobility in Japan, 1916–1975', *Work and Occupations*, vol. 24, no. 1: 17–32.

Chimoto, A. (1986) 'Employment in the Meiji period: from "tradition" to "modernity"', *Japanese Yearbook on Business History*, vol. 3: 135–59.

Chimoto, A. (1989) 'A historical examination of Mitsui's strategies for promoting long-term continuous service', *Japanese Yearbook on Business History*, vol. 6: 45–77.

Clammer, J. (1995) *Difference and Modernity: Social Theory and Contemporary Japanese Society*, London: Kegan Paul International.

Clammer, J. (1997) *Contemporary Urban Japan: A Sociology of Consumption*, Oxford: Blackwell.

Clammer, J. (2001) *Japan and Its Others*, Melbourne: Trans Pacific Press.

Clark, R. (1979) *The Japanese Company*, New Haven, CT: Yale University Press.

Cole, R. E. (1971) *Japanese Blue Collar: The Changing Tradition*, Berkeley, CA: University of California Press.

Cole, R. E. (1978) 'The late-developer hypothesis: an evaluation of its relevance for Japanese employment practices', *Journal of Japanese Studies*, vol. 4, no. 2: 247–65.

CSC (Chōgin Sōken Consarutingu) (1998) *Nijūisseiki no Cōporeeto Shisutemu ni Kansuru Chōsa*, Tokyo: Chōgin Sōken Consarutingu.

Csikszentmihaly, M. (1988) 'The flow experience and its significance for human psychology', in Csikszentmihaly, M. and Csikszentmihaly, I. S. (eds) *Optimal Experience: Psychological Studies of Flow in Consciousness*, Cambridge: Cambridge University Press.

Csikszentmihaly, M. (1997) *Creativity: Flow and the Psychology of Discovery and Invention*, New York: HarperCollins.

Csikszentmihaly, M. and Csikszentmihaly, I. S. (eds) (1988) *Optimal Experience: Psychological Studies of Flow in Consciousness*, Cambridge: Cambridge University Press.

Darbyshire, O. and Katz, H. C. (2000) *Converging Divergences: Worldwide Changes in Employment Systems*, Ithaca, NY: Cornell University Press.

Dore, R. P. (1973) *British Factory, Japanese Factory: The Origins of National Diversity in Industrial Relations*, London: George Allen and Unwin.

Dore, R. P. (1986) *Flexible Rigidities: Industrial Policy and Structural Adjustment in the Japanese Economy 1970–1980*, London: The Athlone Press.

Dore, R. P. (1987) *Taking Japan Seriously: A Confucian Perspective on Leading Economic Issues*, London: The Athlone Press.

Dore, R. P. (1999 [1958]) *City Life in Japan: A Study of a Tokyo Ward*, Richmond, Surrey: Japan Library.

Dore, R. P. (2000) *Stock Market Capitalism: Welfare Capitalism: Japan and Germany versus the Anglo-Saxons*, Oxford: Oxford University Press.

Dore, R. P., Bounine-Cabalé, J., and Tapiola, K. (1989) *Japan at Work: Markets, Management and Flexibility*, Paris: OECD.

Dōshisha Daigaku (1999) *Shūshoku Dētabukku 1999*, Kyoto: Dōshisha Daigaku.

Eades, J. S. (2000) 'Introduction: Globalization and social change in contemporary Japan', in Eades, J. S., Gill, T., and Befu, H. (eds) *Globalization and Social Change in Contemporary Japan*, Melbourne: Trans Pacific Press.

Economic Planning Agency (1996) *White Paper on the National Lifestyle Fiscal Year 1995: Looking back on 50 Post-War Years and Forward, in Search of an Affluent and Diversified National Lifestyle for Japan (Summary)*, Tokyo: Economic Planning Agency.

Economic Planning Agency (1999) *Economic Survey of Japan 1998–1999: Challenges for Economic Revival*, Tokyo: Economic Planning Agency.

Eisenstadt, S. N. (1998) 'Modernity and the construction of collective identities', in Sasaki, M. (ed.) *Values and Attitudes across Nations and Time*, Leiden: Brill.

Feiler, B. (1991) *Learning to Bow: Inside the Heart of Japan*, Boston, MA: Houghton Mifflin.

Flanagan, S. C. (1982) 'Changing values in advanced industrial societies: Inglehart's silent revolution from the perspective of Japanese findings', *Comparative Political Studies*, vol. 14, no. 4: 403–44.

Florida, R. and Kenney, M. (1991) 'Organization vs. culture: Japanese automotive transplants in the US', *Industrial Relations Journal*, vol. 22, no. 3: 181–96.

Fruin, W. M. (1983) 'The taste of success: The democratization and internationalization of the Kikkoman corporation', in Mannari, H. and Befu, H. (eds) *The Challenge of Japan's Internationalization: Organization and Culture*, Tokyo: Kwansei Gakuin University and Kōdansha International.

Fujioka, W. (1989) 'Heisei gannen gurēdo appu e no michi', *Chuo Kōron*, April 1989: 204–18.

Furnham, A. (1997) 'The relationship between work and economic values', *Journal of Economic Psychology*, vol. 18, no. 1: 1–14.

Giddens, A. (1990) *The Consequences of Modernity*, Cambridge: Polity Press.

Giddens, A. (1991) *Modernity and Self-Identity: Self and Society in the Late Modern Age*, Stanford, CA: Stanford University Press.

Giddens, A. (1999) *The Reith Lectures 1999*, BBC Radio 4, April 1999.

Gilligan, C. (1996 [1982]) *In a Different Voice*, Cambridge, MA: Harvard University Press.

Gordon, A. (1998a) 'The invention of Japanese-style labor management', in Vlastos, Steven (ed.) *Mirror of Modernity: Invented Traditions of Modern Japan*, Berkeley, CA: University of California Press.

Gordon, A. (1998b) *The Wages of Affluence: Labor and Management in Postwar Japan*, Cambridge, MA: Harvard University Press.

Gray, J. (1998) *False Dawn: The Delusions of Global Capitalism*, London: Granta Books.

Grönning, T. (1997) 'Accessing large corporations: Research ethics and gatekeeper-relations in the case of researching a Japanese-invested factory', *Sociological Research Online*, vol. 2, no. 4, <http://www.socresonline.org.uk/2/4/9.html>, last accessed: 6 November 2002.

Hamada, T. (1998) *Shigoto to Jikojitsugen no Ii Kankei no Tsukurikata*, Tokyo: Dayamondo-sha.

Hamaguchi, E. (1982) *Kanjinshugi no Shakai: Nihon*, Tokyo: Toyo Keizai Shinpōsha.

Hasegawa, H. (1993) 'Japanese employment practices and industrial relations: The road to union compliance', *Japan Forum*, vol. 5, no. 1: 21–35.

Hasegawa, H. (1996) *The Steel Industry in Japan: A Comparison with Britain*, London: Routledge.

Hasegawa, H. and Hook, G. D. (eds) (1998) *Japanese Business Management: Restructuring for Low Growth and Globalization*, London: Routledge.

Hazama, H. (1997 [1964]) *The History of Labour Management in Japan*, London: Macmillan.

Hendry, J. (1999) *An Anthropologist in Japan: Glimpses of Life in the Field*, London: Routledge.

Herbig, P. A. and Borstorff, P. (1995) 'Japan's Shinjinrui: A new breed', *International Journal of Social Economics*, vol. 22, no. 12: 49–55.

Hirokane, K. (n.d.) *Kachō Shima Kōsaku*, Tokyo: Kōdansha.

Hirokane, K. (n.d.) *Buchō Shima Kōsaku*, Tokyo: Kōdansha.

Hirooka, M. (1986) *Yutakasa no Paradokkusu*, Tokyo: Kōdansha.

Hobsbawm, E. (1983) 'Introduction: inventing traditions', in Hobsbawm, E. and Ranger, T. (eds) *The Invention of Tradition*, Cambridge: Cambridge University Press.

Hofstede, G. (1984) *Culture's Consequences: International Differences in Work Related Values*, Newbury Park, CA: Sage.

Hood, C. P. (2001) *Japanese Education Reform: Nakasone's Legacy*, London: Routledge.

Iki, N., Hiroishi, T., and Mukai, M. (2000) 'Jiko shinkoku seido kitei', *Chingin Jitsumu*, no. 861: 43–7.

Imada, S. (1997) 'Work and family life', Japan Labour Bulletin, vol. 36, no. 8, <http://www.jil.go.jp/bulletin/year/1997/vol36-08/06.htm>, last accessed: 11 April 2003.

Imada, S. and Hirata, S. (1995) *Howaito-Karā no Shōshin Kōzō*, Tokyo: Nihon Rōdō Kenkyū Kikō.

Inghilleri, P. (1999) *From Subjective Experience to Cultural Change*, trans. E. Bartoli, Cambridge: Cambridge University Press.

Inglehart, R. (1982) 'Changing values in Japan and the West', *Comparative Political Studies*, vol. 14, no. 4: 445–79.

Inglehart, R. (1990) *Culture Shift in Advanced Industrial Society*, Princeton, NJ: Princeton University Press.

Inglehart, R. (1997) *Modernization and Postmodernization: Cultural, economic and political change in 43 societies*, Princeton, NJ: Princeton University Press.

Jahoda, M. (1982) *Employment and Unemployment: A Social-Psychological Analysis*, Cambridge: Cambridge Unviersity Press.

Japan Institute of Labour (1998) *Human Resource Development of Professional and Managerial Workers in Industry: An International Comparison*, JIL Report Series no. 7, Tokyo: Japan Institute of Labour.

Japan Institute of Labour (2001) *The Labor Situation in Japan 2001–2002*, Tokyo: Japan Institute of Labour.

Jurgensen, C. E. (1978) 'Job preferences (what makes a job good or bad?)', *Journal of Applied Psychology*, vol. 63, no. 3: 267–76.

Kamata, S. (1983) *Japan in the Passing Lane: An Insider's Account of Life in a Japanese Auto Factory*, London: George Allen and Unwin.

Kameyama, N. (1995) '"Risotura" no shinten to howaito karā no "junan"', in Shakaiseisaku Gakkai, *Gendai Nihon no Howaito Karā*, Shakaiseisaku Nenpō no. 39, Tokyo: Ochanomizu Shobō.

Kato, K. (ed.) (1999) *Raifu Dezain Hakusho 2000–01*, Tokyo: Kokuseisha.

Kato, T. (1994) 'The political economy of Japanese *karoshi* (death from overwork)', *Hitotsubashi Journal of Social Studies*, vol. 26: 41–54.

Kato, T. (2001) 'The end of lifetime employment? Evidence from national surveys and field research', *Journal of the Japanese and International Economies*, vol. 15: 489–514.

Kinmonth, E. H. (1981) *The Self-Made Man in Meiji Japanese Thought: From Samurai to Salary Man*, Berkeley, CA: University of California Press.

Kirinoki, I. (2000) 'Nihongata cafeteria puran – dai-ikkai: Cafeteria puran to wa nani ka', *Rōmu Jijō*, no. 964: 44–7.

Koike, Kazuo (ed.) (1991) *Daisotsu Howaito-Karā no Jinzai Kaihatsu*, Tokyo: Tōyō Keizai Shinpōsha.

Kumazawa, M. (1996a) *Portraits of the Japanese Workplace: Labour Movements, Workers, and Managers*, trans. Andrew Gordon, Boulder, CO: Westview Press.

Kumazawa, M. (1996b) 'Nihonteki nōryokushugi no daryoku', *Kōnan Daigaku Keizaigaku Ronshū*, vol. 36, no. 4: 129–60.

Kuruvilla, S. and Erickson, C. L. (2002) 'Change and transformation in Asian industrial relations', *Industrial Relations*, vol. 41, no. 2: 171–227.

Lebra, T. S. (1976) *Japanese Patterns of Behavior*, Honolulu: University of Hawaii Press.

Lincoln, J. R. and Kalleberg, A. L. (1991) *Culture, Control, and Commitment: A Study of Work Organization and Work Attitudes in the United States and Japan*, Cambridge: Cambridge University Press.

Lincoln, J. R. and Nakata, Y. (1997) 'The transformation of the Japanese employment system: nature, depth and origins', *Work and Occupations*, vol. 24, no. 1: 33–55.

Locke, E. A. and Latham, G. P. (1990) 'Work motivation and satisfaction: light at the end of the tunnel', *Psychological Science*, vol. 1, no. 4: 240–6.

Loiskandl, Helmut (1998) 'Truth, beauty, ethics: notes on Japanese and European frames of appresentation', in Trommsdorf, G., Friedlmeier, W., and Kornadt, H.-J. (eds) *Japan in Transition: Social and Psychological Aspects*, Lengerich: Pabst Science Publishers.

McCormack, G. (1996) *The Emptiness of Japanese Affluence*, New York: M. E. Sharpe.

McCune, J. (1990) '*Sayonara* to lifelong jobs', *Personnel*, vol. 17, no. 11: 11–12.

McGaughey, S. L., Iverson, R. D., and De Cieri, H. (1997) 'A multi-method analysis of work related preferences in three nations: implications for inter- and intra-national human resource management', *International Journal of Human Resource Management*, vol. 8, no. 1: 1–16.

McNeill, P. (1989) *Research Methods*, London: Routledge.

Malcolm, J. D. (2001) *Financial Globalization and the Opening of the Japanese Economy*, London: Curzon.

Markus, H. R. and Kitayama, S. (1991) 'Culture and self: implications for cognition, emotion and motivation', *Psychological Review*, vol. 98, no. 2: 224–53.

Maruyama, Masao (1965) 'Patterns of individuation and the case of Japan: a conceptual scheme', in Jansen, M. B. (ed.) *Changing Japanese Attitudes Toward Modernization*, Princeton, NJ: Princeton University Press.

Maslow, A. H. (1987 [1954]) *Motivation and Personality*, New York: HarperCollins.

Matsuzuka, Y. (2002) *Changes in the Permanent Employment System in Japan Between 1982 and 1997*, London: Routledge.

Merleau-Ponty, M. (1998 [1962]) *Phenomenology of Perception*, trans. Colin Smith, London: Routledge.

Miura, M. (2000) 'Breaking free from stranglehold of wartime regime', *Daily Yomiuri*, 3 May 2000: 11.

Motomiya, H. (n.d.) *Sararīman Kintarō*, Tokyo: Shūeisha.

Mouer, R. E. (1989) 'Japanese model of industrial relations: warnings or opportunities', *Hitotsubashi Journal of Social Studies*, vol. 21: 105–24.

MOW (Meaning of Working International Research Team) (1987) *The Meaning of Working*, London: Academic Press.

Nakajima T. (2000) 'Chōsa kekka ni miru mokuhyō kanri seido no dōkō', *Chingin Jitsumu*, no. 854: 4–15.

Nakamura, K. and Nitta, M. (1995) 'Developments in industrial relations and human resource practices in Japan', in Locke, R., Kochan, T., and Piore, M. (eds) *Employment Relations in a Changing World Economy*, Cambridge, MA: MIT Press.

Nakamura, M. (1992) 'Howaito-karā no rōmu kanri to shokushu gainen', in Tachibanaki, T. (ed.) *Satei, Shōshin, Chingin Kettei*, Tokyo: Yuhikaku.

Nakamura, M. (1995) 'Howaito karā no kyaria haba', in Shakaiseisaku Gakkai, *Gendai Nihon no Howaito Karā*, Tokyo: Ochanomizu Shobō.

Nakane, C. (1972) *Japanese Society*, Berkeley, CA: University of California Press.

Nakanishi, T. (2000) '"Dai-ni no sengo" no kokka mokuhyō', *Chūō Kōron*, February 2000: 50–67.

Nakata, Y. and Takehiro, R. (2002) 'Total labour costs and the employment adjustment behaviour of large Japanese firms', *NBER Working Papers*, <http://www.nber.org/books/otw1-00/nakata.pdf>, last accessed: 6 November 2002.

Nihon Keizai Shimbunsha (1989–2002) *Nikkei Kaisha Jōhō*, Tokyo: Nihon Keizai Shimbunsha.

Nishinarita, Y. (1995) 'An overview of Japanese labor–employer relations from the 1870s to the 1990s', *Hitotsubashi Journal of Economics*, vol. 36: 17–20.

Nishinarita, Y. (1998) 'Japanese style industrial relations in historical perspective', in Hasegawa, H. and Hook, G. D. (eds) *Japanese Business Management: Restructuring for Low Growth and Globalization*, London: Routledge.

Nitto, H. (1993) 'The changing structure of Japanese values', *NRI Quarterly*, Summer 1993: 2–27.

NKSKK (Nihongata Koyō Shisutemu Kenkyū Kai) (1995) *Hōkokusho*, Tokyo: Nihongata Koyō Shisutemu Kenkyū Kai.

Noguchi, P. H. (1983) 'Shiranai station: not a destination but a journey', in Plath, D. W. (ed.) *Work and Lifecourse in Japan*, Albany, NY: SUNY Press.

Nomura, M. (1998) *Koyō Fuan*, Tokyo: Iwanami Shinsho.

Nonaka, I. and Takeuchi, H., (1995) *The Knowledge Creating Company*, Oxford: Oxford University Press.

North, D. (1990) *Institutions, Institutional Change and Economic Performance*, Cambridge: Cambridge University Press.

NRKK (Nihon Rōdō Kenkyū Kikō) (1999) *Henka Suru Daisotsusha no Shokki Kyaria*, Tokyo: Nihon Rōdō Kenkyū Kikō.

NRKK (Nihon Rōdō Kenkyū Kikō) (2000) *Shin-Seiki no Keiei Senryaku, Cōporeeto Gabanansu, Jinji Senryaku*, Tokyo: Nihon Rōdō Kenkyū Kikō.

Ohira, K. (1990) *Yutakasa no Seishin Byōri*, Tokyo, Iwanami Shoten.

Ohmae, K. (1995a) *The End of the Nation State: The Rise of Regional Economies*, New York: Free Press.

Ohmae, K. (1995b) 'Letter from Japan', *Harvard Business Review*, May–June 1995: 154–63.

Okazaki, K. (1996) 'A measurement of the Japanese lifetime employment system', *Keio Business Review*, vol. 33: 105–15.

Okazaki, T. (1994) 'The Japanese firm under the wartime planned economy', in Aoki, M. and Dore, R. (eds) *The Japanese Firm: Sources of Competitive Strength*, Cambridge: Cambridge University Press.

Oswald, A. J. (1997) *Happiness and Economic Performance*, Discussion Paper Series, no. 18, Centre for Economic Performance, University of Oxford.

Parsons, T. (1951) *Toward a General Theory of Social Action*, London: Harvard University Press.

Paul, W. J., Jr, Robertson, K. B., and Herzberg, F. (1969) 'Job enrichment pays off', *Harvard Business Review*, March–April 1969: 61–78.

Pieterse, J. N. (1995) 'Globalization as hybridization', in Featherstone M., Lash, S., and Robertson, R. (eds) *Global Modernities*, London: Sage.

Plath, D. W. (1989) 'Arc, circle and sphere: schedules for selfhood', in Mouer, R. E. and Sugimoto, Y. (eds) *Constructs for Understanding Japan*, London: Kegan Paul International.

Plath, D. W. (ed.) (1983) *Work and Lifecourse in Japan*, Albany, NY: SUNY Press.

Popper, K. (1972 [1959]) *The Logic of Scientific Discovery*, London: Hutchinson.

Pryor, R. (1979) 'In search of a concept: work values', *The Vocational Guidance Quarterly*, March 1979: 250–9.

Roberson, J. E. and N. Suzuki (eds) (2003) *Men and Masculinities in Contemporary Japan: Dislocating the Salaryman Doxa*, London: Routledge.

Robertson, R. (1995) 'Globalization: Time–space and homogeneity–heterogeneity', in Featherstone, M., Lash, S., and Robertson, R. (eds) *Global Modernities*, London: Sage.

Robson, D. (1994) 'The sun also sets', *Work Study*, vol. 43, no. 1: 18–19.

Rōdōshō (2000a) *Howaito-Karaa wo Meguru Saiyō- Senryaku no Tayōka ni Kansuru Chōsa Kenkyū Hōkokusho*, <http://www.jil.go.jp/kisya/index.2d_html>, last accessed: 6 November 2002.

Rōdōshō (2000b) *Rōdō Keizai Hakusho*, Tokyo: Nihon Rōdō Kenkyū Kikō.

Rohlen, T. P. (1974) *For Harmony and Strength: Japanese White-collar Organization in Anthropological Perspective*, Berkeley, CA: University of California Press.

Rohlen, T. P. (1979) '"Permanent employment" faces recession, slow growth, and an aging work force', *Journal of Japanese Studies*, vol. 5, no. 2: 235–72.

Rōmu Gyōsei Kenkyūjo (1999) *Koyō Kanri no Jitsumu*, Tokyo: Rōdōshō Seisaku Chōsabu.

Rosenberger, N. R. (ed.) (1992) *Japanese Sense of Self*, Cambridge: Cambridge University Press.

Roth, J. (1963) *Timetables*, New York: The Bobbs-Merrill Company.

Rowley, C. and Benson, J. (2002) 'Convergence and divergence in Asian human resource management', *California Management Review*, vol. 44, no. 2: 90–109.

Sagie, A., Elizur, D., and Koslowsky, M. (1996) 'Work values: a theoretical overview and a model of their effects', *Journal of Organizational Behaviour*, vol. 17: 502–14.

Sako, M. (1997) 'Introduction: forces for homogeneity and diversity in the Japanese industrial relations system', in Sako, M. and Sato, H. (eds) *Japanese Labour and Management in Transition: Diversity, Flexibility and Participation*, London: Routledge.

Sato, H. (1997a) 'Human resource management systems in large firms: the case of white collar graduate employees', in Sako, M. and Sato, H. (eds) *Japanese Labour and Management in Transition: Diversity, Flexibility and Participation*, London: Routledge.

Sato, H. (1997b) 'Still going! Continuity and change in Japan's long-term employment system', *Social Science Japan*, August 1997: 16–18.

Sato, I. (1988) '*Bōsōzoku*: flow in Japanese motorcycle gangs', in Csikszentmihaly, M. and Csikszentmihaly, I. S. (eds) *Optimal Experience: Psychological Studies of Flow in Consciousness*, Cambridge: Cambridge University Press.

Sayer, D. (1991) *Capitalism and Modernity: An Excursus on Marx and Weber*, London: Routledge.

Scheuch, I. (1998) 'A comparative study of modernization in Germany and Japan', in Trommsdorf, G., Friedlmeier, W., and Kornadt, H.-J. (eds) *Japan in Transition: Social and Psychological Aspects*, Lengerich: Pabst Science Publishers.

Schlosstein, S. (1993) 'High noon for the rising sun', *Journal of Business Strategy*, vol. 14, no. 5: 44–8.

Se, T. (1999) 'A theory of fallibilistic liberalism', MPhil dissertation, University of Sheffield.

Sennett, R. (1998) *The Corrosion of Character: The Personal Consequences of Work in the New Capitalism*, New York: W. W. Norton and Company Inc.

Skinner, K. A. (1983) 'Aborted careers in a public corporation', in Plath, D. W. (ed.) *Work and Lifecourse in Japan*, Albany, NY: SUNY Press.

SKSH (Shakai Keizai Seisansei Honbu) (2000) *Nihonteki Jinji Seido no Genjō to Kadai: Dai san kai 'Nihonteki jinji seido no henyō ni kan suru chōsa' kekka*, Tokyo: Shakai Keizai Seisansei Honbu.

SKSH (Shakai Keizai Seisansei Honbu) (2001a) *Nihonteki Jinji Seido no Genjō to Kadai: Dai san kai 'Nihonteki jinji seido no henyō ni kan suru chōsa' kekka*, Tokyo: Shakai Keizai Seisansei Honbu.

SKSH (Shakai Keizai Seisansei Honbu) (2001b) *Hataraku Koto no Ishiki*, Tokyo: Shakai Keizai Seisansei Honbu.

Smith, T. C. (1959) *The Agrarian Origins of Modern Japan*, Stanford, CA: Stanford University Press.

Sōmuchō (1971–97) *Shūgyō Kōzō Kihon Chōsa*, Tokyo: Sōmuchō Tōkeikyoku.

Sōmushō (2002) *Nihon Tōkei Geppō*, no. 494, Tokyo: Sōmushō Tōkeikyoku.

Sōrifu (2000) *Gekkan Yoron Chōsa*, vol. 32, no. 8, Tokyo: Ōkurashō Insatsukyoku.

Stoetzel, J. (1955) *Without the Chrysanthemum and the Sword: A Study of the Attitudes of Youth in Post-war Japan*, New York and Paris: Columbia University Press and OECD.

Storey, J., Edwards, P., and Sisson, K. (1997) *Managers in the Making: Careers, Development and Control in Corporate Britain and Japan*, London: Sage.

Suehiro, A. (2001) 'An introduction to this issue's special topic: "Atypical" and "irregular" labour in contemporary Japan', *Social Science Japan Journal*, vol. 4, no. 2: 159–60.

Sugayama, S. (1995) 'Work rules, wages, and single status: the shaping of the Japanese employment system', *Business History*, vol. 37, no. 2: 120–40.

Sugimura, Y. (1997) *Yoi Shigoto no Shisō: Atarashī shigoto no rinri no tame ni*, Tokyo: Chūkō Shinshō.

Takahashi, Y. (1997) 'The labor market and lifetime employment in Japan', *Economic and Industrial Democracy*, vol. 18: 55–66.

Takeuchi, Y. (1997) 'The self-activating entrance examination system – its hidden agenda and its correspondence with the Japanese "salary man"', *Higher Education*, vol. 34: 183–97.

Takezawa, S. (1995) *Japan Work Ways 1960–1976–1990*, Tokyo: Japan Institute of Labour.

Tao, M. (1998) *Kaisha Ningen wa Doke e Iku? Gyakufūka no Nihon-teki keiei no naka de*, Tokyo: Chūkō Shinsho.

Tawney, R. H. (1975 [1922]) *Religion and the Rise of Capitalism*, Harmondsworth: Penguin.

Terao, M. (1998) *Denai Kugi wa Suterareru*, Tokyo: Fusōsha.

Tominaga, K. (1990) *Nihon no Kindaika to Shakaihendo*, Tokyo: Kōdansha.

Tominaga, K. (1998) 'A sociological analysis of the modernization of Japan', in Trommsdorff, G., Friedlmeier, W., and Kornadt, H.-J. (eds) *Japan in Transition: Social and Psychological Aspects*, Lengerich: Pabst Science Publishers.

Tsutsui, W. M. (1998) *Manufacturing Ideology: Scientific Management in Twentieth-Century Japan*, Princeton, NJ: Princeton University Press.

Ujigawa, M. and Uemura, T. (1970) *Sararīman Kakumei*, Tokyo: Nihon Seisansei Honbu.

Utsumi, S. (2000) *Sararīman Hōkai*, Tokyo: Mikkasa Shobō.

Vlastos, S. (1998) 'Tradition: past/present culture and modern Japanese history', in Vlastos, S. (ed.) *Mirror of Modernity: Invented Traditions of Modern Japan*, Berkeley, CA: University of California Press.

Watanabe, S. (1997) *Posto Nihongata Keiei: Gurōbaru Jinzai Senryaku to Rīdāshippu*, Tokyo: Nihon Rōdō Kenkyū Kikō.

Weber, M. (1976 [1904]) *The Protestant Ethic and the Spirit of Capitalism*, London: George Allen and Unwin.

Whitley, R. (1999) *Divergent Capitalisms: The Social Structuring and Change of Business Systems*, Oxford: Oxford University Press.

Whittaker, D. H. (1990) 'The end of Japanese style employment?' *Work, Employment and Society*, vol. 4, no. 3: 321–47.

Williams, D. (1996) *Japan and the Enemies of Open Political Science*, London: Routledge.

Yamakoshi, A. (1996) 'Can a new generation change Japan?' *Japan Economic Institute Report*, no. 10A.

Yankelovich, D. (1978) 'The new psychological contracts at work', *Psychology Today*, May 1978: 46–50.

Yano, M. (1997) 'Higher education and employment', *Higher Education*, vol. 34: 199–214.

Yatabe, K. (2000) '"Nenrei-kyū" haishi ni tomonau jitsumu ue no kadai', *Chingin Jitsumu*, no. 853: 4–12.

Index

Abegglen, James 38–40, 59
aesthetics 22, 59, 146; form 156
affluence 39
ageing 73
ancien régime 19
area studies 152
ascription 17, 18, 48, 70
Ashkenazi, Michael 21, 41

Bauman, Zygmunt 17, 19, 34
Big Bang 98, 99
biography 18
Black Ships 26, 149
Bubble Economy 40, 64, 74

Calvin, John 25
capitalism 1–13, 14–37, 150; Japan's 44;
    market 58; modern 145; theoretical
    perspective 14–37
capitalist modernity xv, xvii, 2, 14–37,
    23–5, 27, 33, 37, 40, 68, 72, 108–9,
    149, 152
career chimneys 135
Casey, Catherine 71, 104
chōnan 128–9
Clammer, John 20, 22
Company A 11, 49–50, 62–3, 87, 88, 89,
    92, 93, 130, 132, 138, 139, 140
Company B 11, 46, 48, 56, 64, 87, 88, 90,
    91, 93, 129, 133, 137, 138
Company C 11, 46, 48, 56, 64, 87, 88, 90,
    92, 93, 129, 133, 137, 141, 143
Company D 11, 52–3, 67, 87, 89, 93,
    127–8, 132, 134, 135, 136, 137, 141,
    142, 143, 144
company-hunting 57
compatibility: contrived 67; organic 67
convergence 29, 37, 95–6, 105, 148–51; of
    culture 72

Csikszentmihaly, Mihaly 4, 109–12
cultural modelling 21, 69, 70

Denki Rengō 12
deregulation 94
desires 40
Dore, Ronald 35–6, 43, 45–6, 59, 64, 80

economics 152
Edo period 41–2
eldest son 128–9
employment: adjustment 74; institutions
    and organizations of 5–7; retention
    42
enterprise unionism 39; unions 44

flexibility: numerical 59; functional 59
flow 109–12, 132
fulfilment 55, 58, 68, 110–11, 122

gatekeeper, relations with 12
Giddens, Anthony 16–19, 20, 33, 41,
    152
globalization 1, 10, 15, 18, 23, 29–36, 71,
    86, 146, 148; of competition 35;
    economic 72, 93, 149–51; of
    production 95; of Western capitalism
    104

Hazama, Hiroshi 48, 69, 104
hōkōnin 41–2
hypothetico-deductive model 9–10

ie 21, 43
ikigai 115
imperialism 149
individuation 18–19
industrial paternalism 69
Inglehart, Ronald 6, 29–31, 109

Japan Federation of Employers'
   Organizations *see* Nikkeiren
Japan Institute of Labour *see* Nihon
   Rōdō Kenkyū Kikō
Japan Electrical, Electronic, and
   Information Union *see* Denki
   Rengō
Japanese management system 67
Japanese-style management 43
Japanization 149
job rotation 49
job-changing 55, 117–22
job-hunting 57

kanjinshugi 28
karōshi 60
keieikazokushugi 42

liberalization 98
life-planning 17–18
lifetime employment 7–9, 38–147;
   dependent attributes 73, 76–86; in
   post-war Japan 38–70; system 7–10,
   79–100, 139–40
Loiskandl, Helmut 41, 59
love 43
Luther, Martin 25

management by objectives (MBO) 61
managerial familism 69
manga comics 9
Marx, Karl 28
Maslovian hierarchy 113
Maslow, Abraham 107–9
material affluence 10, 23, 40
Matsushita Electric 85
Meiji: period 41–2; Restoration 41
Ministry of Labour 79
Mitsubishi 41
Mitsui House 41
modernity 1–13, 14–37, 42, 59, 104, 105,
   147, 150; definitions 14; theoretical
   perspective 14–37
modernization 20–1, 24–7, 155; cultural
   25–7; economic 70, 72; in Europe
   24–25; Japanese 28, 34, 42
motivation 69, 107–8, 110
motivations, personal xvi
motives 18

National Mobilization Law 44
needs, desires, and values 5, 40, 45, 57,
   68, 71, 114, 144

needs, hierarchy of 107–9
Nihon Rōdō Kenkyū Kikō 12
Nikkeiren 12

OECD 59, 77
oil shocks 66–7
on-the-job training (OJT) 85

partnership of fate 54–5
pay and promotion 61
pensions 85, 90–2
Perry, Commodore 26, 149
Plath, David 23, 144–5
promotion 85; seniority-based 50;
   structure 81

recruitment 50–3, 73, 79–80, 88–92; of
   mid-career graduates 88
reflexive project of the self 17, 95, 104,
   109, 146, 152
Reformation 24, 27, 31
Renaissance 24, 27, 31
retirement 49–53, 55, 66, 133–4

salary 49–51, 53–5, 129
salarymen 7–9, 51–2, 54, 60, 64, 66, 72,
   100, 107, 122–7, 130, 146, 153–5
satisfaction with work 122–5
Scientific Management 4, 149
Second World War 41
self: and modern society 27–9; Japanese
   22–4, 28, 36; reflexive 22; relational
   22–4; submerged 23
self-actualization 17, 18, 22, 36–7, 46, 57,
   65, 109, 113, 117, 120, 131, 135–6,
   153
self-determination 18–20, 149
self-identity 17–18
sempai 47
seniority 49; promotion 139
seniority system 140
seniority-based pay and promotion
   39–40, 81
shanai kōbosei 84–90
Shunto 99
sociology 152
South Korea 66
Spring Wage Offensive 99
suicide 60
Sumitomo 41

Taisho period 42
Taylor, Frederick 4

Taylorist production practices 43
Tokugawa 26
Tominaga, Ken'ichi 25–7
tradition 16, 38, 70, 72; invention of
　21–2; Japanese 53
transfers 91
trans-rationality 22, 41, 59

unemployment 3

value change 31
values 108–10; young people's 112

wages 49
Weber, Max 6, 24, 28
welfare corporatism 44, 69
Westernization 31–2, 150–5
work 2–11, 14–15, 143; content 114;
　satisfaction with 122–5
work values 3–5; in Japan 112–25

eBooks – at www.eBookstore.tandf.co.uk

A library at your fingertips!

eBooks are electronic versions of printed books. You can store them on your PC/laptop or browse them online.

They have advantages for anyone needing rapid access to a wide variety of published, copyright information.

eBooks can help your research by enabling you to bookmark chapters, annotate text and use instant searches to find specific words or phrases. Several eBook files would fit on even a small laptop or PDA.

NEW: Save money by eSubscribing: cheap, online access to any eBook for as long as you need it.

Annual subscription packages

We now offer special low-cost bulk subscriptions to packages of eBooks in certain subject areas. These are available to libraries or to individuals.

For more information please contact webmaster.ebooks@tandf.co.uk

We're continually developing the eBook concept, so keep up to date by visiting the website.

www.eBookstore.tandf.co.uk